STUDIES IN THE
ANCIENT HISTORY OF
NORTHERN IRAQ

STUDIES IN THE ANCIENT HISTORY OF NORTHERN IRAQ

BY

DAVID OATES

Director of the
British School of Archaeology
in Iraq

Lately Fellow of Trinity
College, Cambridge

PUBLISHED FOR

THE BRITISH ACADEMY

BY THE OXFORD UNIVERSITY PRESS
LONDON
1968

Oxford University Press, Ely House, London W. 1

GLASGOW NEW YORK TORONTO MELBOURNE WELLINGTON
CAPE TOWN SALISBURY IBADAN NAIROBI LUSAKA ADDIS ABABA
BOMBAY CALCUTTA MADRAS KARACHI LAHORE DACCA
KUALA LUMPUR HONG KONG TOKYO

PRINTED IN GREAT BRITAIN
AT THE UNIVERSITY PRESS, OXFORD
BY VIVIAN RIDLER
PRINTER TO THE UNIVERSITY

THIS VOLUME IS DEDICATED
TO THE MEMORY OF
SIR AUREL STEIN, K.C.I.E., F.B.A.
SCHOLAR AND PIONEER

CONTENTS

LIST OF PLATES

b

LIST OF FIGURES

FOREWORD

THIS volume, prepared by Mr. David Oates for the Stein–Arnold Committee of the British Academy, is primarily the report of his own survey and excavation of sites in northern Iraq between 1954 and 1958. But it is at the same time a memorial to the great explorer whose pioneer work in this field during 1938 and 1939 had provided the initial stimulus. In those years Sir Aurel Stein, stirred by the dramatic results of Père Poidebard's air-surveys of the Roman frontier-region in Syria, began a similar enterprise in the adjacent territories to the east with the ready help of the Royal Air Force and the Iraq Petroleum Company. Brief accounts of the preliminary results, which appeared promptly in the *Geographical Journal*, showed something of the potentialities of the project; and, in the disturbed years between 1939 and his death at Kabul in 1943, Stein prepared a fuller manuscript with a view to ultimate publication. In the year of his death—his 81st year—he was still pursuing Alexander the Great through the wastes of Las Bela and 'Gedrosia', and a few months later he at last achieved his lifelong ambition of visiting Afghanistan. Before leaving on his last journey he tried to extract a promise from his friend Lieut.-Col. Kenneth Mason, then Professor of Geography at Oxford, that he would undertake to arrange for the publication of the manuscript. 'My answer', writes Colonel Mason, 'was that he was a wicked old man to go rollicking off into the blue at the age of 80 and to leave a comparative ignoramus to "clear up his mess". But he had the knack of persuasiveness very highly developed!'

Subsequent examination of the manuscript, however, and of such of its illustrations as had survived the war years showed that in fact they were not in a condition for publication, and both Colonel Mason and others of Stein's friends felt that, had the author lived, he would have been of the same mind. Further field-work and a more leisurely assessment were demanded by the range and importance of the subject and by changing perspectives. Worth-while knowledge of a complex problem such as that of the Roman frontier in the deserts of Iraq involves the accumulation of more exact evidence than a somewhat hasty survey, whether from the air or from the ground, can be expected to produce, even though the observer be a genius. Now, working under the inspiration of Aurel Stein, Mr. Oates has begun, in this Memorial Volume, to lay the foundations of a historical structure which will eventually, with much further labour, give a new substance to 'the lost traveller's dream'. His work has been carried out with the aid of grants from Stein's bequest to the Academy and the co-operation of the British School of Archaeology in Iraq.

MORTIMER WHEELER

1967

ACKNOWLEDGEMENTS

THE field-work on which these studies are based was carried out with the aid of grants from the Stein–Arnold Fund of the British Academy and the British School of Archaeology in Iraq. I must record my debt to both these institutions and to my college, which has supported me throughout with a benevolent tolerance of my nomadic habits. I am especially indebted to Sir Mortimer Wheeler, Secretary of the British Academy, who first suggested that I should undertake the completion of Sir Aurel Stein's work in Iraq, gave me the means to do so, and endured the slow gestation of my conclusions; and to Professor M. E. L. Mallowan, then Director of the British School of Archaeology in Iraq, who placed the resources of the School at my disposal and has responded without stint to my demands on his learning, his time, and his energy.

In Iraq I found a unique combination of scholarship and generosity in the Directorate-General of Antiquities, under the direction successively of the late Dr. Naji al-Asil, Sayyid Taha Baqir, and Dr. Faisal al-Wailly. They and their staff exceeded even the obligations of Arab hospitality in their unfailing kindness. I must acknowledge a special debt to Sayyid Fuad Safar, Inspector-General of Excavations, and Sayyid Mohammed Ali Mustafa, who have allowed me to tap their unrivalled knowledge of Mesopotamian archaeology. Outside the Directorate-General I was received with courtesy and co-operation by every government official with whom I came into contact. I remember with especial pleasure my friend, host, and guide on many cross-country sorties, Sayyid Abdul Amir al-Wailly, then Mudir Nahiya of Sherqat and amateur archaeologist.

It is impossible to record all my obligations. Miss Barbara Parker, for many years Secretary and Librarian of the British School, solved my practical problems and told me a great deal about Assyria. Mr. Geoffrey Clarke shared in the discomfort of my first season without a word of complaint and produced beautiful drawings of Beled Sinjar. Mr. and Mrs. Ross Thomas, formerly of the British Council in Mosul, never failed to provide a home for weary and dirty archaeologists.

The first two chapters of this work were read in manuscript by Professor Albrecht Goetze, doyen of Mesopotamian historians, who suggested some improvements. It is superfluous to add that the errors are my own. My wife took part in the excavations at Nimrud and Ain Sinu, and is responsible for the reports on the pottery from both sites. Without her constant help and encouragement the book would never have been written.

DAVID OATES

Trinity College, Cambridge, 1963

I

THE MESOPOTAMIAN SCENE

LANDSCAPE, CLIMATE, AND ECONOMIC POTENTIAL

(Fig. 1)

THE basin of the Tigris and Euphrates rivers is a broad sickle-shaped trough, some 1,200 km. long and up to 400 km. wide, with its long axis running north-west from the head of the Persian Gulf.[1] It lies between the highlands of Anatolia and Iran on the north and east and the Arabian massif on the south-west, and is cut off from the Mediterranean by the coastal mountains of Palestine and Lebanon. A low saddle between the northern end of the Lebanon range and the foothills of Anatolia, opposite the westerly bend of the Euphrates, affords the easiest and most direct link between Mesopotamia and the sea. Within these boundaries the trough has been progressively filled by sedimentary deposits. In the north these are of Miocene date, overlaid at the foot of the mountains by Quaternary outwash material and elsewhere by areas of loess. A low cliff line stretching from Hit on the Euphrates to Samarra on the Tigris marks off the northern plain from the flat alluvium of the south, which is the result of a continuous process of deposition since the Quaternary period by the rivers which discharge into the Persian Gulf.

Historians long believed that the Hit–Samarra line represented the shore of the Gulf in early Holocene times, and that the alluvium was a delta which has since advanced down the Gulf to its present limits. It has recently been demonstrated that this explanation was too simple.[2] The present aspect of the country, including some of its most important features, owes much to geological activity which reached its peak in the Pliocene period but has continued to exercise an important effect down to the present day. This was a movement of the underlying structure of the Anatolian and Iranian plateaux in the direction of the stable Arabian massif, which had two consequences. Firstly, it engendered during the Pliocene a folding process which formed the mountain ranges of southern Anatolia and the Zagros, with their outlying parallel ridges which traverse northern Mesopotamia from west to east and thence swing to the south-east across the Tigris valley and down the western borders of Iran. Secondly, as a continuing result of this process there has been intermittent subsidence of the floor of the basin itself, which has been particularly observed at its south-eastern end. This has caused periodic rejuvenation of the river system, but the silt which the rivers have carried down from the mountains

---

[1] Excellent summaries of the geography of the Tigris and Euphrates basins and its effect on human settlement can be found in R. J. Braidwood and B. Howe, 'Prehistoric Investigations in Iraqi Kurdistan', *SAOC*, 31, ch. ii, and, with reference to modern settlement, D. H. Davies, 'Observations on Land Use in Iraq', *Econ. Geog.* 33 (1957), 122–34.

[2] G. M. Lees and N. L. Falcon, 'The Geographical History of the Mesopotamian Plains', *Geog. Jl.* 118 (1952), 24–39.

has been deposited in an ever-deepening depression. Consequently we must now envisage a geographical development diametrically opposed to earlier assumptions. It is probable that in the glacial conditions of the late Pleistocene period the waters of the Gulf were considerably below their present level, and a much larger area of alluvial plain was then

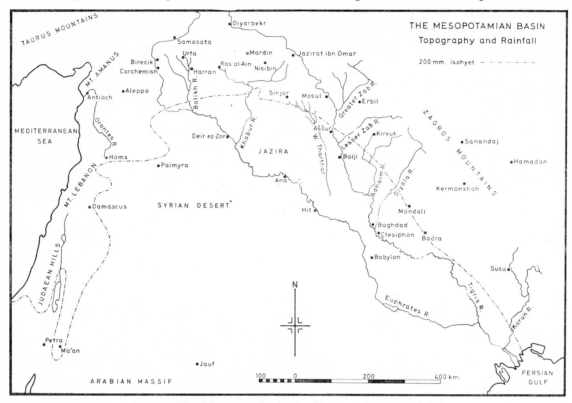

FIG. 1. The Mesopotamian Basin: Topography and Rainfall

exposed. The rise in sea level which resulted from the melting of the great ice-sheets in the early Holocene would have caused a gradual retreat of the shoreline to approximately its present position. Since that time the evidence seems to show that the interaction of subsidence and deposition has produced a rough equilibrium between land and sea levels. Since subsidence has been episodic while deposition was continuous, there have been minor oscillations in the coastline coupled with local inundations inland, some of which may have coalesced into the Flood Legend; but it is significant that the shells scattered over the surface of the alluvium, which were originally taken as evidence for the north-eastward extension of the Gulf in early times, have on examination proved to be of fresh-water origin. We may assume, then, that the physical shape of the basin changed little throughout historic times, and may now consider the different types of landscape which this geological development has produced.

The south-western fringe of the basin, where the Arabian massif slopes gently up from the valley of the middle and lower Euphrates, is overlaid by beds of limestone and marl, with occasional remnants of sandstone, and the surface is a rocky desert with patches of windblown sand, cut up by *wadis* (seasonal water courses) which rapidly drain off the sparse winter rains. Bordering this on the east is the flat silt of southern Mesopotamia. The northern plain is undulating country with sandy gypsiferous soil and patches of loess and Quaternary alluvium, while the eroded hill-chains which surround and intersect it form a mosaic of barren upland and comparatively small but fertile valleys. The use which can be made of these different terrains is, as elsewhere in the Near East, stringently controlled by the climate.[1] This is basically continental in type, with hot summers and relatively cold winters. Rainfall occurs in the winter and spring months, but distribution within that period and the annual aggregates vary considerably; both have a significant effect on the success or failure of crops in marginal areas. The rain is the product of depressions moving eastwards from the Mediterranean, apparently reinforced to a small extent by moisture drawn from the lakes and marshlands of the south and perhaps from the Persian Gulf. Along much of the Mediterranean littoral these rain-bearing depressions are intercepted by the coastal mountains, but the saddle between the northern end of Lebanon and the foothills of the Taurus allows them freer passage along the northern and eastern rim of the basin, which in consequence receives a much higher annual average than the plains to the south and west. The average aggregate in fact decreases progressively from as much as 1,000 mm. per annum in the mountains of Kurdistan to less than 100 mm. in the desert south-west of the Euphrates. The isohyet representing an annual average of 200 mm., regarded in this region as the minimum necessary for the dry farming of cereal crops, describes a great arc across the middle of the northern plain, crosses the Tigris well to the north of its junction with the Lesser Zab, and skirts the foothills of the Iranian mountains. It has been rightly emphasized, moreover, that this line does not accurately represent the realistic limits of potential cultivation, since a farmer depends not on an average of rainfall calculated over a period of years, but on the reliable minimum in any year.[2] This more stringent criterion restricts the area still further.

The economic potential of different parts of the region thus varies greatly. The flank of the Arabian massif produces transient patches of seasonal grazing, which may be supplemented by catch-crops of grain in the *wadi* beds where some moisture remains from the sporadic winter spates; it can be inhabited only by pastoral nomads. A similar situation prevails in the plain immediately to the north and north-east, although its marginally better climate, particularly on the fringes of the rainfall farming zone, encourages a semi-nomadic economy based primarily on sheep rather than on the more resistant camel. Settled agriculture is only possible in this arid area where the entrenched valleys of the

[1] We cannot say with certainty what changes, if any, have taken place in the climate of the Near East in historic times, for this requires analysis of a mass of detailed information which has not yet been collected. Where local studies have been made, relating to particular periods, no evidence of any great change has been observed after the immediately post-glacial period: e.g. H. E. Wright, Jr., in Braidwood and Howe, *SAOC*, 31. 97; S. A. Harris, *Sumer*, 17 (1961), 110. The boundaries of ancient settlement as defined by the distribution of sites nowhere significantly exceeds the limits imposed by the modern climate. It is my impression that where a recession of agriculture has taken place in historic times it can be explained on political and social grounds, although such an explanation is not necessarily the whole truth. To detect marginal variations will require the use of indicators more sensitive, and more accurately datable, than we possess at the moment.

[2] D. H. Davies, *Econ. Geog.* 33, 129 and fig. 4.

Euphrates and Tigris and their major tributaries widen sufficiently to provide irrigable bands of alluvium. At these points irrigation can be practised either by lifting the water from the river, or by digging a canal, with or without some form of barrage to supplement the natural drop in river level. Unless such works are on a very large scale, rare though not entirely unknown before the advent of modern civil engineering, the amount of land that can be brought under cultivation by this means is relatively small, being confined to a narrow strip in the valley bottom. The economic return is, however, high by comparison with the yield of rain-watered land, and one or other system has often been adopted where conditions permit.

In the alluvial plain of the south, lift or natural flow irrigation can be, and since the beginning of agriculture has been, used to water land in the immediate vicinity of the rivers, but its employment on a larger scale gives rise to major problems. Since the drop in level from the northern to the southern extremities of the plain, a distance of 700 km., is little more than 30 m., the head of a large natural flow system must often be sited a considerable distance from the land it is intended to serve. The flatness of the plain also makes the provision of effective drainage extremely difficult; the saline content of the water is high and evaporation rapid in the heat of summer, with the result that irrigation systems on the alluvium have suffered extensively both in ancient and modern times from salination which effectively destroys the fertility of the soil.[1] These problems can be overcome, but to exploit any considerable part of the potentially rich land between the rivers demands the resources of a large and well-organized community. The economy of historic societies dependent on large-scale irrigation was thus peculiarly subject to factors other than the simple dictates of their natural environment. A large labour force was necessary for the construction of extensive supply and drainage canals, and this implies a degree of social cohesion and preferably, although not inevitably, a central authority to organize and direct the work.[2] Once created, the systems must be maintained in the face of the constant natural process of silting, both in the canals and in the rivers which supply them, since flooding is the most destructive of all risks. They must also be defended, in the simple military sense. The cutting of the dykes by the Mongol invaders who overthrew the feeble Abbasid caliphate in the thirteenth century A.D., more than any other single factor, changed southern Mesopotamia from one of the richest regions of the known world into the desert we see at the present day.[3]

That part of the northern plain which lies within the rainfall zone is natural grassland and very suitable for cereal crops, but the dry-farming technique is less productive and the plain cannot, by this means alone, support as dense a population as the alluvium. It is on the other hand less sensitive to political disaster, although, as we shall see, the extent

---

[1] T. Jacobsen and R. M. Adams, 'Salt and Silt in Ancient Mesopotamian Agriculture', *Science*, 128 (1958), 1251.

[2] For a discussion of the significance of irrigation as a factor in the development of community organization, see R. M. Adams in *City Invincible*, 1960, pp. 279–80.

[3] It was not the only factor, and a considerable decline had taken place in some areas long before the Islamic period. For a detailed survey of the rise and decline of irrigated agriculture in the eastern part of the alluvium, see R. M. Adams, 'Agriculture and Urban Life in Early South-western Iran', *Science*, 136 (1962), 109–22.

of settlement on its border with the steppe reflects the degree of security which its government can provide. Here, too, irrigation has often been employed to increase the yield of riverain land, although it is noticeable that the few systems constructed on a more than local scale have not survived the governments which created and maintained them. Beyond the rim of the plain the foothills of Anatolia and the Zagros, with their fertile valleys, perennial streams, and relatively high rainfall, encourage the growing of profitable export crops such as grapes and deciduous fruits as well as cereals. They also afford hill pasture for sheep and goats, a dubious asset since these rank with charcoal burners among the principal agents of deforestation and the resultant erosion.

COMMUNICATIONS

Before we proceed to examine some salient traits of the actual pattern of occupation we must consider a third factor, the natural lines of communication which are the product of geography and climate. This chapter is largely concerned with the effect of the internal character of the region on its history. But many of the most important factors, economic and political, have their origin outside its borders, and it is important to identify the major routes which connect it with the outside world as well as the internal links between its settled areas.

Firstly, two general considerations must be put forward which control the relevance of this description to any particular historical situation. Near Eastern routes, however obvious on the map, have in the past been subject to two major limitations on their use, the availability of an adequate water-supply and the degree of security which they afford. It is a familiar experience to those who have penetrated its remoter regions by motor-car to employ a local guide who knows the track which he would take from place to place on horseback or on foot, but is unable to assess the ability of an unfamiliar vehicle to negotiate particular natural hazards. Similarly, before the days of motor transport, a major highway on the steppe had a certain capacity, dependent on the frequency and amounts of water and forage which it offered, and this capacity varied with the seasons; moreover the water of desert wells is often brackish, sometimes undrinkable except in extremity, and may have ill effects on those unaccustomed to it.[1] Certain of the desert tracks were impassable except to camels by reason of the long distances between reliable wells. Others had ample resources for the passage of a caravan or a military patrol, but were utterly inadequate for an army on the march, a distinction which one suspects was not always apparent to, or was ignored by, the local guides who must have been pressed into service.

The criterion of security affected commercial more than military routes, although we find that the memory of Carrhae long inhibited Roman army commanders from using the main arteries of trade across the northern plain of Mesopotamia. Even on commerce it operates in sometimes unexpected ways, of which a single instance may serve as a warning against too easy assumptions. The Beduin have long constituted the most obvious threat to desert trade. It might be assumed that any route which kept within the boundaries of settled land was *ipso facto* more secure and more likely to be frequented. But if we study

[1] C. P. Grant, *The Syrian Desert*, 1937, pp. 207–9.

the recent history of the Euphrates valley, the natural link between the Mediterranean coast and southern Mesopotamia, we find that the Great Desert Route of the eighteenth and nineteenth centuries consistently kept a day's or even two days' march west of the river, since the regular toll exacted by Beduin was a lesser burden than wanton plundering by the villagers of the riverain land, who enjoyed a particularly evil reputation.[1] So although the general line of traditional highways may be plotted with fair confidence, the precise location of any route at different periods may vary under the influence of local conditions. Such variations greatly affect the fortunes of individual sites, and many generalizations about the history of caravan cities have been based on the use of a small-scale map, on which a tenth of an inch represents a day's march. For this reason the description of the principal routes which follows is couched in general terms, and more specific descriptions of individual roads at particular dates will be given as they become relevant to the subject-matter of later chapters.

The heart of the system is a triangle of three major channels of communication, each composed of a number of alternative roads, which link the modern cities of Aleppo, Baghdad, and Mosul. The first, from Aleppo to Baghdad, runs along or parallel with the Euphrates valley over much of its length, and as a military route had the additional advantage of auxiliary water transport in the south-eastward direction. Between Aleppo and Mosul lies the rainfall zone of the northern plain, and there are essentially two routes, each subject to historic variations. One crosses the Euphrates in the neighbourhood of Carchemish and thence follows the northern rim of the plain through Ras al-Ain to Nisibin or, via the Khabur, to Sinjar; the other leaves the rainfall zone in preference for the upper section of the Euphrates valley, which it follows as far as the junction of the Khabur and thence turns north-east across the plain south of Sinjar. The railway now follows the Nisibin branch of the former route, the latter being the modern motor track through Deir ez-Zor known, at its eastern end, as the Tariq al-Halep. Between Mosul and Baghdad there are again two main possibilities, either the Tigris valley road which has to negotiate broken country in the north and inhospitable steppe in the south, or the long but less forbidding way through Erbil and Kirkuk which keeps within the rainfall zone almost to the Diyala valley at Baquba. Rafts supported on inflated skins were until recently used for river traffic down the Tigris, although rapids at the point where it merges into the plain render it impassable for ordinary craft.

West of the triangle lies the Syrian desert, which is crossed by a web of caravan routes radiating from Tadmor (Palmyra) to Aleppo, Homs, and Damascus in Syria, to the mouths of the Balikh and Khabur, and to Ana and Hit in the Euphrates valley. Water and pasture on these tracks is limited, but the best of them will permit the passage of a very large body of men and animals. The direct track from Damascus to Hit, on the other hand, passes through barren country south of Tadmor and in recent times was only used by the most hardy couriers. The longer and more difficult crossing of the southern desert can be accomplished by a route through Ma'an and the oasis of Jauf at the southern end of Wadi Sirhan, to the head of the Persian Gulf.[2] This formerly departed from Petra, but it

---

[1] C. P. Grant, op. cit., p. 172. [2] C. P. Grant, op. cit., p. 35.

seems probable that Nabataean prosperity depended to a greater extent on the north–south trade, passing between the Hejaz and Damascus on the old Spice Road, now the Darb al-Hajj or Pilgrim Road. The nodal points on the Syrian side of the desert, Damascus, Homs, Aleppo, all have their outlets to the Mediterranean which were the *raison d'être* of the great ports of ancient and modern times. By far the easiest of these is the saddle west of Aleppo, where the Orontes turns down to the sea. Here, too, there is ready access from the plain of Cilicia on the north-west, and it is not surprising that Antioch in the lower Orontes valley, which during the Hellenistic and Roman periods took over from Aleppo the control of this vital gap, became one of the greatest cities of the East.

The principal highway from western Anatolia through Mesopotamia crosses the Euphrates either at Birecik (Zeugma) or at Samosata further to the north, then through Urfa (Edessa) and Harran (Carrhae) joins the northern route from Aleppo to Mosul by way of Ras al-Ain. This was the Achaemenian royal road from Sardis to Susa[1] which from Mosul followed the route described above through Erbil to Baquba, where it crossed the Diyala. It then skirted the foothills of Iran, taking advantage of the oases which occur where river valleys debouch into the alluvial plain, as at Mandali and Badra. In the early second millennium B.C. a slightly different version of its north Mesopotamian sector was the road used by Assyrian traders between Kültepe in Cappadocia and their capital at Aššur, modern Sharqat, on the Tigris below Mosul. At that time it seems to have traversed the upper Khabur basin and passed across the plain south of Jebel Sinjar.[2] A third variant of this section departed from Nisibin, crossed Jebel Sinjar at the pass of Gaulat and followed the well-watered slopes of the hill-chain which continues the Sinjar range south-eastwards across the Tigris valley. This road gained the Tigris at Aššur or at the crossing point of Baiji below the Tigris gorge, from which it could follow either the river southward, or the foot of Jebel Hamrīn east of the river, bringing it eventually to the Diyala valley. Other routes from the north into Mesopotamia are those from central Anatolia through Diyarbekr and Mardin, from Bitlis west of Lake Van down the upper Tigris valley by way of Jazirat ibn Omar, and a difficult track from Van itself through the Hakkiari mountains to Amadiya and thence to Mosul.

On the east there are many passes of varying difficulty through the Zagros. From Erbil there is a way north-eastwards through the gorge of Rowanduz to the district of Lake Urmia and Tabriz. A second route from Erbil leads eastward to Qala'at Dizeh, from which one mule track goes north-east towards Lake Urmia, another south and east to Baneh.[3] A road from Kirkuk enters the plain of Sulaimaniya, from which it is possible to reach Hamadan (Ecbatana) by either of two passes, one leading to Sanandaj (Sinneh), the other south-eastwards by Halabja to Kermanshah. By far the most important route, however, is the road from Baghdad up the Diyala valley and by way of the Halwand pass, to Kermanshah and Hamadan. This was the Khorasan Road which, starting at that time from Ctesiphon just south of Baghdad, was the main artery of the Parthian and Sassanid Empires, and which has been in constant use since prehistoric times. It will be noticed

[1] Herodotus, v. 52.
[2] See below, p. 35 and n. 3.
[3] E. M. Wright, 'The Eighth Campaign of Sargon II of Assyria', *JNES*, ii (1943), 175–6.

that all the great highways meet at the northern end of the alluvial plain, and this has undoubtedly dictated the establishment, within fifty miles of one another, of the most remarkable sequence of historic capitals in the world. Agade, the city of the first Sargon, was certainly in this area although its exact location is unknown, and it was succeeded by Babylon, Dur Kurigalzu of the Kassites, Seleucia on the Tigris, Ctesiphon, and Baghdad.[1]

THE DISTRIBUTION OF POPULATION

The actual pattern of settlement, so long as the region enjoyed a prosperous economy based on agriculture, seems to have reflected the advantages and disadvantages of its component areas as they have been summarized in the first section. It is obvious that estimates of population in antiquity can be no more than intelligent guesses, and more recent population statistics clearly do not, in certain material particulars, reproduce the ancient situation. Two factors especially distort the picture, at least in the territory of modern Iraq. Southern Mesopotamia was heavily depopulated by the Mongol invasion, both as a result of the ruthless character of the conquest itself—800,000 people are said to have been slaughtered by Hulagu at the capture of Baghdad—and through the breakdown of the economy which ensued. Only in the last century has the population recovered and it is probably still below its ancient level. Secondly, its distribution is now affected by essentially modern considerations. Mechanical transport has permitted a great increase in the viable size of cities, and the introduction of industry has engendered a variety of more highly paid employment which attracts a flood of poor peasants from rural areas. In 1888 the population of Baghdad was estimated at 150,000;[2] at the time of the first accurate census in 1947 it was 364,000, by 1957 it had doubled again, and it now verges on a million persons.

Nevertheless, some notion of the main groupings of population may be derived from simple criteria such as the location and size of the principal ancient sites. Although salination had already taken serious toll of the irrigated land of the south before 1000 B.C., yet this area continued to support a concentration of cities, large and small, without parallel in the ancient world. Since no site has been completely excavated we cannot say what part of the total area of any city was occupied at any one time, or how intensive the occupation was. Nor is their impressive aspect founded only on local resources, for they lay at the focus of great trade routes, and some were imperial capitals, symbols of prestige which drew part of their sustenance from their subject provinces. But in the middle of the first millennium B.C. Sippar, Borsippa, Nippur, Lagash, Uruk, and Ur were all

[1] Nothing has been said of the internal communications of the alluvial plain itself, for these have been largely governed by variable factors such as the courses of the Tigris and Euphrates and the extent of the lakes and marshes, as well as by the location of the irrigation canals. But it is worthy of note that much traffic still goes by water, and the proportion must have been considerably higher when the great canals were navigable and there was no railway to carry heavy loads. Certainly a large part of Mesopotamia's external trade has always passed up and down the Persian Gulf, although before the coming of steam it was a seasonal affair, governed by the winds which in late summer, from June to September, brought sailing ships up the Persian Gulf. C. P. Grant, The Syrian Desert, p. 99; A. L. Oppenheim, 'The Seafaring Merchants of Ur', JAOS, 74 (1954).
[2] E. A. Wallis Budge, By Nile and Tigris, i (1920), 192.

important centres, while the Babylon of Nebuchadnezzar covered an area of 850 hectares.[1] Herodotus, writing in the middle of the fifth century B.C., says that Babylonia was the richest of the Persian provinces, and that its wealth came from agriculture; he mentions cereal crops dependent on irrigation, and the omnipresent date palm.[2] Babylon gave way to Seleucia and Ctesiphon as the metropolis, but many of the other traditional sites maintained their importance. Even after the fall of the Sassanid Empire the three original Muslim cities of Kufa, Wasit, and Basra were all sited in the alluvial plain, and Abbasid Baghdad, the greatest capital of all, was founded only 40 km. north of Ctesiphon. Under the early Abbasid caliphate the extensive Nahrawan canal system, which watered the long arc of alluvium east of the Tigris, reached the peak of its development, and the prosperous condition of the country at this time is revealed by the detailed descriptions of Arab geographers.[3]

The riverain lands of the Middle Euphrates and the lower courses of its tributaries, the Balikh and the Khabur, also lie in the irrigation zone. Their cultivable area is comparatively small and its successful exploitation is conspicuously dependent on defence against the nomads within whose territory it lies. In consequence, the people who have occupied these lands have often been of desert origin; their communities, once established, have rarely been large enough to guarantee their own defence against a massive incursion, and their history has reflected the strength or weakness of the larger states whose satellites they were. But they lie on one of the most important highways of the Near East and, given favourable conditions, have at times achieved a prosperity and assumed a cultural importance out of proportion to their size.

The next element to be considered is the people of the steppe, the modern Beduin. They have been the subject of many books which illuminate their character, and of a mystique which has done much to obscure it. Fortunately, we are here concerned less with their philosophy than with their history and, in particular, their constant interactions with their sedentary neighbours. Their only natural resources are seasonal pastures and small unreliable catch-crops of grain, and their existence is traditionally founded on their flocks and herds, on camels in the barren region and on sheep where conditions are more favourable. Water supplies are scarce but vital and, with grazing rights, form the most common cause of the feuds that divide them. Before the coming of motor transport revolutionized both the conduct of desert trade and the maintenance of law and order, this pastoral economy could be supplemented in a number of ways. Raiding was an intermittent source of wealth, with the added attraction of great social prestige; its targets included the livestock of other tribes, the settled lands and the commerce which passed between them. An alternative to robbery, sometimes scarcely to be distinguished from it, was the system whereby the tribes extended protection to their weaker neighbours, or to caravans passing through their territory, in return for payment in money or kind. In time of war between

[1] O. E. Ravn, *Herodotus' Description of Babylon*, 1942, p. 12. These cities varied greatly in size, and the larger capitals contained vast complexes of monumental buildings which distort any estimate of population based on modern densities, as in H. A. Frankfort, *Kingship and the Gods*, University of Chicago Press, 1948, p. 396, n. 23.

[2] Herodotus, i. 192.

[3] G. Le Strange, *Lands of the Eastern Caliphate*, 1905, chs. iii–v. Nahrawan canal and its towns, pp. 57–60.

states on their borders they have never been slow to exact subventions from one or both combatants in return for service which could rarely be enforced. As long as they have remained true nomads, they have not played a more active role in the organization of trade, which their lack of permanently established centres would scarcely permit and their rigid social code has, at least in recent centuries, despised. Once settled, however, they have been among the greatest merchants of history. The Aramaeans of the Euphrates region in the Late Assyrian period were probably of nomadic origin, and migrants from Arabia who settled in Petra and the oasis of Tadmor founded the prosperous Nabataean and Palmyrene kingdoms on their successive monopolies of the desert routes.

The composition of the steppe population has been far from static. Its most striking historical characteristic has been the tidal movement which brought successive waves of Beduin out of Arabia, each great tribe forcing its predecessors ever further to the north and east. This process has often been described, and is graphically embodied in the Arab proverb: 'Yemen is the cradle of the Arab and Iraq his grave.' In default of detailed records it has not been adequately explained, but its effects on the surrounding settled lands have been of great importance, and its nature merits a brief analysis. The evidence can be seen on every side, in the present distribution of the tribes and in the traditions regarding their origin. To take a modern instance, there was a threefold movement from northern Arabia beginning about A.D. 1600 with the migration of the Jubūr, who were followed in the course of the succeeding two centuries by the Shammar and the Anaiza.[1] Today fractions of the Jubūr survive in the northern and eastern fringes of the steppe, as semi-nomadic herdsmen and cultivators in the Khabur region, and as sedentary villagers in the Tigris valley below Mosul, with a smaller enclave to the north of Mosul between the villages of Zummar and Eski Mosul. Small groups of Jubūr are also to be found in the north of the alluvial plains, on the Euphrates near Hilla, the Tigris south of Baghdad, and the Diyala near Delli Abbas. On the upper Khabur and in the Mosul region they live side by side with remnants of the Tayy, one of the most aristocratic of Arabian tribes, who migrated more than a thousand years before them, and from whom some of the citizens of Mosul are proud to claim descent. The steppe now is divided between the Shammar in the north and east and the Anaiza in the south.[2] These great movements probably stem from a variety of causes of which we have only scattered indications in history and legend. To speak of mounting pressure or of overpopulation, as many writers have done, merely describes the problem without elucidating it. The Tayy, like the tribes which formed the confederacy of the banu-Ghassan on the borders of Byzantine Syria in the sixth century

[1] *Tribus nomades*, pp. 115–16, 125. C. P. Grant, *Syrian Desert*, p. 21.

[2] *Tribus nomades*, pp. 125–6; a complementary map of Beduin tribes in Syria is published in H. Field, *An Anthropological Reconnaissance in the Near East*, 1950, p. 4. Maps showing the distribution of tribes in Iraq can be found in *AGH*, figs. 66–71, and Field, *Anthropology of Iraq*, pt. i, no. 1, 1940, Supplement A.

The Tayy in Layard's day were semi-nomadic, occupying the land immediately east of the Tigris between the Greater and Lesser Zabs, raiding the Jubūr and raided by the Shammar, *Nineveh and Babylon*, 1853, pp. 168–72. The southern Jubūr probably came into the alluvial plain directly from northern Arabia rather than from the Jazira as have the Shammar Toqa, now east of the Tigris below Baghdad. An example of a small group in an arrested stage of infiltration by this route is the Tuman Shammar, who range between the Saudi Arabian frontier and the Euphrates below Kerbela, but sometimes attach themselves to one or other of the two major branches of their tribe, in Nejd or in the Jazira, *AGH*, p. 363.

A.D., are said by Arab historians to have left the Yemen after the breakdown of agriculture which followed the destruction of the Ma'rib dam.[1] Similar results might have been produced particularly among pastoral tribes by marginal climatic changes which history does not relate and archaeology cannot yet identify, for the economy of Arabia carries no insurance against a succession of lean years.[2] A contributory cause was the internecine local rivalries of which early Arab literature provides a constant record. These presumably arose in part from economic motives, but a less predictable factor which should not be underestimated in nomadic society is the great influence of the outstanding leader. Any man who can succeed by force or persuasion in overcoming the habitual disunity of a large group wields a powerful weapon for the furtherance of his own ambition. An example here may be drawn from the career of Abd ul-Aziz ibn Sa'ud, who in this century created the kingdom of Sa'udi Arabia and for a long period threatened the Rualla, an Anaiza tribe who were his neighbours on the north, and the Muntafiq of southern Iraq. It is relevant to notice that the situation was only stabilized by the superior military power of the British, who intervened in their temporary role as guardians of the settled lands.

The effect of the migrations on the sedentary communities has varied, as the last instance would suggest, with their ability to defend themselves. Rarely has it taken the form of organized invasion, and perhaps this term should only be applied to the Muslim conquest, which was unique in its speed, cohesion, and purpose. More often it was a gradual infiltration, ever ready to seize the opportunity of local weakness. Although the opportunities have been intermittent, the pressure has been constant; and it is probably reasonable to say that the breakdown of strong government and tribal encroachment go hand in hand, and that in the ill-documented historical situations with which we have to deal, where we find evidence of one we may infer the other. Sometimes, in areas of marginal fertility, this encroachment has taken the form of an episodic extension of the zone of nomadic or semi-nomadic occupation, but when the chance to penetrate into richer land has presented itself, the herdsman has frequently turned farmer. In the pre-Islamic era a successful penetration into civilized territory, particularly if preceded by a sojourn on its borders, was often followed by the adoption of its culture and even of its characteristic personal names, leaving few distinguishing marks by which we can now identify the foreign element or assess its origin and significance. In more recent times the religious and political circumstances of Islam have a contrary effect, and no townsman now fails to claim the prestige of desert ancestry. It is still possible, however, to observe the slow process of assimilation at different stages. Large areas in the south of Iraq have gone out of cultivation through neglect, mismanagement, and political insecurity, and have been taken over by tribes who are still semi-nomadic. But their principal sheikhs have often adopted a twofold existence as gentlemen of leisure in their town and country houses, while remaining tribal leaders with all the trappings of great tents and fine horses among their

---

[1] H. Field, *Anthropology of Iraq*, pt. ii, no. 1 (1951), p. 9. P. K. Hitti, *History of the Arabs*, 1953, p. 65.

[2] There appears, however, to be no evidence of a major climatic change in Arabia, A. Musil, *Northern Nejd*, 1928, pp. 304–19.

own people.[1] Indeed, many whose people have long been settled, and who are themselves prosperous townsmen or rural landlords, retain the habit of passing the summer in a tent pitched in some favoured position on their land. This preference for the open spaces, so characteristic of the transition from the desert to the sown, is of great antiquity. Many of the Umayyad caliphs would not even winter in Damascus but resided in various retreats on the fringe of the desert, at times in converted Byzantine forts, at times in mansions built on a palatial scale. They visited the capital only on business, and Walid II is even stated never to have set foot in a town; his successor Yazid III was forced to promise that he would live in Damascus and build no more, so expensive had these tastes become.[2] In this they merely continued the practice of the Ghassanids, who for long had no fixed capital, and the Lakhmids, whose abode al-Hira took its origin and its name from their encampment. The earliest Muslim cities of Iraq were likewise founded as military camps, and it was not until the secular government of Islam inherited the full grandeur of the Sassanid Empire, with the establishment of the Abbasid caliphate, that we find imperial cities on the Mesopotamian and Persian model.

The population of the rainfall zone, which skirts the northern fringe of the steppe from Syria in the west to the Iranian frontier in the east, has been affected more consistently than that of any other part of the Tigris and Euphrates basin, except the Euphrates valley itself, by the nomadic movements of which some aspects have been discussed above. The settlement of this region at various periods of ancient history forms the theme of later chapters, but we must here observe certain general characteristics, particularly of its north-eastern sector, which provide a background to the examination of specific problems. There are, as we have seen, essentially two types of landscape.[3] The first is the rolling grassland of the plain, the second the more broken country formed by the foothills of the Anatolian and Iranian plateaux, of which the outlying ridges intersect the plain itself in an interrupted chain close to its southern limit (pl. 1, *a*, *b*). The plain, under ideal conditions which have rarely been fulfilled in historic times, is a land of farming villages and small market towns, more densely populated where perennial streams or rivers increase its agricultural potential. Larger settlements occur only where they are artificially encouraged by the presence of an important road or river crossing, and these have normally provided the centres of administration. In the foothills of the plateaux on the north and east there is a dual economy based on small but fertile parcels of land in the valleys and on the pasture of the upper hill-side above the limits of terraced cultivation. There are villagers engaged in growing the crops which are especially profitable in these conditions—grapes, deciduous

---

[1] The tendency of the sheikh to lead a more sedentary life than his tribe is noted in many Syrian instances by *Les tribus nomades*, e.g. pp. 37, 85, 90, 109–10. It is worthy of note that the deliberate settlement of a tribe, a measure acceptable to the government and often in modern times encouraged by the sheikh, has tended to enhance both the latter's position and his income. As the leader of a pastoral tribe his authority is far from absolute and certainly not hereditary, although it usually remains within the limits of a large family group. If his followers turn to agriculture, the ownership of the land is vested in him and passes to his sons, and he assumes the more arbitrary powers of a great landlord. This development has of course been largely nullified by contemporary measures for the redistribution of land in Iraq, but it has been a striking social phenomenon until recent years.

[2] K. A. C. Creswell, *A Short Account of Early Muslim Architecture*, 1958, pp. 93–95.

[3] Braidwood (*SAOC*, 31) prefers a threefold division into plain, piedmont, and hilly flanks. This has obvious relevance in the study of the earliest farming communities but is less meaningful in historic times.

fruits, and, in modern times, tobacco, rice, and cotton—and there are also herdsmen with flocks of sheep, goats, and cattle. The two ways of life are not mutually exclusive although their interests obviously do not always coincide, nor indeed is there a clear distinction between the foothills and the plain. Most villages have their shepherds, and some which are situated on the edge of the hills or in the broader valleys have considerable areas of grain-bearing land as well as irrigated plots and orchards. But the Kurds, who have formed the great majority of the population in recent centuries, have always been divided in varying proportions between sedentary and nomadic tribes.

Two features of this society merit especial notice. Although the internal communications of the area are adequate to the primitive transport and limited needs of its inhabitants, there are few main routes which afford easy access from the plain. Hence military control of its population has always been difficult, and their culture has evinced the conservative tendencies of highlanders the world over. Secondly, they have not been slow to seize the opportunities to raid or to settle which have from time to time been presented by temporary weakness in the political and military organization of their lowland neighbours. Since medieval times there has been considerable penetration of the plains, demonstrated by the presence there of many Kurdish villages and even pastoral tribes. A group of settlers made conspicuous by their religion and the social cohesion arising from it are the Yezidis of northern Iraq and north-east Syria.[1] These are to be found in some villages of the plain east of the Tigris, where the principal shrine of their cult is located, in the hills of Jebel Sinjar and adjacent areas of the plain, and in smaller groups even further to the west. Their language, which is a Kurdish dialect, suggests that they came originally from the hills to the north and east, and although little is known of their history we may surmise that they occupied their present territories during the period of anarchy following the overthrow of the Abbasid caliphate. As an example of pastoral intruders we may cite the most important of the Syrian Kurdish tribes, the Milli.[2] Thirty years ago their zone of transhumance extended from their winter quarters in the hills around Mardin and Diyarbekr to their spring pastures in the plains as far south as Jebel Abd al-Aziz in north Syria. Their own traditions relate that they came originally from the Ararat region, following the conquest of western Kurdistan by Sultan Selim, and maintained themselves in virtually independent control of their new territory despite many Ottoman attempts to subdue them. In the plain they are neighbours of the Tayy, who lie to the south of Nisibin, and of the Jubūr on the lower Khabur, and they were at war in the early years of this century with the Fedān, one of the Anaiza tribes.

The distribution of Arab and Kurdish tribes in an area which for long enjoyed a prosperous agricultural economy brings out very clearly the twofold nature of the pressure to which the settled inhabitants of the northern plain have been subjected, and the inroads that have been made on them when they lacked the protection of a strong government. This is of particular relevance to the historian, since few societies have left records of their weakness and such periods are notoriously ill documented; yet the changes brought

---

[1] H. C. Luke, *Mosul and its Minorities*, 1925, pp. 122 ff.; H. Field, *The Anthropology of Iraq*, pt. 2, no. 1, pp. 67–93.   [2] *Tribus nomades*, pp. 160–2.

about under these conditions have often contributed materially to the subsequent historical and social pattern. The last five centuries afford a classic example of near-anarchy in the northern plain, from which it is only now recovering, and we are provided as never before with the documentary evidence by which its effects can be analysed. In the

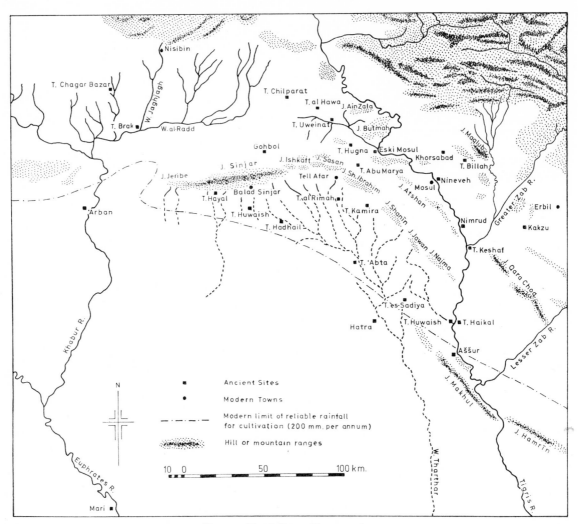

FIG. 2. North Iraq: Topography

sector with which we are primarily concerned, from the Khabur eastward to the Zagros, a closer examination of the geographical factors and of the present distribution of settlement illuminates many ancient problems.

The topography of the area is of prime importance (fig. 2). A glance at the map will show that the plain is everywhere exposed to intruders from the foothills which dominate it on the north and east, but on its border with the steppe there are natural features which have dictated to the Beduin certain well-defined routes of access. As we have already seen, each wave of nomads from Arabia has tended over a long period to force its predecessors

to the north-east across the middle Euphrates. Once past this point their seasonal migrations bring them to the borders of the rainfall zone, and if the opportunity offers they
will enter it, impelled by pressure from behind and attracted by the lure of its richer
pastures and better water supply. In doing so they have usually followed one of two
routes, either up the Khabur valley or eastwards, across the plain south of Jebel Sinjar, to
the Tigris. Direct penetration to the north between the Khabur and the Tigris is barred by
the first outlying range of hills, where Jebel Sinjar, rising as much as 1,000 m. above the
plain, is impassable except at a very few points. It is continued south-eastwards from Tell
Afar to the Tigris at Qaiyara by an intermittent chain of lower ridges, Jebel Sheikh
Ibrahim, Jebel Shanīn, Jebel Jawān, and Jebel Najma, which are less formidable than
Jebel Sinjar but still present a barrier to communication except at well-defined crossings.
The northern sector of this chain is backed by Jebel Atshan, overlooking the Tigris
valley at Mosul; parallel with Jebel Najma but further to the south is the rugged range of
Jebel Makhul, a north-westward continuation of Jebel Hamrīn and separated from it only
by the Tigris gorge. The only point at which communication between the steppe and the
Tigris north of the gorge is virtually unhindered is the saddle, some 30 km. wide, between
Jebel Najma and Jebel Makhul. This serves as a corridor linking the upper Tharthar in
the neighbourhood of Hatra with the river valley between Qaiyara and Sharqat, the site of
ancient Aššur. It is approximately at this point that the outer limit of reliable rainfall
crosses the Tigris.

The distribution of the remnants of formerly nomadic tribes, and even the habits of the
modern Shammar, reflect this geographical pattern very closely. Sections of the Tayy are
to be found at the head of the eastern tributary of the Khabur and also settled to the east
of Tell Afar. The Jubūr are on the Khabur and in villages along the Tigris valley between
Mosul and Sharqat. The northern Shammar still range as far as the Euphrates, but are
divided into two main sections, centred respectively on the Khabur basin and the steppe
south of Sinjar.[1] It is interesting to notice that the Iraqi Shammar have long used Hatra
as one of their principal spring encampments, and that when Ajil al-Yawir, their great
paramount sheikh, decided to build himself a permanent residence he chose a site on the
Tigris near the modern village of Sharqat, 8 km. north of Aššur. The present paramount
sheikh has his house at Qaiyara, where the motor road from Hatra strikes the river, but he
too is frequently to be found encamped in Hatra in the spring. The site of Hatra has other
natural advantages, including a perennial though brackish water-supply in the near-by
Wadi Tharthar, which will later be discussed in more detail. But this brief topographical
survey is sufficient to show that the choice of Hatra as a camping ground and of Sharqat
as a place of residence for the sheikh bears a rational relationship to the overall pattern
of tribal movements which may prove relevant to the ancient occupation of these two
sites.

---

[1] The present division of authority within the northern Shammar is to some extent the result of recent, and
artificial, political development. Ajil al-Yawir was
recognized by the British, who were then the mandatory
power in Iraq, as paramount sheikh, while the French
in Syria accepted Daham al-Hadi. None the less the
division reflects a real difference of migratory habit.

MODERN POPULATION DENSITIES IN NORTHERN IRAQ

The logical conclusion of our study of factors affecting recent settlement must be an examination of the comparative density of modern population in different parts of northern Iraq. For this purpose the most relevant information would, ideally, describe the state of the countryside in the late nineteenth century, for since the First World War the re-establishment of authority has brought about a rapidly accelerating change. For this period, however, no more than the passing observations of travellers are available, and we are forced to rely on the results of the first complete census, carried out in 1947.[1] Let us take as a standard of comparison the *qadha* (administrative district) of Tell Afar, which includes a cross-section of the northern plain from the edge of the steppe in the south to the foothills in the north. It includes little land which is outside the theoretical boundary of possible settled agriculture, although a considerable area was still, at the time of the census, outside the actual boundary as a result of past insecurity. It is one of the principal grain-growing districts of the northern province.[2] Its total area is 8,260 sq. km., with a rural population in 1947 of 25,600. The administrative centre of Tell Afar was a town of 20,400 inhabitants,[3] among whom 75 per cent of the males whose occupation was recorded gave it as agriculture. This is an abnormally high proportion and 50 per cent would probably be nearer the average for such towns;[4] the difference in this case may reflect the historical tendency of the Turcoman population, who are an intrusive element, to live together for mutual protection even at an inconvenient distance from their land. However that may be, there are few trades or crafts in these country towns which are not specifically related to the needs of the agricultural economy, and we may fairly say that it supported directly or indirectly almost the whole population of the *qadha*, some 46,000 people. This gives an overall ratio of 5·6 per sq. km., but the distribution outside the town was strikingly uneven, ranging from 7·2 per sq. km. north of Jebel Sinjar to 2·0 in the south. The *qadha* of Sinjar further to the west contains a significant area of uncultivable land which distorts the figures for its southern part, and has been even more exposed to the intrusion of Beduin from the southern steppe and the Khabur basin; here the overall ratio dropped to 1·9, but north of Jebel Sinjar it remained relatively high at 6·6. In the triangle of land between Tell Afar and Mosul in the north and Sharqat in the south, which is partially shielded from the steppe by the south-eastward continuation of Jebel Sinjar, we find that the ratio diminished progressively from 8·4 in the north to 4·8 in the *nahiya* (sub-district) of Sharqat itself, which lies on the border of the rainfall zone.

The plain east of the Tigris presents a very different picture. The greater part of it has rarely been exposed to the penetration of nomads from the steppe, and such Arab tribal elements as are found there live in villages; these would approximately reproduce the

---

[1] Published by the Directorate-General of Census, Govt. of Iraq, and usefully summarized in H. Field, *An Anthropological Reconnaissance*, 1950, pp. 67–70.

[2] Cf. H. Field, *Anthropology of Iraq*, pt. 2, no. 1, pp. 10–11.

[3] The population of Mosul, the provincial capital, in 1947 was 213,300; in 1889 it was estimated at 63,000 (Budge, *By Nile and Tigris*, ii. 47).

[4] *The Economic Development of Iraq*, International Bank for Reconstruction and Development, 1952, p. 128.

pattern of settlement which existed before their arrival, though perhaps not its original intensity. In the same way the Kurdish villages may be assumed to have taken the place of similar, perhaps larger, units. Here it is interesting to note the modern settlement densities of two *nahiyas* which between them occupy the country east of the river from the first range of foothills in the north to the Greater Zab in the south, and include the immediate territory of three successive capitals of ancient Assyria, Khorsabad, Nineveh, and Nimrud. In the *nahiya* of Tell Kaif, around Khorsabad, the ratio in 1947 was 29·5 persons per sq. km., while in the *nahiya* of Hamdaniya, stretching from Nineveh to the Greater Zab and including Nimrud, the figure was 29·3.[1] Between the Greater and the Lesser Zabs we again approach the limits of the rainfall zone, although parts of the district obtain a marginal advantage from the presence of the massive Jebel Makhmur or Jebel Qara Choq, an eroded ridge some 40 km. east of the Tigris, and there are many villages along the two rivers. The *qadha* of Makhmur yielded ratios of 8·3 and 13·5 in two of its subdivisions, 18·9 in the third *nahiya*, Quwair on the south side of the Greater Zab. It is notable that once again a markedly greater density of modern population coincides, at least in part, with the territory of an Assyrian city, Kakzu.[2]

The geography of Assyrian settlement will be discussed more fully in the following chapters, but it will be useful to conclude this section with a short note on the limitations of such modern evidence as has just been cited. The figures which form the basis of these calculations included the whole population of the countryside in 1947, not only farmers but shopkeepers, artisans, and administrative officials, and their usefulness depends in part on the assumption, stated above, that an insignificant section of the modern population was not directly or indirectly supported by the agricultural economy. The evidence for this is largely personal observation, and any more reliable criterion would involve an exhaustive classification of individuals for which the facts are not available. But since we do not distinguish between the farmer and the shopkeeper, it is not possible to deduce any figures for the average size of peasant holdings in particular areas, which in fact vary in accordance with the dictates of an involved and arbitrary system of land tenure. We cannot therefore say how closely present densities approach the theoretical maxima for particular types of land, and we have no basis for estimating even a maximum figure for the ancient population, still less an actual total at any particular period. The usefulness of these figures lies in the pattern they establish, which can be reasonably regarded as the result of interaction between two variables, fertility and security, both governed to some extent by geographical considerations. This pattern might be called the pattern of

[1] The relative security of settlement in this area is also illustrated by the fact that Tell Kaif and Hamdaniya are the only country districts in the plain where a Christian population of significant size has survived since pre-Islamic times.

[2] The only districts in northern Iraq which approached these figures were those which stretch over the more naturally favoured parts of the Kurdish hills. Amadiya, which includes a part of the upper valley of the Greater Zab in the extreme north-eastern corner of Iraq, showed a ratio of 18·5 persons per sq. km., and Zakho, in the valley of another river called Khabur, an eastern confluent of the Tigris near the Turkish frontier, a figure of 22·0. Shaqlawa, in a particularly rich valley immediately to the north-east of Erbil (ancient Arbela), had a density of 21·6. Here again we may note that both the Greater Zab valley north of Amadiya and the Zakho district have a considerable Christian population.

resilience, for it represents the relative ability of different areas to maintain a prosperous economy through five centuries of virtual anarchy. In this respect alone it may be of value as a standard of comparison in ancient situations, but its value is increased by its relevance to precisely the periods of upheaval for which we have so little contemporary evidence.

II

AŠŠUR, NINEVEH, AND THE ORIGINS OF ASSYRIA

THE SITES OF AŠŠUR AND NINEVEH

SOME facts about the position of Aššur have emerged in the last chapter. It lies on the Tigris, 100 km. south of Mosul, at a point where the valley broadens to a bowl some 5 km. in diameter, affording an expanse of alluvial land which can profitably be cultivated by irrigation. It is, however, close to the edge of the rainfall zone and rain-fed crops are unreliable. The inhabitants of many villages in the bowl consequently rely on outside employment to supplement their income; in particular, some of the men and boys are to be found working as skilled pick men on archaeological excavations all over Iraq. This gives the archaeologist some insight into the workings of their economy, and it is noticeable that the individuals who stay at home are usually those whose families have by fortune or good management acquired a share in an irrigation pump. Many quarrels can be traced to disputes over irrigation, and at times when discipline is lax internal jealousies are often manifested by damage to the pumps. The present population are for the most part settled members of the Jubūr tribe, but sheep still play an important part in their economy and individual members of a family may drive its flock considerable distances in search of summer pastures. The sheikh of this branch of the Jubūr lives at Qaiyara, further up the valley, but at Sharqat itself is a mansion formerly belonging to Sheikh Ajil al-Yawir of the Shammar, the first leader of his tribe to urge upon them the advantages of sedentary life. The relative poverty of the area at the present day is reflected in its low population density (4·8 per sq. km.), although this is naturally higher in the valley itself, and by its present administrative unimportance; the village of Sharqat, 8 km. north of ancient Aššur, is the headquarters of a *nahiya*, the smallest of the administrative divisions.

Some features of its position, however, help to explain the contrast between its ancient and modern status and its special character in the Assyrian period. It is situated on a spur of Jebel Khanuqa, the northern outlier of Jebel Makhul, overlooking the river. Jebel Makhul is a formidable barrier to traffic on the valley road from the south, and the road is obliged to skirt the foot of the range north-westward until it reaches the first crossing point, a saddle which leads it back to the river at Aššur. This is in fact the line taken by the modern highway, from Baghdad to Mosul, which descends from Jebel Khanuqa immediately beneath the west wall of the ancient city. North-west of Aššur lies the corridor between Jebel Makhul and Jebel Najma, which is used by the modern railway to regain the valley just south of Qaiyara. Through the corridor in ancient times passed two important caravan routes, one leading via the upper Tharthar across the plain south of Jebel Sinjar to the Khabur valley, the second skirting the hills north-westwards to the region of Tell Afar and thence to Nisibin. Northwards from Aššur a road runs over broken country, sometimes descending into the river valley, sometimes taking to the hills, to Mosul and Nineveh. A somewhat easier parallel route exists on the east bank, but this involves the crossing of the Greater Zab near its mouth.[1] On the left bank of the Tigris gently undulating country stretches north-east to the foot of the second great hill-chain, Jebel Makhmur or Qara Choq, and eastwards to the valley of the Lesser Zab. Access to Aššur on this side presents few difficulties, and the principal track now leads to the large village of Makhmur in a fold of the hills, and thence to Erbil or Altun Köprü at the crossing of the Lesser Zab. The population of Makhmur district is divided between Kurds from the foothills on the east and Arabs, who claim affiliation with originally Beduin tribes, on the west, suggesting that movements have taken place from both directions.

We can thus deduce certain historical characteristics of the site, which are confirmed by modern observation. Aššur is not an obvious capital for the fertile land of the rainfall zone. It is both geographically and economically on the fringe of the main concentration of population, and it is open to the intrusion of nomads from the steppe, either as raiders or as settlers. Its local resources alone are too circumscribed to permit the establishment of a community large enough to defend itself against this threat. It has, however, positive attractions. To the nomad it is an accessible and pleasant spot for the headquarters of a tribe in the process of settlement, with the additional advantage of profitable control of important routes.[2] Its position on these routes would also recommend it as an outpost for the settled populations of the north or the south. The same considerations gave it military significance at times when political control of the rainfall zone and of the southern alluvium

---

[1] The history of the Tigris valley routes in Islamic times is of some interest. The Abbasid post-road followed the east bank northward from Samarra through Jabiltâ, a little to the north of Takrit, and crossed the Lesser Zab at as-Sinn, the Greater Zab just to the south of Haditha. All these were considerable towns, but none of them now exists. Nor have their sites been certainly identified, although the indications afforded by the route-books locate them within narrow limits. (G. Le Strange, *Lands of the Eastern Caliphate*, p. 91). The reason for their disappearance must be the centuries of insecurity which followed on the downfall of the Abbasid caliphate and laid the Tigris valley open to intruders from the steppe in search of pasture and of booty. Although the west bank route was used by individual travellers, under escort, in the nineteenth century as the quickest way from Baghdad to Mosul, Layard, who took this road in 1851, says that Takrit was then under siege by the Beduin, and food was almost unobtainable. (*Nineveh and Babylon*, p. 579.) In 1847 he had visited Sharqat of which he comments, 'The position of Kalah Sherghat is well suited to a permanent settlement. The lands around are rich, and could be irrigated without much labour. If the population of Mesopotamia were more settled than it now is, the high road between Mosul and Baghdad would be carried along the western bank of the Tigris; and Kalah Sherghat might soon become a place of importance,

both as a station and as a post of defence. At present, caravans, carrying trade between these two cities, are compelled to make a considerable detour to the east of the river. They pass through the towns of Arbil and Kerkouk, and skirt the Kurdish hills, to avoid the Arab tribes of Tai and Obeid.' Of Sharqat itself he also wrote that 'the vicinity is notoriously dangerous, being a place of rendezvous for all plundering parties, whether of the Shammar, the Aneyza or the Obeid'. (*Nineveh and its Remains*, ii. 62, 44–45.) He himself visited it under the protection of a sheikh of the Jubūr. The year was unusually dry, and the Jubūr could find there no pasture for their flocks, so they left a few people to cultivate millet at Nimrud while the sheikh and the greater part of the tribe migrated to the upper Khabur near Nisibin (ibid., p. 67). It has already been noted that in Layard's day much of the Makhmur plain east of Sharqat was occupied by the semi-nomadic Tayy. I know of no better illustration of the effect of insecurity on the Tigris valley in general, and the site of Aššur in particular.

[2] For the exactions of Beduin on this route in the last century, see Layard, *Nineveh and its Remains*, ii. 62; Gertrude Bell, *Amurath to Amurath*, 1924, p. 216. The inhabitants of Takrit in Layard's day levied a burdensome tax on passing rafts taking corn from the Makhmur region to Baghdad (*Nineveh and Babylon*, p. 467).

were, as for the most part they have been until medieval times, in different hands, for it could serve either zone as a frontier fortress.

The position of Nineveh demands less comment, as its claim to be the natural centre of the well-favoured eastern part of the rainfall zone admits less qualification. It lies on one of the best, certainly the most frequented of the Tigris crossings. Its local communications are easy in any direction, and it is the focus of greater routes serving all the other settled regions of the Near East. It is surrounded on all sides by a broad belt of fertile and well-watered country which will support a prosperous economy and a considerable population, and which also serves to insulate the city itself from attack either from the hills on the north and east or from the steppe on the south-west. This has not, of course, ensured complete inviolability. It could obviously be penetrated by armies in times of war, although the resources of the area were normally adequate for its military defence. The effect of such insulation is rather to mitigate the impact of piecemeal incursion, so that intruders who may have taken advantage of temporary weakness become a settled and prosperous part of the economy, able to play a constructive role in its maintenance. Thus we cannot expect that the ethnic composition of the population will remain static, although the economy of the city and its hinterland is not normally subject to drastic changes. This is again borne out by modern conditions. We have observed that the land immediately to the east of Nineveh now supports by far the highest density of population in the north, despite a prolonged period of weak government under the Turkish Empire. Yet among the sedentary population we find the adherents of three different religions, Islam, Christianity, and the Yezidi creed, and four major linguistic groups, Arabic, Kurdish, Assyrian which in the modern sense is a colloquial Syriac, and Turki. Neither of these criteria is evidence for ethnic origin in the strictest sense, but both reflect the different origins of various elements in society and are a valid illustration of the general point. Diversity of language is a particularly relevant indicator, since it is almost our only guide to the composition of early historic societies.

HISTORICAL AND ARCHAEOLOGICAL EVIDENCE

Let us now consider the history and archaeology against this background. The literary evidence is of two types. For a short period of some two centuries we have detailed, though not entirely coherent, evidence from a number of sources. The royal correspondence of Mari,[1] Tell Hariri on the Middle Euphrates, dates in part from the reign of Šamši-Addu I of Assyria, who came to Aššur as a conqueror about 1820 B.C. and later gained control of Mari, where his son Iasmaḫ-Addu was his viceroy.[2] Most of the letters are later, and

---

[1] The Mari letters are in course of publication, *Archives royales de Mari* (texts in transliteration and translation), 1950 ff., under the direction of A. Parrot and G. Dossin.

[2] In this account I have adopted the chronology first suggested by Sidney Smith, *Alalakh and Chronology*, 1940, where the reign of Ḥammurabi of Babylon is dated 1792–1750 B.C. This is still open to objection, however, and B. Landsberger is clearly right is saying

that no final conclusion can yet be reached (*JCS*, viii (1954), 120). In order not to convey an impression of precision which I believe to be unjustified, I have given dates in round numbers except in discussing the figures used by Assyrian scribes (p. 27, n. 3 below). In the latter case arithmetical calculations require that the figures shall be precisely stated, but it is obvious that they are subject to any margin of error that may have been present in their source.

relate to the time when, after Šamši-Addu's death, Mari regained its independence under Zimri-Lim, a member of the original ruling family, but these too give some information about Assyrian affairs. The Mari correspondence is supplemented by a much smaller collection of tablets found at Chagar Bazar in the Upper Khabur basin, which also lay within the domain of Šamši-Addu and may have been his alternate capital, Šubat-Enlil.[1] We also have the business archives of a colony of Assyrian merchants established at Kaniš (Kültepe north of Kayseri) for about two centuries before the time of Šamši-Addu.[2] These documents shed invaluable light on the conditions prevailing in Upper Mesopotamia during the limited time to which they relate, but they also emphasize our ignorance of preceding and succeeding periods. Secondly, a bare skeleton of the history of Assyria is provided by the Assyrian King List, of which extant copies date from the tenth to the eighth centuries B.C.[3] This is in places corroborated and slightly amplified by building inscriptions, of which a small number date from the early period, while others are records of the reconstruction of early buildings by kings of the Late Assyrian Empire who make dutiful reference to the work of their predecessors.[4]

This documentary material has been intensively examined in recent years and its outstanding problems are a matter for the specialists, but it is necessary to summarize the conclusions that have been reached. For the earliest period we have to rely principally on the scanty traditions embodied in the King List, but analysis of these has yielded some interesting results. It begins with a list of seventeen names, followed by an explanatory note: 'Total of seventeen kings who lived in tents.' Unfortunately the linguistic affiliation of these names is not generally agreed,[5] but it seems probable that they are largely, if not exclusively, Semitic. Since the rulers are stated to have been nomads it is unlikely that the names derived from any better source than oral tradition, and probable that the list is far from complete.[6] Indeed the compiler of the King List does not claim to give more than a group of names, with no statement of their relationship one to another, and no

[1] C. J. Gadd, 'Tablets from Chagar Bazar and Tall Brak', *Iraq*, vii (1940), 22 ff. The identification of Chagar Bazar with Šubat Enlil was suggested by B. Landsberger (*Belleten*, 14, 1950, 252). Although not in accordance with Gadd's original view, it is supported by an itinerary published by A. Goetze (*JCS*, vii (1953), 51–72).

[2] An account of the Assyrian trading settlements in Cappadocia appears in A. Goetze, *Kleinasien*, 1957, pp. 67–81; bibliography, pp. 67–69.

[3] A. Poebel, 'The Assyrian King List from Khorsabad', *JNES*, i (1942), 247 ff., 460 ff.; *JNES*, ii (1943), 56 ff. I. J. Gelb, 'Two Assyrian King Lists', *JNES*, xiii (1954), 209 ff. Commentary, with especial reference to chronological problems, B. Landsberger, 'Assyrische Königsliste und "Dunkles Zeitalter"', *JCS*, viii (1954), 31 ff., 46 ff., 106 ff. The King Lists derive some chronological authority from the fact that they appear to have been extracted from lists of eponymous annual officials or *limmu*. The survival of these lists from a very early period is implied by references to *limmu* in surviving copies of the King Lists, but like

all tablets they were subject to damage and some lacunae are admitted by the later scribes. See also M. B. Rowton, *CAH*, i. ch. vi (1962), 24–26.

[4] The latter texts are more reliable than their late date would suggest, since they probably derive their information from original inscriptions found in the course of repairs. In certain particulars, however, they appear to rely on the authority of the current king list, and thus share its occasional misconceptions and defects.

[5] S. Smith, *The Early History of Assyria*, 1928, p. 112, 'it is clear that they are not Semitic'. A. Poebel, *JNES*, i. 252, 'certainly of Semitic origin'. B. Landsberger, *JCS*, viii. 109, n. 206, 'The majority are Akkadian or Akkadianised'. Ušpia and Kikkia occur as the names of private individuals in the Cappadocian texts, S. Smith, op. cit., p. 139.

[6] The name of a ruler of the Agade period, Ititi, occurs in a dedication to Ištar found at Aššur. B. Landsberger considers Ititi to be Semitic, *ZA*, xxxv (1924), 220 ff., but there is no other evidence to indicate his place in the sequence. He may have been an Agade governor.

The Aššyrian King List and related evidence for Assyrian settlement at Aššur

THE KING LIST

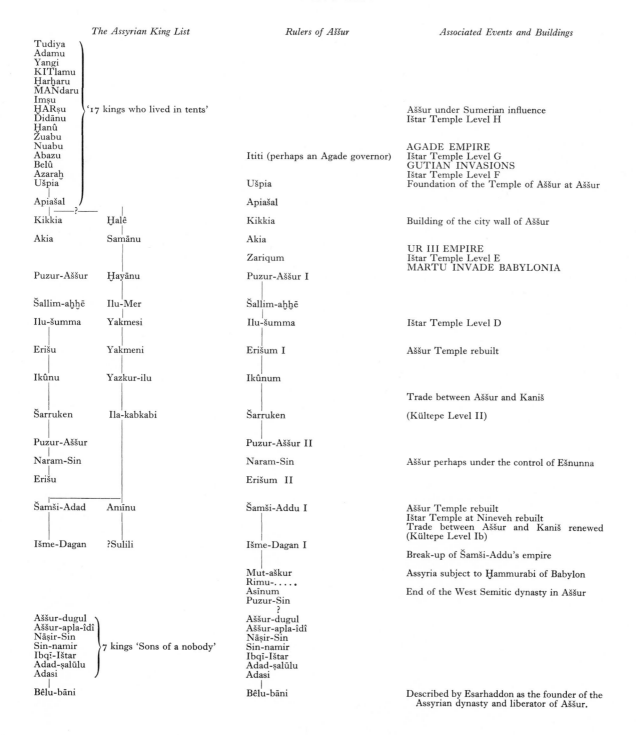

The Assyrian King List		Rulers of Aššur	Associated Events and Buildings
Tudiya			
Adamu			
Yangi			
KITlamu			
Ḫarḫaru			
MANdaru			
Imṣu			
ḪARṣu	'17 kings who lived in tents'		Aššur under Sumerian influence
Didānu			Ištar Temple Level H
Ḫanû			
Žuabu			
Nuabu			AGADE EMPIRE
Abazu		Ititi (perhaps an Agade governor)	Ištar Temple Level G
Belû			GUTIAN INVASIONS
Azaraḫ			Ištar Temple Level F
Ušpia		Ušpia	Foundation of the Temple of Aššur at Aššur
Apiašal	——?	Apiašal	
Kikkia	Ḫalê	Kikkia	Building of the city wall of Aššur
Akia	Samānu	Akia	
		Zariqum	UR III EMPIRE
			Ištar Temple Level E
			MARTU INVADE BABYLONIA
Puzur-Aššur	Ḫayānu	Puzur-Aššur I	
Šallim-aḫḫē	Ilu-Mer	Šallim-aḫḫē	
Ilu-šumma	Yakmesi	Ilu-šumma	Ištar Temple Level D
Erišu	Yakmeni	Erišum I	Aššur Temple rebuilt
Ikûnu	Yazkur-ilu	Ikûnum	
			Trade between Aššur and Kaniš
Šarruken	Ila-kabkabi	Šarruken	(Kültepe Level II)
Puzur-Aššur		Puzur-Aššur II	
Naram-Sin		Naram-Sin	Aššur perhaps under the control of Ešnunna
Erišu		Erišum II	
Šamši-Adad	Amīnu	Šamši-Addu I	Aššur Temple rebuilt
			Ištar Temple at Nineveh rebuilt
			Trade between Aššur and Kaniš renewed
			(Kültepe Level Ib)
Išme-Dagan	?Sulili	Išme-Dagan I	Break-up of Šamši-Addu's empire
		Mut-aškur	Assyria subject to Ḫammurabi of Babylon
		Rimu-.....	
		Asīnum	End of the West Semitic dynasty in Aššur
		Puzur-Sin	
		?	
Aššur-dugul		Aššur-dugul	
Aššur-apla-îdî		Aššur-apla-îdî	
Nāṣir-Sin		Nāṣir-Sin	
Sin-namir	7 kings 'Sons of a nobody'	Sin-namir	
Ibqī-Ištar		Ibqī-Ištar	
Adad-ṣalūlu		Adad-ṣalūlu	
Adasi		Adasi	
Bêlu-bāni		Bêlu-bāni	Described by Esarhaddon as the founder of the Assyrian dynasty and liberator of Aššur.

chronological deduction can be based on such evidence. The interesting fact, however, is that Assyrian tradition firmly believed in the nomadic origin of the early rulers of Aššur.[1] This group is followed in the list by a genealogical table of eleven West Semitic names, beginning with the latest, Amīnu son of Ila-kabkabi, and tracing his descent from Ḥalê, who is stated to have been the son of Apiašal, son of Ušpia; Apiašal and Ušpia are the last two names of the kings who lived in tents. It has been convincingly suggested that the names from Amīnu to Ḥalê are an interpolation, since the father of the later West Semitic king Šamši-Addu I was also named Ila-kabkabi, and this may be an attempt to give Šamši-Addu a lineal connexion with Ušpia and the nomad kings to which he is not entitled.[2] Independent evidence suggests that an Amīnu may have been Šamši-Addu's brother,[3] and it seems probable that the eleven West Semitic names should be deleted from the King List since they were not rulers of Aššur. If this is done, we find three names of uncertain, though again possibly Semitic, type—Sulili, Kikkia, and Akia—following directly on Apiašal, and then three unmistakably Akkadian names, Puzur-Aššur I, Šallim-aḫḫē, and Ilušumma. Of these six the compiler states that 'Their names appear on bricks but their eponyms are unknown'. Puzur-Aššur I, Šallim-aḫḫē, and Ilušumma are, however, established as father, son, and grandson by a building inscription.[4] The list continues with six more Akkadian names, Erišum I, Ikūnum, Šarruken (Sargon), Puzur-Aššur II, Naram-Sin, and Erišum II, who are all stated to be in direct line of descent from Ilušumma. Here

[1] The original objection to this view was put forward by S. Smith, *Early History of Assyria*, pp. 108–17, long before the King Lists containing this statement came to light, and has since been followed by S. A. Pallis, *Antiquity of Iraq*, Copenhagen, 1956, p. 584. One of the grounds on which the objection was based was the existence of a calendar, in which the names of the fourth and fifth months, *Kuzalli* and *Allanate*, were translated by S. Smith (p. 117) 'the month of the gourd' and 'the month of the terebinth', and regarded as evidence that the Assyrians were engaged in specialized agriculture before their appearance in the Tigris valley. These translations do not appear to be widely accepted; see B. Landsberger, 'Der Kultische Kalendar der Babylonier und Assyrer', *LSS*, vi (1915), 89; S. Langdon, *Babylonian Menologies and the Semitic Calendars*, Schweich Lectures, British Academy, London, 1934, pp. 33–34; J. Lewy, 'The Assyrian Calendar', *Archiv orientální*, xi (1939), 37–41. It must be emphasized, however, that the simple view of nomad settlement, against which Smith inveighed, bears very little relation to reality as it can be observed in the present or reconstructed at certain periods in the past. The Muslim conquest was a special case, and even then the transition from nomadic to settled life was by no means as rapid or as complete as it is often represented. In circumstances when these special considerations were not present, the process has been even more gradual and subject to variable political factors that might accelerate, halt, or reverse it at any time. Simple statements about the way of life of the true Beduin are often both inaccurate and irrelevant, for their society represents a complex adjustment to a highly specialized and rigorous economy, much of which cannot be carried over into settled life. Modern analogy suggests that it is in the intermediate stage, when a particular group of nomads is on the borders of and in close contact with the settled land, that they have most influence on its history and are themselves influenced by its economic and social order, and it is this important and often prolonged period of interaction and assimilation that has been neglected by historians. A fundamental study of the literary evidence for nomad tribes in this period is J.-R. Kupper, *Les Nomades en Mésopotamie au temps des rois de Mari*, 1957; reviewed by I. J. Gelb, 'The Early History of the West Semitic Peoples', *JCS*, xv (1961), 27 ff.; a summary account by Kupper may be found in *CAH*, ii, ch. i (1963), 26–30; also 'Le rôle des nomades dans l'histoire de la Mésopotamie ancienne', *JESHO*, ii (1959), 113–27.

[2] B. Landsberger, *JCS*, viii, 33–34. It has recently been pointed out that many of the names in this section of the King List are in rhyming pairs, a circumstance which casts a further doubt on their usefulness (W. W. Hallo, 'Zariqum', *JNES*, xv (1956), 221). Šamši-Addu was regarded by his later successors as one of the great kings of Assyria, and they would naturally have wished to establish his legitimacy.

[3] B. Landsberger, *JCS*, viii. 34 and n. 20; Kupper, *Nomades*, p. 211, n. 1.

[4] *LAR*, i. 13; an inscribed brick from Aššur.

an error is suspected, for there is some reason to identify Naram-Sin with the ruler of that name from Ešnunna, Tell Asmar in the Diyala valley, and we may plausibly regard Naram-Sin as representing at Aššur the foreign domination of Ešnunna.[1] After the name of Erišum II, who was probably a member of the native dynasty, follows the longest of the rare historical notes in the King List.

> Šamši-Addu, son of Ila-kabkabi at the time of Naram-Sin to Karduniaš (Babylonia) he went. In the eponymy of Ibni-Adad Šamši-Addu from Karduniaš he came up, Ekallāte he seized, and three years in Ekallāte he resided. In the eponymy of Atamar-Ištar Šamši-Addu from Ekallāte he came up, Erišu son of Naram-Sin he deposed from the throne, the throne he seized, and thirty-three years he ruled.

The next entry records the reign of Išme-Dagan, son of Šamši-Addu and, as we know from the Mari letters, viceroy of Ekallātum during his father's lifetime. Then followed, according to the two complete versions of the King List, a period of confusion; seven kings are named and each is described as 'Son of a nobody', the customary designation of a usurper. Another version, however, which is preserved only in a fragmentary text from Aššur, gives after Išme-Dagan the names of two further kings of this family, and this is supported by a building inscription from Aššur in which Puzur-Sin, a name unknown to the King List in this period, records the overthrow of the grandson of Šamši-Addu, 'a foreigner not of Assyrian blood', who had according to Puzur-Sin desecrated a temple precinct by the erection of his palace.[2] These conflicting accounts can plausibly be reconciled by supposing that there were at the same time rival claimants to the throne and that the divergence of later records reflects different traditions of legitimacy. However that may be, the significant feature of Šamši-Addu's dynasty is that all its members, and the whole line of his ancestors, bore West Semitic names. From this point onwards the King List presents no major problems. The last of the usurpers whom it names was Adasi, succeeded on the throne by Bêlu-bāni his son and thenceforward by a long list of kings bearing Akkadian names. It was to Adasi that Esarhaddon in the seventh century ascribed the foundation of the Assyrian kingship,[3] and although this may involve an element of special pleading for the legitimacy of his own immediate forebears, there seems little reason to doubt that the succession did from the time of Adasi stay within the limits of one family, even if on occasion it passed to a collateral branch.[4]

---

[1] A. Goetze, *JCS*, vii. 59; cf. B. Landsberger, *JCS*, viii. 35, n. 24.

[2] Both texts are cited by B. Landsberger, *JCS*, viii. 31–33.

[3] Adasi, who came to the throne about 1700 B.C., is described by Esarhaddon as a son of BAL.TIL[ki], an ideogrammatic writing which was regarded in later times as the Sumerian equivalent of the city name Aššur: A. Poebel, *JNES*, i. 263; J. Lewy, *HUCA*, xix (1946), 467 ff., esp. n. 305. The Sumerian writing seems to have been commonly employed by Late Assyrian scribes as a conscious archaism in many contexts and may have no special significance here, but the point of Esarhaddon's reference is surely to claim that Adasi, last of the usurpers, was of the old Assyrian stock. Precisely what he meant may have been no clearer to him than it is to us.

[4] A possible exception to this continuity is the accession of Tiglath-Pileser III, Esarhaddon's great-grandfather (*AfO*, ix (1933–4), 79). There is no evidence who Tiglath-Pileser was, but he may have been a member of the royal house; it is characteristic of Assyrian history that we know virtually nothing of the family antecedents of its great men apart from the king himself. His son Shalmaneser V is described as of the dynasty of BAL.TIL (Babylonian King List A, col. iv, *ANET*, p. 272).

EARLY LEVELS AT ASŠUR

The archaeological evidence complements the King List. Both at Asšur and at Nineveh it suffers from the limitations common to large city sites with a long period of occupation, for the early levels are buried beneath an accumulation of later monumental buildings which it is often undesirable and always expensive to remove. Nevertheless both sites have yielded relevant stratigraphic and epigraphic information. On the site of the temple of Ištar at Asšur Andrae identified a succession of five early building levels dated to the third and early second millennia B.C.[1] The first two, Levels H and G, together represent a temple with a wealth of statuary which has many parallels in the Third Early Dynastic period at Khafaje and Tell Asmar on the Diyala and at Mari. One find, however, a small alabaster head from Level G, is in the style of the succeeding Agade period and must prove that Level G lasted into this time.[2] It was destroyed by fire, and the ruins of the temple were overlaid in Level F by the stone foundations of small and poorly constructed buildings. Then in Level E the temple was rebuilt on an impressive scale, and we find the first epigraphic evidence in the form of a dedication by Zarīqum, governor of Asšur, for the life of his sovereign Amar-Sin, third king of the Third Dynasty of Ur. We know from the records of the great storehouse of this dynasty at Tell Drehem that Zarīqum, as governor of Asšur, was making deliveries to the government commissariat from the forty-eighth year of Šulgi to the fifth year of Amar-Sin, and that after this date he was transferred to the governorship of Susa.[3] The reconstruction of the Ištar temple of Level E may thus be dated before the fifth year of Amar-Sin, that is about the middle of the twenty-first century B.C. The next reconstruction, Level D, is attested by a building inscription of one of the kings named in the King List, Ilušumma son of Šallim-aḫḫē, whose date is discussed below but may be given as approximately a century after Level E. The upper levels do not add to our information about this period, since Level C is undated, and Level B was the work of Adad-nirari I about 1300 B.C.

The early history of two other structures, the temple of Asšur and the city wall, is also relevant since they are important features of the settlement and might be expected to reflect its development. Andrae was hampered in his exploration of the archaic Asšur temple by the presence of a Turkish police post which partially covered the site,[4] but a number of inscriptions were found which reflect, at the least, later notions of its history founded on tradition or on early records. It was said to have been founded by Ušpia who appears in the King List as the last but one of the nomad kings, and it was restored after his time by Ilušumma and his son Erišum I, and by Šamši-Addu I.[5] The city wall was frequently strengthened and repaired throughout the history of the city, and it is difficult to ascribe particular elements of a complicated architectural sequence to their builders, but the inscriptions again yield a number of early names. Its original construction was ascribed to Kikkia, second of the sedentary rulers and the third after Ušpia in the order of

[1] W. Andrae, *Das wiedererstandene Assur*, 1938, pp. 72–79.

[2] W. Andrae, op. cit., *Taf.* 36, d, e.

[3] W. W. Hallo, *JNES*, xv. 220–5.

[4] W. Andrae, op. cit., pp. 82–88. Gertrude Bell, *Amurath to Amurath*, pp. 222–3, visited the site while excavations were in progress.

[5] *LAR*, i. 18, 41.

the King List, as amended by the deletion of Šamši-Addu's genealogy. Later additions and repairs were made by Ilušumma and Erišum I, Ikûnum and his son Sargon I, and Šamši-Addu I.[1]

This evidence, although incomplete and subject to the possible defects of tradition, leads to certain general conclusions. There was a settlement at Aššur from the Third Early Dynastic Period onwards, it was large and prosperous enough to maintain at least one major temple, and its cultural connexions were originally with the south, although this of course implies nothing about the mass of its population. We should certainly expect this early settlement to have had a city wall. It came to a violent end at some time after the beginning of the Agade dynasty, and was succeeded by a relatively impoverished period of occupation. A revival of prosperity came under the political control of the Third Dynasty of Ur, and not long after this time we find the first of a long line of kings of Aššur attested by contemporary documents. The major problem is clearly the date of Ušpia and Kikkia, and the significance of the belief, implicit in the King List and building records, that these two rulers coincided with the first settlement at Aššur of the nomad dynasty whom the later Assyrians regarded as their forebears.

DATE OF THE FIRST ASSYRIAN SETTLEMENT

The combined framework of archaeological and documentary evidence leaves little room for the original Assyrian settlement between the end of the Ur III hegemony about 2020 B.C. and Šamši-Addu I, since the chronological statements of later Assyrian kings imply the use of a source, compiled at least as early as the thirteenth century, which made it possible to calculate the dates in Assyrian terms of Šamši-Addu's predecessors Ilušumma and Erišum I. This source was not necessarily accurate and certainly cannot be regarded as incontrovertible proof of the real dates of these rulers or of Šamši-Addu himself. On the other hand, it was probably an annual eponym list, or a king list derived from it, and must carry some weight; the figures it yields should not be radically altered without very much better external evidence than we at present possess.[2] If we make the single assumption that one thirteenth-century scribe was guilty of a logical error in the use of his king list, then it can be shown that the data used by all the scribes were mutually consistent, and that they yield a date for Erišum I about 2020–1980 B.C. in our reckoning.[3]

---

[1] *LAR*, i. 19.

[2] Cf. M. B. Rowton, *CAH*, i, ch. vi. 24–26.

[3] The sources for this calculation are building inscriptions of Shalmaneser I (*LAR*, i. 41), Tukulti-Ninurta I (*LAR*, i. 62), Tiglath-Pileser I (*LAR*, i. 88), Esarhaddon (*LAR*, ii. 272–3); see also B. Landsberger, *JCS*, viii. 41. There is a notable discrepancy between the figures given for the interval Šamši-Addu I–Shalmaneser I by Shalmaneser himself and by Esarhaddon six centuries later; Esarhaddon's lower figure approximates closely to that given by the late-eighth-century copies of the King List which we possess, and we may assume that Shalmaneser was using a fuller version which, in view of its much earlier date, is more likely to be correct. Tiglath-Pileser I says that

Šamši-Addu reigned 641 years before Aššurdan (1178–1133 B.C.), which gives a date of 1819 B.C. for either the beginning or the end of Šamši-Addu's reign. Shalmaneser I states that the interval between Šamši-Addu and himself was 580 years, giving a date of 1852 B.C. Since the reign of Šamši-Addu lasted 33 years, it seems reasonable to suppose that the two kings were using the same source which, rightly or wrongly, assigned Šamši-Addu to the years 1852–1819 B.C., and that Shalmaneser's scribe calculated his interval from the beginning of Šamši-Addu's reign, while Tiglath-Pileser's scribe, as was more usual, took the end of the reign as a point of departure. Shalmaneser makes the further statement that there were 159 years between Erišum I and Šamši-Addu, whereas Esarhaddon gives 126 years for the same

This cannot be reconciled with the complicated nexus of chronological indications which bear on the dating of the First Dynasty of Babylon, and no final answer to this much disputed problem seems possible at present. But for our purposes we need only remark that a reduction of these figures by the margin necessary to meet every requirement of the Babylonian sources would do a violence to the Assyrian tradition which, in view of its apparently detailed nature, is very difficult to justify.[1] The long reign of Erišum I must at least be placed in the twentieth century B.C., and Puzur-Aššur I, who is shown by contemporary inscriptions to have been his great-grandfather,[2] must have followed very closely on the end of the Ur III domination. It would in fact be a not unreasonable conclusion that the line of kings bearing Akkadian names and headed by Puzur-Aššur I came directly after the liberation of Aššur from the control of Ur. This would also serve to explain the great difference in character between these names, which look as if they have been preserved in written records, and those of their predecessors in the King List, which seem to show the distortion caused by oral tradition, for it is easy to believe that surviving records began after the end of foreign domination. It does not seem possible that the early kings were contemporary with Ur III. The name of the only governor known to us, Zarīqum, does not occur in the King List and he is never mentioned by later monarchs who restored the Ištar temple. Clearly the sources of the list did not include the Ur III governors as kings of Aššur and there must be a chronological gap in the list corresponding to this period of foreign rule. Thus Ušpia and Kikkia should be placed some time before the conquest of Aššur by the Third Dynasty of Ur.

Ušpia is said by Assyrian tradition to have been a nomad and also to have founded the temple of Aššur, Kikkia to have constructed the first city wall. It may be noted here that the two statements concerning Ušpia, so far from being contradictory, carry conviction precisely because they represent nomad settlement at Aššur as a gradual process, in which the site was used first as a religious centre and perhaps a seasonal residence, and only later as a permanent capital, an interpretation which is entirely consistent with the practice of tribal leaders as we can observe it in later and better documented periods. On the other hand, the identification of Kikkia as the first builder of a city wall can hardly be

interval. Again the difference is the length of Šamši-Addu's reign, and it seems that Shalmaneser's scribe this time counted to the end of the reign, so counting the reign twice in his total. Thus 126 years seems the more probable figure for the period from the death of Erišum I to the accession of Šamši-Addu in the sources used by both scribes, which would place the death of Erišum I in 1978 B.C. Tukulti-Ninurta I says that Ilušumma reigned 780 years before his time, and if he is referring to the end of Ilušumma's reign, then Ilušumma died, according to his source, in 2022 B.C. The 44-year interval between the deaths of Ilušumma and of Erišum accords well enough with the statement of the later King List known to us, which gives Erišum a reign of 40 years. Thus if we assume that Shalmaneser's scribe made one error, all the other thirteenth- and twelfth-century statements are consistent and they point to a common

source, presumably the version of the king or eponym list which placed Erišum I between 2020 and 1980 B.C.

[1] In particular the synchronism Ilušumma=Sumu-abum of Babylon, which appears as a catch-line in the 'Sargon Chronicle' (*ANET*, p. 267) seems incompatible with Assyrian evidence. Šamši-Addu of Assyria is generally thought to have come to the throne about 20 years before Ḫammurabi of Babylon (30 years, A. Parrot, *Archéologie mésopotamienne*, ii (1953), pp. 344–6). Sumu-abum died only 89 years before Ḫammurabi's accession, i.e. 69 or 59 years before Šamši-Addu. But the interval between Erišum and Šamši-Addu is given by Assyrian sources as 126 years, with Ilušumma 40 years earlier still, and whatever the interval in years, it contains four generations and six reigns, including Erišum I. Obviously concessions must be made on both sides.

[2] *LAR*, i. 13, genealogy of Erišum I.

taken literally, for he would then be placed early in the third millennium, before or contemporary with the building of the Early Dynastic Ištar temple, and this would imply that the Assyrians retained a memory of one royal ancestor from that time and lost the names of all his successors, except Akia, until the reign of Puzur-Aššur I. Clearly later tradition preserved only the memory of builders who were members of the accepted royal line, and did not concern itself with buildings erected by others, even if their existence and authorship were known.

At this point general considerations once again become relevant. The occupation of Aššur by nomads from the steppe is most likely to have taken place at a time when discipline was weak in the country as a whole, and when Aššur was no longer shielded by the power of some external ruler or patron. Here the archaeological record points to the phase intervening between the powerful Agade dynasty and the rise of the Third Dynasty of Ur, when the Ištar temple of Level G lay in ruins beneath the hovels of Level F. This corresponds in Mesopotamian history with the Gutian invasions which had splintered the south into its component city states, bickering among themselves, the period when the Sumerian chroniclers ask in rhetorical despair: 'Who was king, who was not king?'

One further factor may be taken into account, since it throws some light both on the historical question and on the assumptions underlying the compilation of the King List. The name Aššur was applied to the city as early as the Agade period, for it occurs in tablets of that date from Nuzi, Yorgan Tepe near Kirkuk.[1] On the other hand, theophoric names containing the element Aššur, attesting the worship of the god Aššur, have not yet been identified before the time of Ur III.[2] This evidence may in the future be set aside by the discovery of other texts, but as it stands it would seem to imply that the god was a personification of the city, and that his cult originated not long before the Ur III period. Certainly Aššur in later times shared a precinct with the Sumerian Enlil, and may well have been an intruder, established there in the first instance by the desire of a new dynasty to emphasize its independence with a local cult. Šamši-Addu I in his inscription commemorating the reconstruction of the temple of Aššur refers to both shrines without appreciable distinction of emphasis,[3] but it is certain that Aššur was always regarded as the immediate divine overlord of Assyrian kingship, and he takes the place of Marduk of Babylon in the Assyrian version of the Babylonian Creation Myth. This goes far to explain the distortion of the King List by the inclusion of Šamši-Addu's West Semitic forefathers. The compiler was obviously anxious to prove that this great king was of the true lineage of Aššur's viceroys, and there could be no more effective way of doing this than by making his earliest known ancestor a grandson of Ušpia, founder of the temple and cult of Aššur.

Nineveh presents a very different picture. There R. Campbell Thompson explored the lower levels of the Ištar Temple and M. E. L. Mallowan was responsible for a deep sounding from the highest point of the mound, which penetrated to virgin soil.[4] The latter yielded an accumulation of stratified debris 22 m. high, dating from the Hassuna to

[1] T. J. Meek, 'Old Akkadian, Sumerian and Cappadocian Tablets from Nuzi', HSS, x. p. xi.

[2] M. B. Rowton, CAH, i, ch. vi. 33, n. 1.

[3] LAR, i. 16–17.

[4] R. Campbell Thompson and R. W. Hamilton, 'The Temple of Ishtar at Nineveh, 1930–31', AAA, xix (1932), 55 ff.; M. E. L. Mallowan, 'The Prehistoric Sondage of Nineveh', AAA, xx (1933), 127 ff.

the Ninevite V periods, which shows that Nineveh had been one of the earliest agri-cultural villages in the plain and was already a considerable town before 3000 B.C. The third millennium is ill documented. A complex of vaulted tombs has been tentatively ascribed to the Second Early Dynastic period, and can hardly be earlier, but their contents had been robbed and the ascription rests only on an amulet found near by which may have come from them.[1] Other finds, out of context, suggest contact with the south at this time, although there is nothing to prove foreign domination. A cylinder seal found in the upper Ninevite V level should be attributed either to the Third Early Dynastic or, more probably, the Agade period.[2] An inscription of Šamši-Addu I records the construction of the temple of Ištar by Maništusu, son of Sargon of Agade, and the excavators identified foundations which they believed to be those of Maništusu's temple.[3] This building had been de-stroyed by fire, and was replaced by another, plausibly attributed to Šamši-Addu I.[4] The chronological gap in the evidence between the Agade period and Šamši-Addu I may imply a decline in the status of the site, but it does not prove a break in occupation, for we must bear in mind that only a very small fraction of the total area of the mound has been explored to this depth. Indeed, a part of the site which was already more than 20 m. above ground level would have afforded an impressive foundation for monumental buildings or, in times of insecurity, for a citadel, but would appear unnecessarily inconvenient for ordinary occupation.[5]

The history of Nineveh is in marked contrast to that of Aššur in two particulars, in the presence of massive evidence of prehistoric occupation and in the absence from the build-ing record of any Assyrian king before Šamši-Addu I. The former bears out what has

---

[1] R. C. Thompson, *AAA*, xix. 78–80; A. L. Perkins, 'The Comparative Archaeology of Early Mesopotamia', *SAOC*, 25 (1957), 179.

[2] *AAA*, xx, pl. lxv. 18.

[3] Inscription, *AAA*, xix. 105–7; remains of early structures, pp. 58–62. A fragmentary stone tablet, ascribed to Naram-Sin of Agade, is said to have been acquired in Nebi Yunus, the southern mound within the later city wall of Nineveh; C. F. Lehmann-Haupt, 'Materialen zur Älteren Geschichte Armeniens und Mesopotamiens', *Abhandlung der Königlichen Gesell-schaft der Wissenschaften zu Göttingen, Phil.-hist. Klasse*, N. F. Band IX (1907), 6–7; W. W. Hallo, 'Early Mesopotamian Royal Titles', *AOS*, 43 (1957), 50. Nothing is known of the early history of Nebi Yunus, which became the arsenal of Nineveh in the seventh century B.C., because excavation has been prevented by the presence of the shrine and modern cemetery. If it was occupied in the Agade period, it seems possible that it may, during the succeeding centuries down to the time of Šamši-Addu I, have dis-placed Kuyunjik as the principal settlement, and this would explain the apparent break in the archaeological record on the latter mound. Note, however, that an inscription of Šulgi cited by Lehmann-Haupt as origin-ating from Nineveh has been shown to relate to the restoration of a temple in Kutha (*ZA*, iii (1888), 94).

[4] It is interesting that both the building ascribed to Maništusu at Nineveh and Level G of the Ištar Temple at Aššur were destroyed by fire. Of course the two destructions were not necessarily contemporary, but they accord very plausibly with the anarchic conditions which followed the downfall of the Agade Empire.

[5] I do not believe that 'breaks in occupation' of a well-favoured site are as common as the evidence of incomplete excavation often seems to suggest, and it is worth emphasizing that excavation is always incom-plete. Anyone who has observed local building practice in a mud-brick village will know that occupation oscillates from one end of the general site to the other, simply because it is easier to build a new house on the site of one abandoned many years before, and con-sequently levelled by the natural process of decay, than to undertake the labour of levelling a newly abandoned building. Obviously the excavation of a part of such a village would reveal many levels of apparently inter-mittent occupation, which do not give a true picture of the history of the site as a whole. Religious consider-ations clearly tended to maintain continuity of use on a temple site, but failure to rebuild a temple may reflect the poverty or insecurity of a community rather than its complete disappearance. The relevance of security to the occupation sequence of a mound is discussed below, p. pp. 58-9.

already been said of the geographical advantages of its location. The latter constitutes an argument *ex silentio*, which is dangerous ground for the interpretation of archaeological evidence, but there are special considerations in this case. The building record, though incomplete for the site as a whole, does at least relate to its most important early shrine. Moreover, Šamši-Addu in his foundation cylinder for the Ištar temple states:

The ancient building which Maništusu, son of Sargon, king of Agade, built went to ruin; the building over which after the End of Agade until my reign, until the capture of the land of Nurrugum, seven generations passed and among the kings preceding me n[one had restored][1]

and later kings, Shalmaneser I and Aššurnasirpal II, regarded Šamši-Addu as the founder.[2] It would be surprising if any record or tradition of restoration by an early Assyrian king before the Third Dynasty of Ur had been ignored, and the seven generations who preceded Šamši-Addu must, on any count, include the kings who came after the fall of the Third Dynasty, among whom were some notable builders; Ilušumma and Erišum I restored all three buildings of which we have any record at Aššur in this period, including the Ištar temple there.[3]

There is in fact reason to suspect that Nineveh was part of a separate principality, which may perhaps have owed allegiance to the more powerful rulers of Aššur, but did not until the time of Šamši-Addu come under the direct control of the Assyrian kings, who were thenceforward responsible for the maintenance of its principal shrine. In this connexion Šamši-Addu's reference to the capture of the land of Nurrugum is significant, for it was obviously a great event which was in some way connected with the restoration of the Ištar temple at Nineveh. Nurrugum is known from several references in the Mari letters as both a city and a district, and although its capital cannot be located at present, the district included the city of Apqum.[4] Two towns of this name are known, one at the source of the Balikh, the other at Tell Abu Marya, some 50 km. west of Nineveh.[5] Conquest of the territory around Abu Marya would obviously be a vital step toward the control of the river crossing at Nineveh, and it seems reasonable to suppose that the land of Nurrugum incorporated this area between modern Tell Afar and the Tigris. Its actual boundaries may of course have been larger, and it is possible that it included Nineveh, if Nineveh was not a capital city at this time.

THE ECONOMY OF AŠŠUR

This speculation leads to one important question. If Aššur, as the capital of an apparently prosperous, independent principality under the predecessors of Šamši-Addu I, did not directly control the agricultural land on which the later Assyrian kingdom so obviously depended, and if its own immediate resources were as limited as they now seem, what was the basis of its prosperity? Fortunately a partial answer can be given by a review of the

---

[1] *AAA*, xix. 106.

[2] *AAA*, xix. 95, 111.

[3] Šamši-Addu's 'seven generations' after the End of Agade are difficult to interpret; the King List would suggest that, being himself a contemporary of Naram-Sin, he was in fact counting from Puzur-Aššur I, i.e. from the end of Ur III.

[4] *ARMT*, v. 43, 61, 62.

[5] A. Goetze, *JCS*, vii. 57, 61. *Apqum ša Baliḫa* would seem to be irrelevant in this context.

trade, with its headquarters in Aššur, which is documented by the archives of Assyrian merchants established in various centres in Cappadocia at this time, notably by the texts discovered in one of their principal centres at Kaniš, modern Kültepe between Kayseri and Sivas. Level II at Kültepe is equated approximately with the period from Puzur-Aššur I to Puzur-Aššur II; then the Assyrian trading station was destroyed by fire and, after a break in occupation which seems to correspond with the domination of Ešnunna at Aššur, was replaced by a new settlement, Level 1b, at the time of Šamši-Addu I.[1] There is as yet no evidence of this trade before or during the Ur III period, for Level 3 at Kültepe has produced no tablets, but it seems unlikely that it came into being suddenly with the setting up of the only trading station, Kültepe 2–1b, that has been fully explored, although it may have been intensified at this time for political reasons.[2] From the tablets we discover that there were regular donkey caravans carrying exports from Cappadocia, notably copper, to Aššur and returning with woven fabrics of various grades and another metal, probably tin.[3] The use of silver as currency permits us to estimate the relative values of the objects of trade where their prices are recorded in the regions linked by the trade route, and thus to reconstruct in outline the pattern of demand and supply which underlay the exchange.[4] This is an important step, since Aššur itself may well have been a primary

[1] K. Balkan, 'Observations on the Chronological Problems of the Kārum Kaniš', *Türk Tarih Kurumu Yayınlarından*, vii/28 (1955), 59–60. For a general account of these trading stations, see A. Goetze, *Kleinasien*, 1957.

[2] The origin of the Assyrian communities in Cappadocia, and even their precise later status, is not clear. I find it difficult to accept J. Lewy's argument (*HUCA*, xxvii (1956), 53 ff.) that they represent a direct Assyrian administration of large parts of Cappadocia during the period preceding Šamši-Addu I. The evidence he puts forward might well be explained on the assumption that these economically important centres enjoyed some form of extra-territorial privilege combined with considerable local influence, as did the 'factories' of East India merchants 200 years ago. For the view that the territory in which the trading stations were situated was governed by local rulers, see A. Goetze, *Kleinasien*, p. 76. Even if it existed in the Ur III period, the trade would probably have expanded as a result of the break-up of the Ur III Empire, which seems to have dislocated the trade of Aššur's southern rivals (see below, p. 34).

[3] The metal in question, Akkadian *anakum*, has been variously translated 'lead' or 'tin'. Whatever may be its meaning in other contexts, I do not believe either that merchants used the same name for both metals, thus inviting a confusion which would have lost them many customers, or that the Assyrians carried lead from Aššur to Cappadocia where there were plentiful supplies in the Taurus mines. J. Lewy suggests that they carried lead ore to be smelted in Cappadocia because there was no wood for smelting furnaces in Aššur (*JAOS*, lxxviii (1958), 92). If this was their only

problem it would surely have been simpler to bring wood down the Tigris to Aššur. In my view 'lead' does not make sense in the context of this trade, 'tin' does. For other arguments and references, see J. Laessøe, 'Akkadian Annakum: "Tin" or "Lead"?', *Acta Orientalia*, xxiv. 83–94.

[4] A. Goetze, *Kleinasien*, p. 78, has shown that in the Cappadocian texts tin, which had been bought at prices varying from 12 to 20 shekels for 1 shekel of silver, was sold at 6 to 10 shekels for 1 of silver, yielding a gross profit on this operation of 100 per cent. Whether this in fact represents a high net profit margin depends on the overhead expenses of the trade, and it would be interesting to know whether the tablets give sufficient information to enable us to estimate, for instance, the total cost of running a caravan. However, the total profit to the merchant must have accrued from operations conducted in both directions. This presents a more difficult problem. The cloth trade must be left out of account for lack of data concerning the cost price of the goods, although wool was one of Aššur's staple products. In the case of the metal trade, the evidence from the eastern end of the trade route is rather unsatisfactory, but it seems worth presenting a tentative conclusion in the hope that it may be corrected.

In any discussion of this problem certain considerations must be kept in mind. The use of silver as a medium of exchange and accountancy permits easy comparison of prices in the same locality at the same moment, for it is then a common factor between different commodities and its intrinsic value can be eliminated from the equation. But silver was primarily a currency, not a commodity in demand for its usefulness; expressed in cash or credit, it essentially represents

producer of wool but has no native source of tin and must have acted as an entrepôt in this trade, dependent on the profit that could be made by the middleman.

The Kültepe texts give the value of copper in terms of silver as a ratio varying, probably in relation to the quality of the copper, from 46:1 to 70:1, and the value of tin, again in terms of silver, between 6:1 and 10:1. Thus tin was about seven times as expensive as copper, which was relatively cheap at Kaniš because of the supplies locally available in the Taurus mines.[1] There are no comparable figures of this date from the eastern end of the trade route, but some three centuries later we find that at Nuzi, near Kirkuk, the ratio of copper to silver lay between 340 and 480:1, while the ratio of tin to silver was 216:1; in fact, tin was one and a half to two times as expensive as copper.[2] It is obvious that tin was worth three or four times as much, in terms of copper, at Kaniš as it later was at Nuzi. We cannot, however, accept the comparison as valid, because of the long interval of time which separates the evidence from the two sites, unless it can be shown that the availability of tin at Nuzi was not due only to a recent improvement in supply. Here we are assisted by a letter discovered at Šušarrā, now Tell Shemshara in the Ranya plain east of Erbil, which dates from the time of Šamši-Addu I. It is a request to the ruler of Šušarrā

purchasing power. In the case of modern currencies it is obvious that the maintenance of equilibrium between purchasing power and the supply of goods involves complicated manipulation of the supply of money and credit, and this is an important element in price stability. We do not know what methods were used to limit the amount of silver in circulation in the ancient Near East, although some governmental control may be inferred from the fact that it rarely if ever appears as an article of trade in private hands. It seems unlikely, however, that these methods were based on any very consistent economic principle, and certain that there was no international standard. Consequently fluctuations in the supply of silver in different areas and at different times might have affected the prices of commodities in a way unrelated to their real value based on supply and demand. An apparent drop in prices might, for instance, reflect either an increase in the supply of essential goods or a fortuitous decrease in the amount of silver available, leading to the inflation of its exchange value. Ideally it would be possible to relate the value of units of currency, such as the shekel of silver, to a 'cost-of-living index' based on wages and the prices of staple foodstuffs, but the evidence of the tablets relevant to a particular situation is rarely adequate for such an analysis. In face of this uncertainty it seems best, where certain commodities are being directly exchanged in the course of trade, to assess their relative values in the places linked by the trade route as if the operation were simple barter.

[1] For sources of copper in Anatolia see R. J. Forbes, *Metallurgy in Antiquity*, Leiden, 1950, p. 303. I have here used the figures given for the most valuable quality of copper, described as 'washed' or 'refined' (*masium, dammuqum*, A. Goetze, loc. cit.), since it

yields the lowest ratio of relative value and hence provides the most conservative estimate of profit. It is interesting to note that a direct comparison may be made between the price of 'washed' copper in Cappadocia at this time and its price in Ešnunna according to the Law Code (A. Goetze, 'Laws of Ešnunna', 1956, pp. 24–25). The latter give a ratio of 120 shekels of copper to 1 of silver. This may be a propaganda statement designed to represent costs below their true level, but it compares closely with actual prices recorded in economic texts of the Ur III period, and the similarity was one of the reasons for Goetze's proposal to date the composition of the Laws close to the Third Dynasty of Ur. This argument gains force from the comparison with Cappadocian prices, which are twice as high. Even allowing for a degree of misrepresentation in the Ešnunna price, it cannot be contemporary with the Assyrian copper trade, the existence of which presupposes that the price of copper was substantially higher in the Tigris region than in Cappadocia.

[2] Dorothy Cross, 'Movable Property in the Nuzi Documents', *AOS*, x (1937), 44–47. It will be noticed that both metals were much cheaper in terms of silver than they had been earlier in Cappadocia. This may arise from an improvement in supply rather than inflation of the value of silver, for the silver price of barley at Nuzi was much higher than it had previously been in southern Mesopotamia. But barley, although a staple food, is not in itself a good price index because of the fluctuations in its value which are difficult to discount when the total number of tablets is small; at Ur in time of famine its price went up to sixty times the normal level (T. Jacobsen, 'The Reign of Ibbi-Suen', *JCS*, vii (1953), 42).

from his overlord, probably Išme-Dagan, for the supply of a large quantity of tin for the manufacture of weapons, and it implies that Šušarrā was a depot for tin at this period.[1] We may therefore suppose that the comparative cheapness of tin at Nuzi reflects the existence of a source of supply which had been available for some centuries.[2] This source cannot have been a local one. Although it cannot certainly be identified, the position of Šušarrā, close to the western end of practicable mountain routes through the Zagros from Iran,[3] suggests that the metal may have been brought from one of the known sources east of the Zagros, perhaps the southern slopes of the Elburz range.[4] It could also have reached the Kirkuk district from the same source, either by this route or through the more southerly pass east of Sulaimaniya.

It seems, then, that Aššur profited by the purchase of tin which was imported from Iran through the mountains on the east and could be resold at a much higher price in Cappadocia on the west. The disposal of the copper which was taken in exchange presents a separate problem. It is unlikely that any quantity was passed on in payment to the producers of tin, since they had access to other sources in Iran. Some of the metal was doubtless worked in Aššur, which was a notable centre of the craft; in later times one of the city gates was known as the Gate of the Metal-Workers. It can be shown, however, that considerable amounts were re-exported in a third direction, down the Tigris valley to Babylonia. During the third millennium copper had been imported into Sumer from the Persian Gulf. It appears that this source of supply was cut off, at least in the north of the alluvial plain, after the collapse of the hegemony of the Third Dynasty of Ur.[5] This may have stimulated imports from Assyria, to which a few texts bear witness.[6] A tablet from Tell ed-Der near Sippar, written in the Old Assyrian dialect, details amounts of copper delivered by various individuals which were lying in the *babtum* of Aššur.[7] The presence of the list at Tell ed-Der suggests that the metal was at the disposal of agents in that city. The existence of the mercantile connexion is further attested by two letters written by

[1] J. Laessøe, *Acta Orientalia*, xxiv. 85–88; for Išme-Dagan as the writer, see Laessøe, 'The Shemshara Tablets', *Arkaeologisk-kunsthistoriske Meddelelser Danske Vid. Selsk.* 4, no. 3 (1959), 55.

[2] It is worth remarking that the discovery of a small number of Cappadocian texts at Nuzi proves a connexion with that site in the relevant period, although the nature of the connexion cannot be reconstructed from five tablets of which four are illegible (T. J. Meek, *HSS*, x, pp. xxiv–xxv).

[3] J. Laessøe, 'The Shemshara Tablets', p. 20.

[4] R. J. Forbes, *Metallurgy in Antiquity*, p. 238 and map opp. p. 232.

[5] Leemans, *Foreign Trade*, pp. 121–3.

[6] Texts in Leemans, *Foreign Trade*, pp. 99–102.

[7] The word *babtum* denoted a 'quarter' of a city, its inhabitants, or its administration (A. Goetze, *Laws of Ešnunna*, p. 135, n. 4 and refs.), but Leemans' suggestion that it has some etymological connexion with a city gate is not incompatible with this meaning. The quarters of Near Eastern towns are often even now described by reference to 'gates' which in many cases have long since ceased to exist. The modern usage is appropriate, since the bazaars engaged in the manufacture or sale of different commodities tended in the walled town to grow up in the vicinity of the various gates, and the name of the gate still serves as a good description of a homogeneous commercial district. The present reference suggests that the *babtum* included a depot for metal in transit; it may be relevant to note that one of the officials in charge of a *babtum* at Mari functioned as a tax-collector (*ARMT*, vii. 226).

It would be interesting to know what Ilušumma meant by the phrase, in an inscription in which he claims to have restored the freedom of many southern cities, 'I washed the copper of the Akkadians' (*ZA*, NF ix (1936), 114 ff., ll. 49–65). Although Erišum I, son of Ilušumma, is said to have actively encouraged the Cappadocian trade and even to have had a financial interest in it (J. Lewy, *JAOS*, lxxviii. 99–101 and n. 68), Ilušumma's apparently commercial statement seems inappropriate to its high-flown political context.

Assyrians to their agent in Sippar concerning the disposal of a sum of money belonging to them; and some indication of the type of goods which Babylonia sent to Aššur in return may be obtained from a business letter from a merchant in Aššur to his correspondent in Kaniš:

> Regarding the purchase of garments of the Akkadians about which you wrote me. After you had left, the Akkadians did not come any more to the city; their country is in trouble.[1]

We have in these varied sources an outline of the life of Aššur as a trading community taking advantage of its position at the junction of great natural routes, but it is worth observing that the site was not without possible rivals in the east–west trade. To north and south lay alternative highways. The road through Nineveh does not seem to have been much used at this time, although it must have been, from the point of view of climate and terrain, more attractive. On the south, Iranian tin could, and probably did, pass from Elam into Babylonia and thence up the Euphrates valley to northern Syria,[2] but this route does not seem to have challenged the Assyrian monopoly in Anatolia, although it again passed through settled lands where water was plentiful. The road used by the Assyrian merchants has been reconstructed from the evidence of the Kültepe tablets by A. Goetze. Its general course has been described above, but its noteworthy feature is that, by contrast with the Nineveh and Euphrates valley road, it appears to have traversed the northern plain of Mesopotamia in an almost direct line from Aššur to the valley of the Khabur, keeping as close as possible to the edge of the rainfall zone.[3] The advantages of a direct route to

---

[1] 'Garments of the Akkadians' are frequently mentioned in the Cappadocian texts and were obviously a product of high quality; Leemans, *Foreign Trade*, p. 98.

[2] Leemans, *Foreign Trade*, pp. 123–4; cf. *ARMT*, vii. 293–5. The price of tin at Mari seems to have been ten or even fifteen times that of copper, although we are apparently dealing here with ingot tin on the one hand and granulated copper on the other.

[3] A. Goetze, 'An Old Babylonian Itinerary', *JCS*, vii (1953), 65–70 and map, 72. I have personal knowledge only of that part of the route which lies within the boundaries of modern Iraq, and can add nothing to Goetze's excellent commentary elsewhere. Even in the sector between Aššur and the Khabur I can propose no certain identifications, which must await the discovery of epigraphic evidence from the sites; ancient place-names do not appear to have survived in the Jazira, probably because of the discontinuity of settlement. Topographical considerations do, however, suggest probable locations for some of the stations on the route. Firstly, a general point must be mentioned. Since some of the stations are shown by references in the Mari letters to have been towns of considerable size, they must have lain within the rainfall zone, the modern boundary of which coincides approximately with the limit of distribution of ancient sites, and the road must have deviated slightly to the north of a direct line joining Aššur with the Khabur valley north of 'Arban,

where Goetze locates the site of Ḫabura. The road-stations are (Goetze, chart, 65)

Aššur—Saduatum—Razamā ša Burama-x— Abu-Tiban—Gad/tara—Razamā ša Uḫakim —Ḫabura.

The total distance from Aššur to Ḫabura is about 250 km. If this was accomplished in six stages, the average length of each stage was rather more than 40 km., appreciably longer than the average of 25–30 km. observed between Ḫabura and the Euphrates, but not impossibly so.

The first part of the road must have run north-westwards between Jebel Makhul and Jebel Najma. The modern track from Aššur to Hatra follows this line for c. 38 km., then bends south-west to join the Qaiyara–Hatra track before crossing the Wadi Tharthar. If it were to continue on its original alignment, it would intersect the track coming from Qaiyara where the latter now crosses a *wadi*. On the west bank of the watercourse at this point, some 44 km. north-west of Aššur, is a mound 10–15 m. high with, at its foot, a scatter of surface pottery suggesting an area of occupation about 200 m. across, and ranging in date from the prehistoric period to the second millennium. The name of the mound, Tell es-Sadiya, suggests a possible identification with *Saduatum*, but against this it must be noted that *Sanduwātum* of the Mari letters, which as Goetze points out must be the same site, was a fortified

slow-moving pack animals are obvious, but its use argues a confidence in the security of the region which is borne out by the absence in the Kültepe texts of any mention of highway robbery, although the payment of tolls was an accepted part of travelling expenses. The situation, in fact, is strikingly reminiscent of that which prevailed in the eighteenth century A.D. when caravans found it more profitable to pay the tolls exacted by nomad tribes than to face the more frequent and less predictable demands of their sedentary neighbours,[1]

town used as a place of refuge for the local population (*ARMT*, v. 43). Tell es-Sadiya hardly seems large enough for this purpose, unless it is bigger than it appears; the indented slope of the *wadi* makes it difficult to distinguish between natural and artificial features.

From this point the Early Assyrian road would have continued towards the bend of the Wadi Tharthar north of Hatra, some 40 km. distant, and *Razamā ša Buramᵛ-x* might be expected in this neighbourhood, which was still considered capable of supporting a newly founded city in the eighth century B.C. (Dur Bel-ḫarran-bel-usur, Tell 'Abta, see p. 55 below). For the next stage, *Abu-Tiban*, I can make no suggestion. The line of the road must have passed close to Tell Hadhail, a walled city of second-millennium date 27 km. south-east of Beled Sinjar. But Tell Hadhail itself is an obviously important site which should be one of the cities mentioned in the Mari letters, where Abu-Tiban does not occur. It must be noted, however, that negative evidence of this sort is inconclusive, and in general that surface examination cannot define precisely historical fluctuations in the importance of a site.

For *Gad/tara*, Qatarā of the Mari correspondence, we have a valuable piece of evidence in *ARMT*, iv. 29, from which we learn that Išme-Dagan, presumably coming from the direction of Aššur or Ekallātum, arranged for an official from Šubat-Enlil, Chagar Bazar, to meet him at Qatarā, which must have lain at, or south-east of, the junction between the Aššur–Ḫabura road and a route crossing Jebel Sinjar from the north. Since the Kültepe texts place Gad/tara only two stages east of Ḫabura, the only possible pass which this route can have used is the Bara gap between Jebel Sinjar and Jebel Jeribe. Two sites suggest themselves: Tell Hayal, just south-east of the pass, which under the name of Alaina or Hileia was the Roman road junction (see below, p. 78), or Tell Huwaish, a walled city 23 km. south-east of Tell Hayal and 15 km. south of Beled Sinjar. If the Aššur–Ḫabura road passed through Tell Hayal, it would then have skirted the southern side of Jebel Jeribe westwards, reaching the Khabur in two stages of about 35 km. each. If Gad/tara was Tell Huwaish, then it may have taken a more southerly line and the total distance would be *c.* 90 km. It can hardly have been east of Tell Huwaish unless there is a missing stage on the route.

Certain other consequences for the topography of the Mari correspondence follow from these observations.

Karanā, which figures as a provincial capital in the empire of Šamši-Addu and later as an independent principality, is to be looked for near Qatarā (e.g. *ARMT*, ii. 39 and v. 37) and was clearly the more important of the two places. It might be Tell Huwaish if this is not Qatarā, or Tell Hadhail. *ARMT*, ii. 39, anticipates an attack on both sites, then under the protection of independent Mari, by Išme-Dagan, who was at Razamā, probably Razamā ša Burama-x near the Wadi Tharthar; in this case he was advancing up the Aššur–Ḫabura road and preparing to dispute control of the plain south of Jebel Sinjar with the Mari forces, a very plausible situation from the geographical standpoint. Another site, *Zanipa*, is mentioned as a fortress city in the province of Nurrugum together with *Apqum*, Tell Abu Marya (see above, p. 31 and n. 5 and below, p. 54, n. 3), and is also attested as a station on another road leading from Šubat-Enlil to Babylonia (Goetze, p. 64). This route does not include Qatarā or Apqum, and probably used the crossing of Jebel Sinjar intermediate between these two sites, at the pass of Gaulat; it would have corresponded approximately in this sector with the Roman route from Zagurae to Hatra through Vicat (see below, p. 79). Near the line that it must have taken is a walled city of second-millennium date, Tell al Rimah (Tell Irmah), 20 km. south-west of Tell Abu Marya and 13 km. south of Tell Afar. North-west of the Gaulat pass in the direction of Šubat-Enlil lies another prominent mound, Gohbol, surrounded by a walled enclosure nearly 1,500 m. square. The pottery indicates occupation of the mound and its immediate vicinity from the second millennium and perhaps earlier down to the Hellenistic period, and again in Islamic times, but the walls cannot be dated. Gohbol might be one of the sites listed on Goetze's itinerary between Šubat-Enlil and Zanipa. I must emphasize, however, that these are only tentative suggestions, since our limited knowledge of second-millennium pottery does not permit more than approximate dating of the sites and, as I have said before, the results of surface survey are at best imprecise evidence.

[1] See above, p. 6. Cf. also Strabo, xvi. 748, who remarks that in his day the desert route was preferred to the Euphrates valley because the regular tolls paid to the Scenite Arabs ensured security, by contrast with the exactions of phylarchs in the settled land. He specifically mentions, however, that camels were in use; donkeys could hardly have been employed on the open steppe where water and forage were relatively scarce.

and it may be suggested that similar motives dictated the choice of the Assyrian caravan leader. Another factor must have been familiarity with the terrain, and this may perhaps reflect the background of the Assyrians themselves who, by their own account, had not long abandoned the life of the steppe at the time when this route first came into use.

The activity of the Assyrian trading post at Kaniš was temporarily interrupted at a time which seems to correspond with the reduction of Aššur to provincial status under Naram-Sin of Ešnunna, who campaigned widely in the north and north-west. There is not yet sufficient evidence to show whether the expansion of Ešnunna was in part inspired by a desire either to suppress a commercial rival or to reap the profits of the northern trade route. None the less the motive is plausible, and it is worth remembering that throughout this period the territory of Ešnunna in the Diyala basin included, in addition to a rich area of agricultural land, a section of the easiest route from Mesopotamia to Iran through the Halwand pass. The interest of its rulers in the north-west continued after the time of Naram-Sin and is frequently attested by the Mari letters, while there was a continuing rivalry between Aššur under Šamši-Addu I and Ešnunna for the control of the district between Erbil and the Lesser Zab through which ran the eastern road from Aššur.[1] Meanwhile the intervention of Šamši-Addu brought to Aššur a period of independence under its second dynasty of nomad origin and even, during Šamši-Addu's lifetime, a brief pre-eminence which may fairly be regarded as the first Assyrian empire. This episode is a unique illustration of the importance of individual genius in the history of the land bordering on the steppe, both in the intruder's meteoric rise to power and in the extension of his control over the agricultural zone which alone could provide that power with an enduring foundation. On both counts it is a fitting climax to this brief survey of Assyrian origins.

THE WEST SEMITIC DYNASTY

The documentary evidence for this period is unusually rich. We possess a large selection of the administrative correspondence that passed between Šamši-Addu and his son Iasmah-Addu, viceroy of Mari, as well as letters between Iasmah-Addu and Išme-Dagan, exchanged while the latter was viceroy in Ekallatum and, after his father's death, king of Aššur. It must be noted, however, that neither Šamši-Addu's own archives, nor those of Išme-Dagan, have come to light, and many questions raised by the Mari letters can hardly be answered without them.[2] There are also references to Assyrian affairs in the much larger bulk of the Mari correspondence pertaining to the reign of Zimri-Lim, a member of the earlier ruling family of Mari expelled by Šamši-Addu, who regained the throne a short time after Šamši-Addu's death. This mass of detailed information cannot be

---

[1] The conquest of this district, of which the capital was Qabarā (A. Goetze, RA, xlvi (1952), 156), demanded the personal attention of Šamši-Addu, and it was apparently regained by Ešnunna five years before his death (J. Laessøe, 'The Shemsharā Tablets', p. 17 and n. 15). Qabarā lay on the road to Šušarrā: Laessøe, op. cit., pp. 50, 52.

[2] Two tablets from Chagar Bazar (C. J. Gadd, Iraq,

vii. 49 and 58, nos. 932 and 991) seem to form part of the records of Šamši-Addu, since they consist of returns of personnel from Ekallātum, which would hardly have been sent to the Khabur unless their destination was the administrative centre of the empire. This seems a powerful argument for the identification of Chagar Bazar as Šubat-Enlil, confirming the indications of the itineraries. See also p. 22, n. 1.

assembled into an entirely coherent narrative since individual documents can rarely be dated. But although the sequence of events remains confused, the letters present a vivid picture of the political and social circumstances of the time. To them can be added the statement in the Assyrian King List describing Šamši-Addu's rise to power, and his own building inscriptions for the temple of Aššur in Aššur and the temple of Ištar at Nineveh.

The King List states that Šamši-Addu, son of Ila-kabkabi, went down to Babylonia in the time of Naram-Sin, thence he proceeded to the capture of Ekallātum and three years later to the conquest of Aššur where he reigned thirty-three years. A reference to Ila-kabkabi has been identified in a tablet from Ischali on the Diyala, then under the control of Ešnunna, which records an issue of rations to an agent of Ila-kabkabi.[1] In the Mari letters he is found at first in treaty relations, and then in conflict, with Zaggid-Lim, king of Mari.[2] The site of his capital is unknown, if indeed he was a sedentary ruler, which is by no means certain. It has been suggested that Amīnu, also described as his son by the King List, was the elder brother of Šamši-Addu, who had thus no hereditary expectations of kingship and was driven to seek his fortune elsewhere, a neat hypothesis though incapable of proof.[3] Be that as it may, it is interesting to notice the geographical pattern of Šamši-Addu's progress to the throne of Aššur, in the course of which he was successively established within the cultivated land of Mesopotamia at precisely those points where they lie open to incursion from the steppe, and where the distribution of formerly nomadic tribes, both ancient and modern, shows that such incursions have frequently taken place. The modern analogy has already been described, and recent work on the distribution of nomads attested in the Mari letters has shown that the ancient and modern patterns are strikingly similar. At this time the tribes of the steppe spoke a West Semitic dialect, and their personal names are readily recognizable among the East Semitic Akkadians who had preceded them into Mesopotamia some centuries before. We have observed that Šamši-Addu's own family bore West Semitic names. So, at the same period, did the rulers and many of the inhabitants of the Middle Euphrates cities, and the kings of the First Dynasty of Babylon, descended presumably from nomads who infiltrated into the north of the alluvial plain in the late third millennium. West Semitic-speaking tribes can also be traced from references to them or from places named after them, in the Tigris valley north of Baghdad and across the river to the east, between the Diyala and Jebel Hamrīn. It is of particular interest to observe that some tribes such as Iamutbal and Idamaras are found, in separate fractions, both to the east of the Tigris and on the Euphrates or in the upper Khabur basin, reflecting the pattern of fragmentation which exists at the present day.[4] Ekallātum, Šamši-Addu's first capital, has not been precisely identified but must lie not far to the north of Aššur,[5] and it was from Ekallātum that he mounted his conquest of Aššur.

[1] Kupper, *Nomades*, p. 208, n. 1.
[2] *ARMT*, i. 3.
[3] Kupper, *Nomades*, p. 211; see above p. 24 and n. 3. For the career of Šamši-Addu, see now Kupper, *CAH*, ii, ch. i (1963), 3–10.
[4] Idamaras: Kupper, *Nomades*, p. 10; Iamutbal: ibid., pp. 216–17.

[5] *ARMT*, xv. 123. Its identity with Late Assyrian Ekallāte, below p. 55, can hardly be in doubt. I cannot help being struck by the similarity of the name to modern Tell Haikal, on the east bank of the Tigris 15 km. north of Aššur. I have unfortunately been unable to visit this site, which is said to be a large mound with evidence of Late Assyrian occupation. Since this note

Šamši-Addu subsequently adopted the Assyrian royal title,[1] but he did not settle down to sedentary life in his new city in the manner to which his fellow rulers of Babylon, Mari, and Ešnunna were accustomed.[2] Judging from the extent of his military activities he must have spent a considerable part of his life on campaign, but even when he was not so engaged he seems to have divided his time between Aššur and a second capital, Šubat-Enlil, on the upper Khabur.[3] The list of palace personnel from Ekallātum, found at Chagar Bazar, demonstrates that certain administrative operations relating even to the Tigris area were centred on Šubat-Enlil rather than on Aššur. His military operations in the Khabur region are mentioned in the Mari letters before Mari came under his control, and it seems likely that his interest there was a hereditary one.[4] Too much reliance should not be placed on the reconstruction of his hypothetical motives, but his constant displacements of residence afford a striking parallel with more recent rulers, such as the early Umayyad caliphs or on a lesser scale the paramount sheikhs of modern times, who have adopted the responsibilities of sedentary government without fully accepting its restriction on their nomadic habits. Certainly it is at least a curious coincidence, unless his family were originally nomads established in the Khabur region, that he chose to conduct his early enterprises in precisely those areas where we might expect to find tribal fractions related to those of the Khabur valley.

Little evidence for the process of consolidation of Šamši-Addu's kingdom around Aššur can be gleaned from the Mari letters, but this in itself is not without significance. This area was divided into a number of administrative districts which are mentioned from time to time in the later Mari correspondence. Their location cannot yet be precisely determined, but it seems probable that Nurrugum lay in the north near Nineveh, certainly on the west bank of the Tigris and perhaps on the east as well.[5] Sanduwātum was north-west of Aššur on the road to the upper Tharthar, and Razamā between Sanduwātum and Jebel Sinjar.[6] Near Razamā were Karanā,[7] which seems to have served on occasion as a

was written the position of Ekallātum north of Aššur has been established by the discovery of a complete copy of the 'Illinois Itinerary' (A. Goetze, *JCS.*, vii (1953), 65. The new text places Ekallātum between Aššur and Apqum (Tell Abu Marya). See W. W. Hallo, 'The Road to Emar' *JCS*, xvii (1964).

[1] In his foundation inscription of the temple of Aššur, *LAR*, i. 16–17, he uses the title *šar kiššati*, which is usually rendered 'king of the world' but clearly has some more precise implication. On his bricks from the Aššur temple he employs the customary designation of his predecessors, 'Viceroy of Aššur', *LAR*, i. 15. In the Nineveh inscription, *AAA*, xix. 105–7, he adds to these *danum*, 'legitimate (king)', first used in the Akkadian form by Naram-Sin of Agade (W. W. Hallo, *AOS*, 43. 65); *šakin* *d*Enlil, 'prefect of Enlil'; and *naram* *d*Ištar, 'beloved of Ištar', thus virtually completing the standard range of titles used by his successors.

[2] The 'Old Palace' tentatively attributed to Šamši-Addu by the excavators of Aššur may date from long before his time; M. E. L. Mallowan has pointed out

that it resembles closely the palace of Naram-Sin at Tell Brak (*Iraq*, ix (1947), 27–28).

[3] See p. 37, n. 2 above.

[4] Kupper, *Nomades*, p. 212.

[5] See p. 31 above, and M. Falkner, *AfO*, xviii/1 (1957), 22. I do not feel happy about a number of Miss Falkner's other proposals because they ignore the boundary of the rainfall zone which must govern the location of sites in the Jazira.

[6] Probably Razamā ša Burama-x, see above p. 35, n. 3. There were at least four places called Razamā: Razamā ša Iamutbal, east of the Tigris and north of Ešnunna (*ARMT*, ii. 18); Razamā ša Burama-x, in the vicinity of the upper Tharthar; Razamā ša Uḫakim, perhaps south of Jebel Chembe; and a Razamā near Larsa in southern Mesopotamia (A. Goetze, *JCS*, vii. 64).

[7] Sometimes placed east of the Tigris on the assumption that *ARMT*, vi. 23, is an itinerary. If it is, it is a remarkably circuitous route, for it would take the messengers in question from Babylon to Mari via

headquarters for the whole area, and Qatarā. Qabarā was the capital of the country between the Lesser Zab and Erbil, probably at or near Altun Köprü.[1] Some of these districts, for instance Sanduwātum, may have been dependencies of Aššur which automatically came under Šamši-Addu's control after his conquest of that city; but others are unlikely to have done so, either because their separate conquest is specifically recorded, like Nurrugum or Qabarā, or because they reappear as apparently independent principalities after Šamši-Addu's death, as for instance Razamā and Karanā. It is notable that none of the campaigns which led to their subjugation, with the exception of Qabarā, is recorded in the published letters between Šamši-Addu and Iasmaḫ-Addu, and it is a reasonable inference that they were conquered before the surviving correspondence began. It would indeed have been prudent for Šamši-Addu to affirm his position in the upper Tigris valley before engaging in more extended schemes of conquest, since it afforded him security and vastly greater local resources than Aššur alone could provide. At all events, his building inscription from the temple of Ištar at Nineveh emphasizes the vital significance of the capture of Nurrugum, and this is best explained as the success which set the seal of unity on the country that we later come to recognize as Assyria.

When the situation is first revealed to us in more detail by the archive of Iasmaḫ-Addu, the kingdom embraced all the land between the Tigris and the Euphrates from the north of Babylonia to the foothills of Anatolia, and was being extended eastwards beyond the Tigris. The foundation inscription of the new temple of Aššur probably shows us Šamši-Addu at the peak of his power, when he claims to have received the tribute of the kings of the north and to have set up his stele in Lebanon on the shore of the Mediterranean; these statements, and the royal titles of the Nineveh text, 'Legitimate king, king of the world', foreshadow the pretensions, true or false, of many of his successors on the Assyrian throne, and do much to explain the reverence they had for him. It is not entirely clear how the administrative responsibilities of the kingdom were divided in his lifetime, largely because we have only one section of its records. It would appear, however, that Iasmaḫ-Addu as viceroy of Mari was responsible for the administration of the riverain cities of the Middle Euphrates, and for the maintenance of order among the nomads who pastured their flocks on either side of the river. Iasmaḫ-Addu himself owned large numbers of sheep, as we learn from a request which he made to Ishi-Addu, king of Qatna north of Aleppo, that they should be allowed to use the latter's pastures in time of drought at Mari.[2] He was evidently a weak character, often berated by Šamši-Addu for his supine failure to set his house in order. By contrast, his brother Išme-Dagan inherited some part of his father's military ability and seems to have spent a great part of his time extending Šamši-Addu's

---

Ešnunna on the Diyala, Ekallātum on the Tigris, Karanā, Qabarā near Altun Köprü, and Arrapḫa (Kirkuk). It seems to me more likely that a list of individual messengers coming from these different places is indicated, and in this case it has no bearing on their location.

[1] See p. 37, n. 1 above.

[2] *ARMT*, v. 16. Cf. also the elaborate arrangements made for shearing, for which 300–400 men were required. *ARMT*, v. 67. Wool was cheap at Aššur by comparison with barley. The prices given by Šamši-Addu I and Sin-kashid of Uruk yield equivalents of 7½ *minas* of wool to 1 *kor* of barley in Aššur against 4 *minas* of wool to 1 *kor* of barley in Uruk (A. Goetze, 'Laws of Ešnunna', 29). Actual prices may be distorted, but there is no reason to question the relative values given.

conquests to the east of the Lesser Zab, although we also hear of his administrative activity, in particular of his local responsibility in a census which was evidently being carried out on Šamši-Addu's orders throughout the kingdom.

After Šamši-Addu's death the situation changed with startling suddenness. Of the letters that can be assigned to this period, only the first, in which Išme-Dagan informed Iasmaḫ-Addu of his accession and assured him of protection against Ešnunna and Elam, sounds a note of confidence, and almost at once we find the kingdom on the defensive, with Išme-Dagan making valiant efforts to hold it together.[1] At this time the adminis- tration of the districts of Nurrugum, Karanā, Qatarā, and Sanduwātum seems to have passed into Iasmaḫ-Addu's hands, for we find the governor of Karanā reporting to him on measures which have been taken to secure their population and flocks against attack by con- centrating the one in the fortress cities and sending the other into the desert.[2] Although the circumstances are obscure, it is none the less interesting that both the Middle Euphrates valley and the north-eastern border of the Jazira towards the Tigris should apparently have been placed under unified command, for such a measure anticipates a very similar arrangement under the Late Assyrian Empire.[3] Within a short time, however, the kingdom disintegrated. Šubat-Enlil was lost, and Iasmaḫ-Addu was ousted from the throne of Mari by Zimri-Lim, whose reports from his governors reflect the confusion of succeeding years. We see Išme-Dagan struggling to retain by force or diplomacy even the districts in the vicinity of Aššur itself. Razamā, Qatarā, and Karanā are independent principalities alternately held or threatened by the troops of Mari and Assyria, while the rulers of Elam and Ešnunna and the great Ḫammurabi of Babylon seem to play power politics with the lesser princes as their pawns. The King List credits Išme-Dagan with a reign of forty years. If this is not a gross exaggeration, he must have acknowledged the supremacy of Ḫammurabi during a part of this time, but the Tigris valley from Nineveh to Aššur seems to have remained united in his hands. Although this strip of country alone survived the wreck of Šamši-Addu's dominions, it was the heart of Assyria and the kernel of its future expansion.

---

[1] It is possible that the tide turned before Šamši- Addu's death; P. Van der Meer, *RA*, xlvii (1953), 16–18, and J. Laessøe, 'The Shemshara Tablets', pp. 73–74.

[2] *ARMT*, v. 36, 37, 40, 43. Cf. the function of Late Roman fortresses in the same region, Ammianus Marcellinus, xviii. 7. 3, 'compulsuri agrestes cum familiis et pecoribus universis ad tutiora transire'. See below, p. 94.

[3] See below, p. 55, n. 1.

III

THE RISE AND FALL OF THE GREAT CITY

FOR a large part of the second millennium B.C. Assyria was a satellite of more powerful kingdoms, Mitanni on the north-west and the Kassite dynasty in Babylonia. So little is known of the history of this period that it would be unprofitable to discuss it here. Assyrian independence was re-established by Aššur-uballiṭ (c. 1366–1330 B.C.), and some of his successors in the thirteenth and twelfth centuries brought about an extension of Assyrian authority over neighbouring lands which foreshadowed the achievements of the Late Assyrian Empire. During this time Aššur remained the capital and royal residence, but it was too far removed from the main concentrations of agricultural land, and presumably of population, to be a convenient administrative or military centre, and was later to be abandoned in favour of sites which were in this respect more suitable, although it always retained its religious pre-eminence as the home of the national shrine. Detailed evidence concerning the fortunes of Assyria becomes available once more with the royal annals of the late tenth century B.C., and from that time onwards is augmented by an increasing flow of administrative and personal documents which illuminate many facets of public and private life. In this chapter we shall first consider some aspects of the information provided by these sources, and by archaeology, which particularly illustrate the local foundations of Assyrian power and the restrictions they imposed on Assyrian policy; and shall then attempt to summarize the sparse evidence at present available for the second half of the first millennium B.C., after the documentary record had been abruptly cut off by the final destruction of Assyria as a political entity.

The most obvious single feature in the settlement pattern of the Late Assyrian kingdom is the great metropolis. For the first time in the history of Northern Iraq we find royal capitals rivalling in size the largest cities of the alluvial plain. Three sites were used in turn as the royal residence and administrative centre by the kings of the ninth to the seventh centuries B.C. The first was Kalḫu, modern Nimrud,[1] which had been founded as a town of moderate size by Shalmaneser I on the site of an early third millennium village on the east bank of the Tigris some 8 km. above its junction with the Greater Zab. Here Aššur-nasirpal (884–859 B.C.) at the beginning of his reign laid out a citadel 20 hectares in extent, with an outer wall enclosing an area of some 360 hectares. Kalḫu remained the capital until the reign of Sargon II (722–705 B.C.), who built himself a new city, Dur Šarrukin (now Khorsabad), north-east of Nineveh under the northern end of Jebel Maqlub; here the total area enclosed within the walls was nearly 320 hectares, the citadel over 20 hectares. It was not completed until just before Sargon's death, and his son Sennacherib chose to move to Nineveh, which thereafter remained the seat of government until the fall

[1] For recent discoveries at Nimrud, see M. E. L. Mallowan, annually in *Iraq*, xii–xxi (1950–9), except xvii (1955); D. Oates, *Iraq*, xxiii–xxv (1961–3).

of Assyria in 612 B.C. The citadel of Nineveh in the seventh century covered more than 20 hectares, the whole city about 750 hectares.

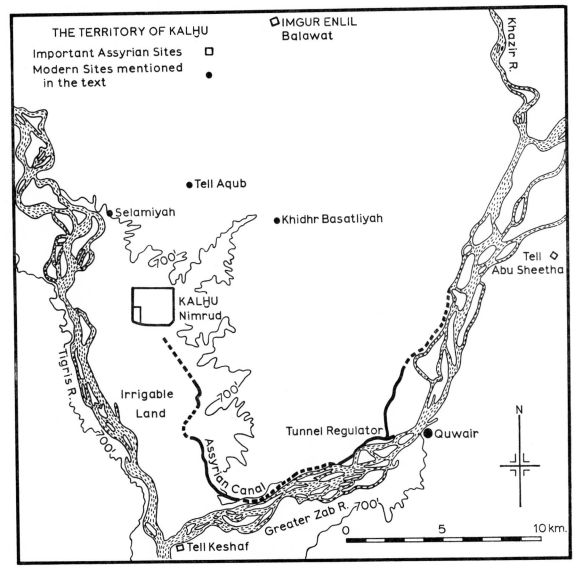

FIG. 3. The Territory of Kalḫu

THE POPULATION OF KALḪU

In the case of Kalḫu we have some contemporary figures for its population. After the completion of his palace there Aššurnasirpal held a great feast which is described in detail on his stele discovered in 1951.[1] He lists over 69,000 guests in four categories: 16,000, the population of the city, presumably its former inhabitants, 47,074 who had been brought there to labour on the new building programme, 5,000 distinguished visitors from

[1] D. J. Wiseman, *Iraq*, xiv (1952), 24–32; see discussion, M. E. L. Mallowan, *Iraq*, xiv. 20–22.

the provinces, and 1,500 officials from other royal establishments in the empire. It seems likely that the workmen, and women who are specifically included in the total of 47,074, subsequently remained to form part of the population of the new city, which would then have totalled more than 63,000. This figure has been compared with the obviously more approximate one of 120,000 given by the Book of Jonah for the population of Nineveh, which has about twice the area of Kalḫu.[1] A direct comparison between these figures and the population of modern cities, such as Aleppo of which the settlement density is known, may be misleading, for virtually the whole of the citadel in each case was given over to grandiose administrative and religious buildings, and large parts of the outer city seem to have been occupied by the mansions of the nobility, in which the households would have been comparatively small in relation to their size.[2] No representative quarter containing smaller private houses, with a higher population density, has ever been excavated although they must obviously have existed. There is, however, another possible approach to the problem, which cannot provide a check on the accuracy of the ancient figures, but does throw some light on their plausibility and suggests general conclusions which may be drawn from them. This is a comparison with the estimates we can make of the population that might have been supported on the agricultural land available in the locality (fig. 3).

Virtually all the land surrounding Kalḫu may be regarded as cultivable. An obvious limiting factor on the size of the territory which is likely to have been cultivated by people living on one site, before the coming of modern transport, is the length of the daily journey which the farmer is prepared to make in order to reach the most distant part of his land. In practice the lure of employment on the excavations at Nimrud draws men daily from villages about 7 km. away, and those who come from more distant villages do not normally return to their homes at night. Probably this distance, which represents one to one and a half hours' travelling time, should be regarded as a maximum, and even this would not be acceptable unless life in the urban community was especially attractive either for the amenities or the security which it offered. If we then take a radius of 7 km. from Kalḫu as the limit beyond which the land would not be farmed by families who lived in the city and could be strictly described as part of its population, and also exclude land beyond the Tigris,[3] we obtain a very approximate figure of 100 sq. km. for its territory. Of this about 75 sq. km. consists of undulating country above the level of the river valleys, while the remainder is low-lying alluvial land in the flood plain of the two rivers below Kalḫu.[4]

[1] Jonah xi. 4; Wiseman, op. cit., p. 28.

[2] This comparison, as a basis for the approximate calculation of ancient city populations, was suggested by H. Frankfort, *Kingship and the Gods*, 1948, p. 396, n. 23. Frankfort, however, initiated the comparison by reference to the residential quarters of cities such as Ur, where small private houses had been excavated, and in such cases it has a certain validity.

[3] It cannot be assumed with certainty that the territory of Kalḫu did not extend across the Tigris to the west, particularly as the river at that time followed a course immediately beneath the citadel on the eastern

edge of its flood plain, and there was presumably a strip of alluvial land some 3 km. wide on its western bank. If this was included, it would increase the total area by 20–25 sq. km.

[4] These suggested limits are approximately confirmed by the distribution of ancient sites in the neighbourhood. One Assyrian village site has been identified about 6 km. to the south, another 7 km. to the north. Selamiya, on the river bank 5 km. above Nimrud, was a considerable walled town, but the pottery seems to be mainly Islamic; earlier occupation cannot be proved, since the site of a possible earlier settlement is

It is difficult to determine the relationship of land to maximum population with any accuracy, but some indication may be obtained from recent estimates of the requirements of a family and of the productivity of land under varying conditions. It is said that a family of six persons can exist, very near subsistence level, on an annual income of 3,000 kg. of barley, which is more tolerant of marginal climatic conditions and gives larger, as well as more reliable, yields than wheat.[1] Of this 1,000 kg. or more would be kept for food, 1,000 kg. would serve as seed or be used to pay for assistance at the harvest, and 1,000 kg. remain to be sold in order to buy the bare necessities of life. The average yield of barley is c. 150 kg. per donum (1/400 sq. km.) on rain-fed land,[2] and the area necessary to produce the annual 3,000 kg. is therefore 20 donums. The almost universal system of crop and fallow in alternate years, rendered necessary by the absence of artificial fertilizers and consequently likely to have been practised in the Assyrian period, raises the total area necessary to meet the requirements of each family to 40 donums or 1/10 sq. km. Without irrigation the territory of Kalḫu as defined above might have supported some 1,000 families directly engaged in agriculture, a total of perhaps 6,000 individuals. We have seen earlier that in the small Iraqi market town of the present day the average proportion of the population directly engaged in agriculture has been estimated at one-half, although it may rise to as much as three-quarters.[3] It seems that without any external stimulus to its economy which might cause an artificial increase in the total population, the original city of Kalḫu might have numbered at most 12,000 inhabitants. The difference between this and Aššurnasirpal's figure of 16,000 must represent an artificial element, but it is not inexplicably large. The city was a royal foundation of Shalmaneser I and as such presumably had some administrative or military significance. It also lay on the road from Nineveh down the east bank of the Tigris, which crossed the Greater Zab at Tell Keshaf, and close to a second important route from Nineveh to Arrapḫa, modern Kirkuk, which forded the Greater Zab at Tell Abu Sheetha, 20 km. east of Kalḫu and thence ran through Kakzu to the crossing of the Lesser Zab at Altun Köprü. There must also have been considerable river traffic past Kalḫu and down the Tigris to Aššur.

The great accretion of population under Aššurnasirpal II must have exceeded the local resources of agricultural land by a substantial margin, and this provides a possible motive

covered by the modern village. On the small mounds near the wells of Khidhr Basatliyah, 8 km. to the north-east, both prehistoric and post-Assyrian pottery have been found, and there may well have been an Assyrian village also. The nearest Assyrian site of any size, however, is the small town of Imgur-Enlil, modern Balawat, 15 km. to the north-east. Naturally I do not preclude the possibility that farmers living in Kalḫu might have spent some time, during seasons of greatest agricultural activity, living in temporary quarters closer to their land as they still do in some areas, but such ephemeral settlements would leave little trace and are hardly relevant to the general point at issue, since these people would certainly have been included in the population of Kalḫu.

[1] *The Economic Development of Iraq*, International Bank for Reconstruction and Development, 1952, pp. 132-3.

[2] It is very difficult to obtain reliable figures for the average yield of crops at the present day, partly because under the prevalent share-cropping system the peasant has an interest in underestimating, the landlord in overestimating, the yield. 150 kg. per donum, equivalent to 5 cwt. per acre, is quoted by authorities, e.g. *The Middle East*, Royal Institute of International Affairs, 1951, without specifying whether it applies to irrigated or unirrigated land or both. The yield for irrigated land is certainly higher, and 150 kg. accords with my own local information for rain-fed land. We have, of course, no means of knowing how ancient and modern yields compare.

[3] See p. 16 above.

for the irrigation scheme which was undertaken in conjunction with the building of the new city. Aššurnasirpal says:

I dug a canal from the Upper Zab, cutting through the mountain to its summit, and called its name *Patti-Hegalli*. The meadow-land by the Tigris I irrigated abundantly and planted gardens in its area. All kinds of fruits and vines I planted and the best of them I offered to Aššur my lord and to the temples of my land.[1]

The line of this canal can still be traced over much of its course, in a rock-cut channel along the bank of the Greater Zab, then following the contours northwards along the eastern rim of the alluvium to a point close to the south-east corner of the outer walls of Kalḫu. During part of its existence it took its water from the Greater Zab through a rock-cut tunnel, formed by linking two shafts sunk from the surface, which passes from east to west through a prominent conglomerate bluff on the north bank of the river opposite the modern village of Quwair (pls. II–III). Across the line of the tunnel at the foot of the first vertical shaft is a low barrier carved out of the natural rock and pierced by three round-headed openings which clearly served as sluices. Steps down the sides of the shafts gave access to the sluices and to the bed of the tunnel. A branch tunnel off the river which pierced the southern edge of the bluff is now entirely filled with silt and its original function is difficult to determine. As far as can be seen it was also provided with sluices and served as an alternative regulator and feed to the head of the canal. It is hard to see what useful purpose would have been served by constructing the two tunnels simultaneously and they probably represent successive solutions of the same problem. It is doubtful, however, whether either branch of the tunnel was the head of Aššurnasirpal's original canal. At the point where they both emerge from the bluff there is a third, open channel which cuts through the bluff at a point some 500 m. north of the tunnel and can be traced as a well-marked canal for another 3 km. upstream. Beyond this point the unnaturally straight line of the western channel of the river suggests that it has cut its way into the bed of the old canal, which may have originated as much as 17 km. above the position of the tunnel, at the confluence of the Greater Zab and its tributary the Khazir.[2]

[1] There follows a list of trees, collected in the course of Aššurnasirpal's campaigns, which were planted in these irrigated orchards including date palms, which do not now bear fruit north of Samarra and cannot even survive a severe winter in Mosul. It seems doubtful whether they were any more successful in the Late Assyrian period, for they are not mentioned in the descriptions of estates that have come down to us; *JADD*, iii–iv, *passim*, and Johns, *An Assyrian Doomsday Book*, 1901, pp. 21–22. The tree *beluṭ*, translated 'lady-palm' in *JADD*, is most probably the dwarf oak, *quercus infectoria*, which produces the galls used in tanning and still an important Mesopotamian product, R. C. Thompson, *Dictionary of Assyrian Botany*, 1949, pp. 249–50; the number of these trees cultivated in the Late Assyrian period throws an interesting light on the continuing importance of herding in the economy, also attested by the numbers of sheep recorded in the Harran census, *Assyrian Doomsday Book*, pp. 22–23. An intriguing problem is the frequent mention of date palms in Assyria in the late first millennium A.D.; G. Le Strange, *Lands of the Eastern Caliphate*, p. 90, Bashīqa; p. 98, Beled Sinjar; p. 99, Tell Afar, accompanied at Bashīqa and Beled Sinjar by oranges and lemons. Does this indicate a warmer climate in the Early Islamic period? The description of the Wadi Tharthar by Tukulti-Ninurta II, father of Aššurnasirpal, *LAR*, i. 128, accords well with its present arid character and suggests that the fringe of the Jazira was not very different in the early first millennium B.C., from which we may suppose that the limits of possible cultivation were much the same.

[2] I am indebted for a discussion of this canal to Mr. C. R. Mann of Binnie, Deacon, & Gourlay, Ltd., with whom I visited the tunnel in 1960. In particular, Mr. Mann pointed out to me the possible continuation of the canal in the line of the river bank upstream of the point where it is still visible.

Neither of these major alternative schemes for feeding the canal can be directly dated. The use of the longer open channel, although it would have given a better head of water and thus might be explained as a method of compensating for the accumulation of silt in the canal, would have been subject to serious difficulties because of the constant changes in the course of the river and its erosive power, which has in fact destroyed the upper section. One or other version of the regulator tunnel through the bluff, if it afforded a sufficient head of water, would seem to be a more satisfactory solution, since the canal below this point is partly cut through rock which would protect it from the river. Moreover the bluff itself projects some distance into the flood plain as a natural breakwater and the river almost inevitably skirts its foot; any tendency to recede from it could be corrected with comparatively little labour. There is some evidence to suggest that the two tunnels were in fact successive later additions to the scheme. The canal was restored by Tiglath-Pileser III (745–727 B.C.) and by Esarhaddon (681–669 B.C.). Tiglath-Pileser's work is only briefly mentioned in a broken text on the wall slabs from his palace at Kalḫu,[1] but Esarhaddon left his record inscribed on a stone tablet in the tunnel itself, where it was seen by Layard.[2] Again the surviving text is incomplete, but it is difficult to see why Esarhaddon should have set up his memorial in the tunnel if he was responsible for the longer canal which would, in this case, have superseded it. It seems possible that Tiglath-Pileser III dug the first regulator tunnel on the south side of the bluff, that this was rendered useless by the silt which now completely fills it, and that Esarhaddon replaced it by the longer tunnel which was cut by linking the vertical shafts sunk from east to west across the bluff. A parallel for this technique of construction can be found in the aqueduct by which Sennacherib, father of Esarhaddon, brought water from the Bastura Chai to Erbil,[3] and it has been suggested that it may have been inspired by the Urartian *qanat* system of underground watercourses seen by Sargon II during his eighth campaign in the region of Lake Van.[4]

The area of land which might have been brought under more intensive cultivation by means of this canal has been estimated at 25 sq. km. Recent survey has enabled us to delineate closely the course of the canal itself, but the courses of the Tigris and the Greater Zab which bounded the irrigated area on the west and south have been subject to substantial variations which cannot be dated, and it seems doubtful whether a much more accurate measurement is possible. Aššurnasirpal says that he planted orchards on this land. It seems unlikely that the whole of the available ground was so employed, since the produce would have been disproportionate to local requirements; the large groves of fruit trees which exist in some favoured parts of Iraq today reflect the accessibility of distant markets through the medium of modern transport. The produce of orchards is now and probably was then a luxury rather than a staple of diet, and would have been dependent on local demand from the wealthier section of the population, government and temple officials, merchants and landowners as well as the palace itself. We may perhaps

[1] *LAR*, i. 270. [2] *LAR*, ii. 279.
[3] Fuad Safar, 'Sennacherib's Project for supplying Erbil with water', *Sumer*, iii (1947), 23–25.
[4] J. Laessøe, 'The Irrigation System at Ulḫu, 8th Century B.C.', *JCS*, v. 21–32. See below, p. 81 n. 1.

guess that a third of the land was used in this way, and the rest as irrigated plough land.[1] If modern statistics are any guide this would not have provided employment for a very large proportion of the increased population. The yield of irrigated barley has been estimated at a minimum of 300 kg. per donum, at least twice that of rain-fed crops. To obtain the 3,000 kg. accepted as a subsistence standard for a family of six persons would then require a minimum holding of 20 donums, of which half would be allowed to lie fallow each year; this practice is now common to both rain-fed and irrigated land, since in the latter case it helps to control the process of salination. This figure is independently confirmed by a provision of the modern law regulating *Lazmah* tenure of irrigated land, which sets 20 donums as the minimum size for a family plot.[2] Seventeen sq. km. of irrigated plough land might then absorb 340 families or approximately 2,000 persons. The intensity of settlement on land planted with fruit trees can be eight times as great, for here the modern law prescribes a minimum of 5 donums and there is naturally no fallow season. The possibility that some of the orchard area constituted a royal park does not materially affect the number of persons employed in its maintenance, and in all 8 sq. km. might support or find occupation for some 600 to 650 families, rather less than 4,000 people. In addition there would still be the 75 sq. km. of rain-fed land above the level of possible irrigation, supporting as before 750 families or 4,500 people. The effect of the construction of the canal would then be to increase the potential population directly engaged in agriculture from 6,000 to a maximum of 10,500 people and the natural size of the community from 12,000 to somewhat over 20,000. If the land on the west bank of the Tigris was also brought under irrigation with water from the Tigris itself, then the grand total might exceed 25,000.

Whatever may be the defects of these calculations, and they are intended only as a very approximate guide to the ancient situation, it is difficult to see how many more families could have worked land within a practicable distance of Kalḫu even after the completion of Aššurnasirpal's irrigation scheme, since the figure adopted for the size of holdings is based on a series of minimal estimates and confirmed by modern practice. It takes no account, for instance, of the possible existence of a share-cropping system which would have expanded the viable minimum size of individual holdings by the proportion necessary to produce the landlord's share. Such a system is less likely in the initial stages of a new settlement scheme, but may well have been in force where a traditional pattern of land tenure prevailed. We know from the records of land sales and grants found at Nineveh,[3] and from the Harran Census, that peasants were frequently tied to, and transferred with, the estate on which they worked. In such cases the land must provide not only subsistence for the farmer but a considerable income in kind for his master, and the population ratio in the countryside is reduced accordingly, although a large part of the lord's income may have

[1] Some of the land was used for growing barley which was issued as rations to workmen: D. J. Wiseman, *Iraq*, xiii (1951), 107, tablet no. ND. 416. For the issue of materials for horticultural operations, B. H. Parker, *Iraq*, xxiii (1961), 24, tablet no. ND. 2424.

[2] *AGH*, p. 453. *Lazmah* tenure was a form of perpetual leasehold instituted to legalize possession by tribesmen of land on which they had long been settled: 'Reports to the Council of the League of Nations on the Administration of Iraq', London, H.M.S.O., 1932, p. 25.

[3] *JADD*, iv (1923), 200–12.

served indirectly to support retainers, artisans, and traders of all kinds, thereby increasing the possible size of urban communities.

We are forced to the conclusion, then, that some 35,000–40,000 of the 63,000 people who formed the combined population of Kalḫu, at least during the period of its construction, were an artificial element in the sense that their subsistence could not be provided from the immediate agricultural resources of the area. It must be remembered that their employment did not cease with the completion of Aššurnasirpal's palace in 879 B.C. His programme included the restoration of all the city temples, and, although these are listed in his stele inscription, the Ninurta temple, which he regarded as the principal shrine of Kalḫu, was not completed until his eighteenth year.[1] The great ziggurrat which adjoined it was still being built in the time of his son, Shalmaneser III, whose inscribed ziggurrat bricks are common on the site.[2] The greater part of the city wall was probably completed before Aššurnasirpal's death, but additions were made by Shalmaneser III, and during his reign a great arsenal and royal palace were erected in the south-east corner of the outer city as well as one or perhaps two palaces on the citadel.[3] Under Adad-nirari III (811–783 B.C.) the temple of Nabu was rebuilt on a grand scale together with an adjoining palace, additions were made to the arsenal, and a mansion erected to the north of the citadel.[4] The excavations which have been made on five sites in the outer city outside the limits of the citadel and the arsenal have revealed three mansions of this kind, and although two were of seventh-century date[5] we may reasonably assume that the Assyrian nobility would also have been provided with palatial town houses in the ninth century when the capital was at Kalḫu, and that many remain to be discovered. Obviously the century following the accession of Aššurnasirpal II was a period of intense building activity at Kalḫu, which would have given continuous employment to a large labour force.

NINEVEH AND ITS IRRIGATION SYSTEM
(Fig. 4)

Inscriptions relating to Nineveh give no information about its population, and the figure of 120,000 given by the Book of Jonah is at best based on a contemporary guess; we know nothing of the situation before the seventh century. On the other hand, we have a detailed description of Sennacherib's great undertaking for the enlargement of its water supply and the purposes for which it was intended, and this provides a useful complement to the study of Kalḫu. This work was on a much larger scale than that of Aššurnasirpal, and seemed to have been accomplished in four main stages:

(i) The canalization of the Khosr river for the irrigation of orchards and of a royal park planted with a great variety of trees, collected in the course of Sennacherib's campaigns. Some at least of the orchards were parcelled out in small plots among

[1] *LAR*, i. 138 ff.
[2] *LAR*, i. 252.
[3] D. Oates, *Iraq*, xxv, and xx. 112. A fragmentary inscription of Shalmaneser also appears on broken reliefs on the façade of a palace in the middle of the mound.
[4] D. Oates, *Iraq*, xix. 35; M. E. L. Mallowan, *Iraq*, xviii. 20 and xvi. 70.
[5] M. E. L. Mallowan, *Iraq*, xix. 21–25.

the citizens of Nineveh. This stage was completed in or shortly after the second year of Sennacherib's reign (c. 703 B.C.) and is first described in the cylinder which commemorates the foundation of his new palace.[1]

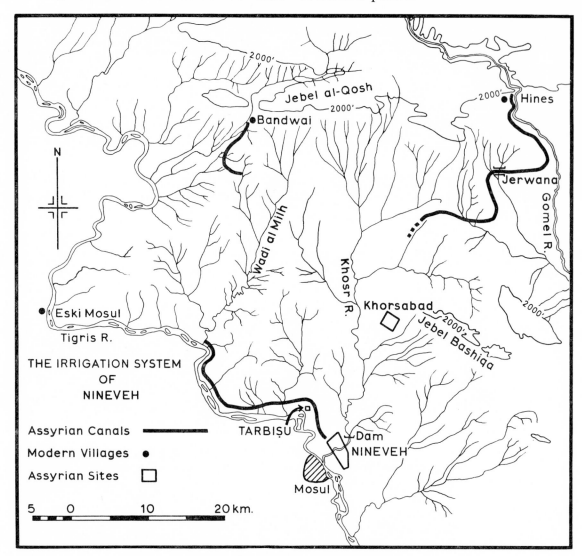

FIG. 4. The Irrigation System of Nineveh

(ii)   The clearance and canalization of the sources at the western foot of Jebel Bashiqa, north-east of Nineveh, which were then led into the Khosr. First mentioned in 700 B.C.[2]

(iii) The diversion into the Khosr of a part of the waters of the Gomel river, by the construction of a canal from the point where the Gomel emerges from the mountains, about 50 km. north-east of Nineveh. This major work included the

[1] *LAR*, ii. 162.   [2] *LAR*, ii. 172.

construction of a stone aqueduct to carry the canal across a watercourse near the modern village of Jerwana, and was completed about 695 B.C. An inscription accompanying rock-reliefs of Sennacherib on the cliff face above the head of the canal, near the present village of Hines, includes an account of his first eight campaigns, and also summarizes the whole work carried out up to that time.[1]

(iv) The diversion of a stream which emerges from the same mountain chain, Jebel al-Qosh, at the modern village of Bandwai, some 30 km. west of Hines (pl. IV). This water was carried by a recently identified canal which makes a broad sweep south-eastwards to join the Wadi al-Milh, which it enters $2\frac{1}{2}$ km. south of a village named Sharafiya. The Wadi al-Milh is a seasonal watercourse which now joins the Tigris some 20 km. east of Eski Mosul, but was then diverted close to its mouth into a second canal following the contours on the left flank of the Tigris valley for a distance of some 16 km. to the north end of Nineveh. This part of the scheme is not attested by any surviving inscription, but the two canals can be traced on the ground and it seems to be the logical complement of Sennacherib's known work. A defaced relief near Bandwai village probably served the same commemorative purpose as those at Hines. The work is not mentioned in the Hines inscription and for this reason has been placed at the end of the sequence, which seems to have been executed in geographical order from east to north.[2]

Several statements in the inscriptions throw light on the purpose of this great reorganization, which tapped the resources of the whole area between Nineveh and the mountains. Sennacherib says that the Khosr was used to water all the orchards in the hot season and, in the winter, a thousand fields of alluvium around and below the city.[3] Winter irrigation must have been intended for grain crops, and we learn from the Hines inscription that the land between Nineveh and Tarbiṣu, now Sharif Khan near the Tigris bank 3 km. north-west of the city, grew grain and sesame. Even the royal park, which was in part a botanical garden and a pleasure resort and included an artificial swamp, served a practical purpose: reeds from the swamp, cypress and mulberry from the plantations, were cut for use in the construction of the new palaces.[4] Cotton, which made its appearance in Assyria for the first time, was no mere curiosity: 'The wool-bearing trees they sheared and wove into garments.'[5] It is clear that although the size of the undertaking reflects the notion of grandeur so characteristic of the Late Assyrian kings and it cannot have been an economic proposition, yet it had a practical motive, 'To increase the productivity of the low-lying fields'.[6]

The location of the land which was brought under intensive cultivation can be inferred from the inscriptions, the position of the canals, and the topography of the ground. Some of the orchards which depended on the Khosr and the waters of Jebel Bashiqa must have lain to the east of Nineveh in the narrow valley between the inner and the outer ramparts.

---

[1] *LAR*, ii. 149–51. An account of this work, and a discussion of the whole system up to this point, is given by T. Jacobsen and S. Lloyd, 'Sennacherib's Aqueduct at Jerwan', *OIP*, xxiv (1935).

[2] These canals were observed by the writer in 1957–8.
[3] *LAR*, ii. 172.
[4] *LAR*, ii. 150.
[5] *LAR*, ii. 172.
[6] *LAR*, ii. 177.

The remains of a dam in this valley probably mark the site of Sennacherib's swamp,[1] and the dam may also have served to regulate the water supply for the lower part of the valley and a small area of land south of the city. The Hines inscription states that the Khosr was also used to irrigate the grain crops between Nineveh and Tarbiṣu, and there must have been a canal along the north wall leading to this section of the Tigris flood plain. The rest of the flood plain north of Tarbiṣu was evidently supplied with water by the fourth stage of the scheme which diverted the Wadi al Milh and its artificial tributary from Bandwai around the northern rim of the Tigris valley. Unfortunately this area, which represents a considerable proportion of the whole, has varied so greatly with the changes in course of the river itself that no useful estimate can be made of the amount of land under cultivation in Sennacherib's time. But the flood plain of the Tigris at this point is considerably narrower than at its junction with the Greater Zab, and even the inclusion of some land east and south of Nineveh can hardly have raised the total to a higher figure than the corresponding estimate for Kalḫu. In fact, it would have supported a larger agricultural element among the inhabitants of the city and to some extent was intended to do so, but the increase, in proportion to the total population in the seventh century, was even less than at Kalḫu and the number of people who had to be maintained on resources other than those of the immediate agricultural territory of Nineveh was much higher.

POPULATION, RESOURCES, AND STRATEGY

These cities represent a highly artificial element in the economy of northern Iraq. A complete discussion of this phenomenon would require an analysis of the whole of Late Assyrian history, but some of its implications are particularly relevant to the pattern of settlement in this period and merit a brief survey. We must first consider the possibility that they derived a substantial part of their income from trade. In the case of Kalḫu this may be virtually discounted, since the site does not command an important river crossing or a natural road junction. Nineveh, however, does enjoy both these advantages and its successor, Mosul, was long a merchants' city supported largely on the profits of its own manufactures and an extensive commercial connexion with Baghdad, Aleppo, Trebizond, and Tabriz. As such it maintained, even in the comparatively unfavourable conditions of the late nineteenth century, a population of over 60,000.[2] Trade had been a vital element in the economy of Aššur, and probably also of Nineveh, in the Early Assyrian period, and at any time Nineveh was bound to profit by its local position at the point of interchange between the population of three different geographical regions, the nomads of the steppe and the farmers of the plain and of the hills. Yet the administrative correspondence of the Late Assyrian kings, the great bulk of which was found at Nineveh, reveals no concern at all with commerce, although the prices of staple foodstuffs are the subject of a proper interest.[3] Such business documents as we possess may be uncharacter-

---

[1] R. C. Thompson and R. W. Hutchinson, *Archaeologia*, lxxix, 114–16, plan (fig. 1) and pl. lviii.

[2] E. Wallis Budge, *By Nile and Tigris*, ii. 47.

[3] Prices: H. W. F. Saggs, *Iraq*, xxi. 162, letter no. lii; harvest prospects: loc. cit. lvi and *Iraq*, xviii. 40, letter no. xxiv.

istic, for they have usually been excavated in or near administrative buildings and often belong to officials, but the financial transactions involved seem to reflect the working of an agricultural economy and there is nothing to suggest that the parties had any trading interest beyond the normal exchange of land, slaves, animals, and crops.

It is in fact abundantly clear, both from the royal annals and administrative records, that the main preoccupation of an active king was the maintenance of Assyrian control over large subject territories. This control was dependent on efficient organization coupled with ruthless military action. The operation of the machinery of government can be seen on the one hand in the correspondence between the king and his officials, on the other in the archives of great administrative buildings such as the North-West Palace and the arsenal at Kalḫu.[1] The letters embodied the day to day questions and decisions affecting every aspect of government, while the central archives, even in their fragmentary state, illustrate the detailed assessment of resources which was the foundation of the system; we find here records of the receipt and issue of foodstuffs and raw materials for the construction and repair of military and other equipment, of the annual census of men, animals, weapons, and supplies at the disposal of the government. The individual features of this organization are not new. Ḥammurabi of Babylon corresponded with his governors on administrative matters, and the earliest known example of the imperial arsenal is the depot established at Tell Drehem near Nippur by the kings of the Third Ur Dynasty.[2] But the great kings of the Late Assyrian Empire brought it to an unrivalled pitch of efficiency which must have been a great factor in their military success. It was not, however, an achievement which was celebrated by their official propaganda. In their annals and in their sculptures, which together one may fairly regard as the self-portrait of the régime, there is a constant emphasis on two themes, war and tribute. The theory implicit in this presentation, over-simplified as it may be, is self-evident. Royal grandeur, of which the great cities were a material expression, could only be supported on the tribute of territories far beyond the natural borders of Assyria, and the tribute could only be exacted by the threat, and often the presence, of overwhelming military force. The successful application of this theory, intermittent as it may have been and, no doubt, exaggerated by the partisan reports that we possess, is none the less a striking historical fact which has never been adequately explained. Indeed, no useful analysis of it is possible without an answer to one primary question, the size of the native Assyrian population from which the army was drawn, and this cannot at present be attempted. But there is no apparent reason why it should have exceeded the population of comparable areas in Syria or southern Anatolia which Assyria came to dominate in the course of the ninth century. For this reason it is likely that the total number of Assyrians was much smaller than the total of their subject peoples, and this numerical inferiority seems to be reflected in their military policy.

[1] The royal correspondence from Nineveh is translated in L. Waterman, *Royal Correspondence of the Assyrian Empire*, 1930–6. For administrative letters from Nimrud, see H. W. F. Saggs, *Iraq*, xxi (1959), 158–79. For ration issues, establishment returns, etc., from Nim-rud, see B. H. Parker, *Iraq*, xxiii (1961), 15–67, and for a summary of material from the arsenal, D. Oates, *Iraq*, xxiv (1962), 20–22.

[2] See p. 26, n. 3 above.

A discussion of Assyrian strategy based only on literary evidence has one important defect, that it relates only to the periods when such evidence is available, in fact to the reigns of those kings who were successful soldiers. The situation before the time of Adad-nirari II (912–891 B.C.) is little documented, and the same may be said of the period of relative weakness from the death of Adad-nirari III in 783 B.C. to the accession of Tiglath-Pileser III in 745 B.C., and of the last thirty years of Assyria before its downfall in 612 B.C. Moreover, the evidence that does exist deliberately presents a record of successful attack, ignoring for reasons of prestige any possibility of invasion or consideration of defence. A survey of the geographical situation and of the distribution of sites helps to correct this distortion. We have seen that Assyria is open to penetration, in times of weakness, from the south-west and from the highlands on the north and east. In the tenth century B.C. the Aramaeans, West Semitic-speaking peoples of Arabian origin, had long been established on the Middle Euphrates and had penetrated up the Khabur to occupy the land on the west side of the Tigris around modern Diyarbekr.[1] The highlands were in part controlled by the kingdom of Urartu, with its capital near Lake Van, and in part occupied by smaller communities recognizing no external allegiance. Defence against intruders is a natural prerequisite of security and although, as we have observed, later Assyrian records do not admit the necessity, the location of cities on the approaches to Assyria itself often suggests that their function was partly military.

This is most clearly seen where the possible routes of access are best defined by natural features, as they are on the west side of the Tigris. On the north-west, in the region of Nisibin, there lay in the time of Adad-nirari II the small state of Ḥanigalbat, the last remnant of the Mitanni kingdom. From Nisibin the stages on the high road to Nineveh are marked by town sites, many of prehistoric origin and all occupied in the first millennium B.C.—Tell Roumeilan, Tell Chilparat, Tell Hawa, Tell Uweinat, Tell Hugna. From Tell Hugna there have been in historic times two traditional routes to Mosul and Nineveh, the first gaining the Tigris valley at Eski Mosul, the second passing through or near Tell Abu Marya. How much of this road was under direct Assyrian control before the time of Adadnirari II is not known and cannot be learnt from superficial examination of the sites, but the long-established territory of Assyria certainly extended as far as the Eski Mosul–Tell Abu Marya line. Eski Mosul was a Late Assyrian town by the name of Balata,[2] while Tell Abu Marya was the Assyrian Apqu. Apqu would appear to have been the more important of the two sites at this period, for Adad-nirari II built a 'palace' there.[3] It would appear that the 'palace' was not so much a royal residence as an administrative and especially a military base, for he records its construction immediately before the account of five successive campaigns against Ḥanigalbat. West of Tell Abu Marya the

---

[1] For a recent summary of the evidence concerning Aramaean penetration, see Kupper, *Nomades*, pp. 112 ff. The best general account of the history of this period is still S. Smith, *CAH*, iii (1925), chs. i–v. The standard work of reference for Assyrian geography is E. Forrer, *Die Provinzeinteilung des assyrisches Reiches*, 1921, which is, however, open to correction on the basis of more recently discovered evidence.

[2] E. Forrer, op. cit., p. 106.

[3] *LAR*, i. 362. For the identification of Apqu with Tell Abu Marya, see F. J. Stephens, *JCS*, vii (1953), 73–74. An earlier 'palace' had been begun by Aššur-reš-iši (1133–1116 B.C.) and completed by one of his successors, possibly Aššur-bel-kala (1075–1057 B.C.). Aššurnasirpal II either added to the building of Adad-nirari II or erected another.

saddle between Jebel Sasan and Jebel Sheikh Ibrahim provides the most northerly access to the Assyrian plains from the Jazira, and this was dominated by Tell Afar, commonly identified with Assyrian Nimit-Ištar.[1] The next gap in the hill chain south-east of Tell Afar, at the modern village of Muhalabiya between Jebel Sheikh Ibrahim and Jebel Shanīn, was guarded in the Middle Assyrian period by a small fortified town, Tell Kamira, of which the ancient name is unknown.[2] Its circuit of massive walls, disproportionate to the area they enclose, suggests a military function, but we do not know how long it remained in use. Between this point and Aššur lay the provincial capital of Isana, which has not yet been identified. There is indeed no obvious Assyrian site controlling the western end of the corridor which leads from the Wadi Tharthar to the Tigris; the location of Isana may solve this problem, but the foundation of Tell 'Abta on the Wadi Tharthar north of the later site of Hatra during the troubled period of the mid-eighth century suggests that this gap may have been a conspicuous one.[3] Aššur itself and Ekallāte served to guard the Tigris valley route from the south. On the east of the river the direct road from the crossing of the Lesser Zab to Nineveh ran through Kakzu, used by Aššurnasirpal II as a base for his operations in the mountains south-east of Assyria, while Erbil controlled the more easterly road. The organization of the area east and north-east of Nineveh remains somewhat obscure, but Šibaniba, now Tell Billa at the foot of Jebel Bashīqa, was a considerable Middle and Late Assyrian town containing a government arsenal and would

[1] With the westward expansion of Assyrian control in the ninth century Apqu and Nimit-Ištar were incorporated in a larger province under the governor of Rasappa, the extent of which in the reign of Adad-nirari III is shown by an inscription of Nergal-ereš, who described himself as governor of Nimittu-Ištar, Apqu, Marē, Rasapu, Katni, Dur Karpati, Sirku, the lands of Lakē and Hindanu, Anat, the land of Suḫi, and another city of which the name is broken (LAR, i. 261; see Forrer, Provinzeinteilung, pp. 14 ff.). The province thus included both Aramaean states on the Middle Euphrates and Assyrian cities separated from them by the expanse of the northern Jazira. This appears to be an administratively inconvenient combination, although it recalls Iasmaḫ-Addu's very similar sphere of responsibility a thousand years before (see above, p. 41). Nergal-ereš appears on the list of limmu as governor of Rasappa in 804 and again in 775 B.C., which suggests an exceptionally long term of office. His very extensive command may have been a temporary arrangement ad hominem, and indeed it seems doubtful whether the constantly changing boundaries of the Assyrian empire would have permitted any permanent definition of the frontier provinces at this time; the later provincial boundaries were the work of Tiglath-Pileser III. Rasappa, however, remained an important province, for its governor held limmu office immediately after the chief government officials in the eighth century (LAR, ii. 436–7). Its capital is usually thought to be in the Sinjar region, but my survey revealed no site which obviously of exceptional importance at this time, although one of the second-millennium sites mentioned

above (p. 35, n. 3) may, in fact, have been Rasappa. It seems just possible that the name is a later form of Razamā, but if so, Razamā ša Burama-x should lie north-west of the bend of the Wadi Tharthar, and there must be a stage missing between it and Aššur on Goetze's itinerary; in this case Tell Hadhail would suggest itself. I do not believe Rasappa was Beled Sinjar (Forrer, op. cit., p. 15); see below, p. 99. The identification with later Resafa, proposed by A. Musil, The Middle Euphrates, 1927, pp. 210–11, is open to the objection that no sign of an Assyrian settlement has been reported from Resafa. It would also require the removal of Apqu and Nimit-Ištar further to the west. This seems unlikely in this context but not impossible since there was an Apqum ša Baliḫa in the Early Assyrian period and the name means 'pool' (Goetze, JCS, vii. 57), and I have been unable to find any positive evidence for the location of Nimit-Ištar at Tell Afar. The only other evidence I know that has any bearing on the location of Nimit-Ištar is RCAE, 814, where it is evidently a collecting point for timber being delivered to Khorsabad, but this is hardly specific.

[2] A brief and uninformative sounding was carried out here by A. H. Layard (Nineveh and Babylon, pp. 241–2).

[3] Dur Bel-ḫarran-bel-usur, named after its founder who was successively high chamberlain to Shalmaneser IV and Tiglath-Pileser III, and who in the earlier reign so far usurped the royal prerogative as to establish freedom from taxes and feudal service for its inhabitants (LAR, i. 295–6).

probably have played some part in it, while Kurba'il, an unidentified city north of Nineveh, is later mentioned in connexion with the Urartian frontier.[1]

This inner ring of cities did not constitute a system of linear defence, but they would have served a double military purpose as well as the social and economic functions common to all small Near Eastern towns. They would have exercised disciplinary control over their immediate neighbourhood, and furnished bases from which, under a strong king, could be mounted the raids which were at once the most effective and the most profitable reminder of Assyrian power. Under Adad-nirari II and his successors, who proved to be a remarkable series of energetic warriors, these expeditions led to the establishment of the formal empire of which Kalḫu was designed to be a worthy capital. It is at this point that we must ask whether the resources of Assyria, particularly in man-power, were equal to the ambitions of her rulers for foreign conquest and domestic magnificence. The logical extension of earlier strategy was the establishment of more distant fortresses manned by sufficient garrisons to keep the provinces in check. But the greater part of the army remained, as it had always been, an annual levy, and it seems unlikely that the available manpower under any system could have furnished standing forces of the necessary size. New fortresses were indeed established and garrisoned, but their effect had to be reinforced by a most significant measure, the deportation of substantial numbers of the conquered peoples, who could themselves be kept under more effective surveillance away from their homelands, and who served as hostages for the good behaviour of their kinsmen who remained.

The steps taken during the reign of Aššurnasirpal II and his son Shalmaneser III (859–824 B.C.) for the control of the Middle Euphrates and Northern Syria provide a good example of the application of this technique, which was copied and extended by later rulers. Aššurnasirpal reports the establishment of two royal cities, Kar Aššurnasirpal and Nibarti-Aššur, straddling the Middle Euphrates valley, and the settlement of an Assyrian garrison in Aribua, a royal city of Ḫattina, beyond the Euphrates in North Syria.[2] We learn from the inscriptions relating to the building of Kalḫu that the 47,000 workmen and women whom he settled there were drawn from Suḫi, Lakē, and Sirku on the Middle Euphrates and from Bit Adini, Ḫatte, and Ḫattina in North Syria; the other subject population represented at Kalḫu were inhabitants of Zamua, south-east of Assyria around Sulaimaniya, where he also founded a fortress city, Dur Aššur (modern Bakrawa).[3] His son Shalmaneser III encountered stiff opposition in Bit Adini, and after his final victory he turned the royal capital, Til Barsip (now Tell Ahmar), into an Assyrian fortress under the name of Kar Shalmaneser, and established Assyrian garrisons in three other cities.[4] The king of Bit Adini was deported to the city of Aššur with 17,500 of his people.[5]

Whether, as has sometimes been suggested, this policy envisaged the creation of a

---

[1] Tell Billa: E. A. Speiser and C. Bache, *BASOR*, xl (1930), 12 ff., and *MJ*, xxiv (1935), 33–48. On the location of Kurba'il or Kurban, see *Iraq*, xxiii. 31; xxiv. 16, n. 26; xxiv. 98–99; for its connexion with the Urartian frontier, *RCAE*, 123.

[2] *LAR*, i. 163, 166.

[3] *LAR*, i. 154. The deported inhabitants of Zamua are specifically stated to have been used as forced labour in Kalḫu.

[4] *LAR*, i. 218.

[5] *LAR*, i. 229.

cosmopolitan society within the empire seems very doubtful; like the ideas of universal citizenship attributed to Alexander, the notion is too sophisticated for the man. But it was an ingenious and, for the time, successful solution of two problems, the maintenance of control over territories larger than Assyria itself, and the provision, for the construction of the great cities, of labour forces greater than Assyria alone could furnish. Yet in both respects it reflects the inadequacy of Assyrian manpower for the tasks that were being thrust upon it, and it had a number of obvious consequences which cannot have failed to influence the course of Assyrian history. The instances quoted above record the settlement at Kalḫu and Aššur alone of nearly 65,000 foreigners in the space of forty years; our examination of the resources of Kalḫu has shown that the greater part of the new population there must have been fed from outside the territory of the city, and it seems certain that they were ultimately supported on the revenues of the provinces. Thus one result of employing the device of deportation in the creation of a military empire and an imperial establishment was to render the maintenance of the empire essential to Assyrian survival, while another was the progressive dilution of the native population of Assyria from whom the army was drawn. This was hardly a serious cause of weakness in the ninth century. But the constant and probably inevitable expansion of this policy led, in the seventh century, to absurdities which are barely cloaked under the bombastic language of the royal annals.[1] We do not know how many people Sennacherib brought to Nineveh to perform forced labour on his new capital. His own claim, in the earliest building inscription, to have brought 208,000 captives to Assyria can hardly be taken literally, but it does give some indication of the terms in which he thought.[2] When, on the other hand, he founded the fortress city called by his own name, Kar Sennacherib, he settled in it not an Assyrian garrison but a colony of provincials deported from other parts of the empire, which as a guarantee of security can only have been acceptable *faute de mieux*. In the annals of his son Aššurbanipal (669–c. 627 B.C.) we find the same situation exaggerated

---

[1] The instances I have chosen here are an arbitrary selection from a mass of evidence. A great extension of the system of wholesale deportations coincided with the revival of Assyrian expansion under Tiglath-Pileser III; S. Smith, *CAH*, iii (1925), 34 and 41–42. The resettlement of subject peoples in Syria in the reign of Sargon is conveniently summarized in a table of events in that area published by H. W. F. Saggs, *Iraq*, xvii (1955), 148–9. Saggs has rightly pointed out that the government concerned itself with the welfare of both Assyrian and foreign settlers, *Iraq*, xviii (1956), 55, citing letters nos. xxiv–xxvi, ibid., pp. 40–43; letter no. xxvi relates to the provision of wives for Aramaean settlers. On the other hand letter no. xxii (*Iraq*, xvii) casts a grimmer light on the ultimate sanction which ensured the loyalty of captives taken into Assyrian service; it seems to refer to an argument between two officials, one of whom wished to conscript some prisoners while the other maintained that they should be killed, since they were unreliable soldiers.

It is tempting to compare this system with the recruit-ment of the fighting men of hostile tribes as auxiliaries in the imperial army which became a regular feature of Roman practice, but there is an important difference. The pacification of a Roman province was accompanied by a deliberate process of Romanization, and army service opened the way to citizenship, a position of prestige and some privilege in this new society which was worth fighting for. When the king of Assyria says of a conquered population, 'With the people of Assyria I counted them', it seems to mean that they were thenceforward privileged to share the increasingly heavy burdens of forced labour and military service. In such circumstances they would be loyal as long as the military success of Assyria assured them a certain prosperity, but they had no visible motive for risking their lives in its defence if it was hard-pressed. Once the weakness of Assyria became apparent, then the subject peoples had little to lose by changing sides, and their defection would accelerate its collapse.

[2] *LAR*, ii. 133.

to an even greater extent by the insupportable inflation of Assyrian military responsibilities. Garrisons in Egypt were drawn from newly conquered lands east of the Tigris, enemy troops from Elam and the coast of Palestine were incorporated directly in the Assyrian army.[1] Within twenty years of the death of Aššurbanipal Assyria had ceased to exist as a political entity. This sudden reversal of fortune cannot be explained in the absence of historical evidence from Assyria itself in the last thirty years of its existence. But the two Median invasions of 614 and 612 B.C.[2] which brought about its final downfall do not represent the sudden appearance of a new and overwhelming military power on the Assyrian horizon, but rather a tribal coalition of the type with which Assyria had long been accustomed to deal. It seems that internal weakness must have been an important contributory cause. A study of the population and resources of the homeland of Assyria suggests that their inadequacy may have dictated the policies which created the empire and compelled its maintenance, while their exhaustion contributed to its collapse.

ASSYRIA AFTER THE FALL OF NINEVEH

The history of Northern Iraq after the destruction of Assyria must be reconstructed almost entirely from archaeological evidence, supplemented by sparse and for the most part uninformative literary references. The post-Assyrian period has, moreover, suffered from the neglect of archaeologists who regarded it, not without reason, as the impoverished descendant of more illustrious forebears, and it has only recently been the subject of serious study. Any account of it must therefore acknowledge historical and geographical gaps in knowledge, but it is of importance to a general study of the area because the breakdown of authority permitted a significant change in the pattern of settlement. The ambition of Assyrian kings no longer maintained their great cities in defiance of local economic restrictions and, the artificial stimulus removed, the population seems to have reverted to a condition dictated to a greater extent by its immediate environment.

The Assyrian population cannot have disappeared overnight, and there is in fact evidence from Kalḫu to suggest that some of the inhabitants of the city returned after its sack in 612 B.C. to seek shelter in the ruins. The character of this temporary resettlement is significant. It was confined to the fortified areas, the citadel and the arsenal in the south-east corner of the outer city. In the case of the arsenal a deliberate attempt was made to put the building in a posture of defence by rebuilding the north gate, which had been dismantled for repair in 614 B.C. and had not been re-erected at the time of the final onslaught in 612 B.C.[3] We have no means of knowing what authority was responsible for this work, but it was not the Assyrian government, which lingered on in Harran until 608 B.C. but never again exercised control over the homeland. But it clearly reflects insecurity in the countryside, which is indeed demonstrated by the fate of these refugees. Three levels of post-Assyrian occupation have been identified within the walls of the arsenal. None of them could be precisely dated, but all produced pottery identical with that of the latest Assyrian occupation from which they cannot have been far removed in

[1] *LAR*, ii. 326, 311, 319.
[2] D. Oates, *Iraq*, xxiii (1961), 9.
[3] D. Oates, *Iraq*, xxiii. 10–11 and xxiv. 11–13.

time. All in turn came to a violent end. It seems likely that the hill tribes who had suffered so much at Assyrian hands were now taking their revenge, and the suggestion is borne out by the fact that the Babylonians, who had fallen heir to Assyrian military responsibilities in this area, found it necessary to campaign in the hills north-east of Assyria in 608 and 607 B.C.

After the final disappearance of these last remnants of the city population of Kalḫu we have very little archaeological evidence until the Hellenistic period. This probably reflects a degree of stability and security re-established under Achaemenid rule, for the huge mounds of ruins which now represented the citadels of Assyrian cities were unattractive to later settlers except in time of danger, when their inaccessibility might be considered an advantage, and it is precisely these citadels which have attracted the almost exclusive attention of modern excavators. We obtain a passing glimpse of Achaemenid organization from an interesting document found in Egypt, relating to Nehtihur, a subordinate of Aršam who was probably the satrap of Egypt of that name in the late fifth century.[1] Nehtihur was travelling to Egypt on business from Babylon, where Aršam was resident at the time (411/10–408 B.C.), and was provided with a letter from his master to officials along his route, authorizing them to issue rations to the travelling party from Aršam's estates in their districts. For reasons unknown to us Nehtihur took the road across Northern Mesopotamia rather than the more direct Euphrates valley route. His letter of authority was addressed to the officers responsible for La'ir, for Arzuḫin, for Arbel, Ḫalsu, and Mat-al-Ubaš, for Sa'lam, and for Damascus. It cannot be assumed that he passed through all these towns, only that he was expected to draw supplies within their administrative districts, but his journey can be reconstructed with fair accuracy on this supposition, for a number of the places mentioned were Assyrian cities of which the precise or approximate location is known. La'ir was Assyrian Laḫiru, probably Eski Kifri on the line of the modern railway from Baghdad to Kirkuk via the Diyala valley.[2] Arzuḫin (Assyrian A/Urzuḫina) has been plausibly located at the large mound of Chemchemal, 40 km. east of Kirkuk.[3] Arbel is now Erbil (Assyrian Arba'ilu, Sumerian Urbillum), Ḫalsu was probably an Assyrian site but its location is unknown,[4] and Mat-al-Ubaš obviously corresponds with the Assyrian Ubaše, of which the name has suggested an identification with Tell Huwaish, overlooking the Tigris 20 km. north of Aššur.[5]

---

[1] G. R. Driver, *Aramaic Documents of the Fifth Century B.C.*, 1957, p. 28.

[2] For earlier references bearing on the location of these places, see Driver, op. cit., pp. 57–58. Laḫiru is identified with Eski Kifri on the *Map of Ancient Sites in Iraq*, issued by the Directorate-General of Antiquities, Republic of Iraq, but I have been unable to discover the positive grounds for this identification.

[3] H. W. F. Saggs, *Iraq*, xx (1958), 209.

[4] The proposed identification of Assyrian Ḫalsu or Barḫalza with Hazza, an important settlement in the Sassanid period (E. Herzfeld, *Memnon*, i (1907), 123 ff.) is supported by Strabo's mention of Χαζήνη as one of the four districts in the plains around Nineveh (xvi. 736); Hazza lay in the direction of Erbil (Hoffmann,

Auszüge, p. 210). This is further corroborated by the location of the gate of Nineveh called 'The Gate of the land of Ḫalsu' at the south-east corner of the city (R. C. Thompson and R. W. Hutchinson, *Archaeologia*, lxxix. 111), but the actual site remains unidentified.

[5] The site of Tell Huwaish (not to be confused with Tell Huwaish south of Beled Sinjar, see p. 35 n. 3 above) lies on a tongue of elevated land between the Tigris valley and the Wadi Jirnaf, overlooking the modern railway station of Jirnaf. It has no obvious citadel mound. A conglomerate bluff at the southern tip of the ridge may originally have served this purpose, but there seems to be no great accumulation of artificial debris on its summit, which is now heavily eroded. There is a considerable scatter of pottery, including

Nehtihur's route seems at first to have followed the Royal Road from the Diyala valley northward as far as the crossing of the Lesser Zab, and then turned across the Tigris to join one of the roads which ran north-west into Syria via the Khabur basin. Two points of interest emerge from this document. Firstly, Laḥiru, Arzuḥina, Arbela, Ḥalsu, and Ubaše were administrative centres in the fifth century. Secondly, a Persian nobleman owned estates in all these districts, presumably by royal grant. The extent of his holdings is perhaps explained by the suggestion that he was a member of the royal family, and it may be that the land had originally formed part of the estates granted to high Assyrian officials, whose wide domains in different parts of the country are attested by surviving royal charters of the seventh century.[1]

The existence of estates belonging to members of the royal house is also recorded by Xenophon, who notes that some villages near the Tigris four days' march south of the River Zapatas, the Greater Zab, belonged to Queen Parysatis, mother of Artaxerxes II and of Cyrus the Younger. Xenophon's account of his march through Assyria,[2] although it naturally describes only that part of the region which he happened to see, is nevertheless an interesting reflection of the state of the country in his day (401 B.C.), for its resources were a matter of immediate concern to him and are frequently mentioned. Passing the former site of Kalḥu he refers to the people of villages in the neighbourhood who took refuge on top of the ziggurrat at the approach of the Greek army, although the city itself was deserted and he knew neither its name nor that of its former inhabitants, whom he describes as Medes. Nineveh was similarly identified as a ruined Median city, but here he reports the existence of a town, Mespila, near by. From that point until the army entered the mountains he refers only to groups of villages, with in one case 'a kind of palace' where flour, wine, and barley for horses had been stored for the satrap of the country.

post-Assyrian types, on the slopes of the bluff and on the low mounds on the undulating ground to the north. The most prominent feature of the site is the north wall, which runs across the neck of the promontory about 1 km. from its southern end. This is still up to 8 m. high on the exterior face, with traces of a ditch. An opening near the middle of the wall seems to mark the site of a gate, and from this point the faint trace of an ancient road can be followed across country for some 18 km., running north-west in the direction of Tell Afar. At intervals of some 4 km., where the road crosses the crest of a ridge, there are small mounds between 5 and 10 m. in diameter. On these only a few sherds of indeterminate character were found. Their purpose is obscure; they are well sited for signal stations but seem unnecessarily close to one another. Only four were identified and their siting may be fortuitous. Clearly, however, an important north-west road has at some time gained the Tigris valley at Tell Huwaish, and the site itself was important enough to warrant the construction of an imposing rampart on the north, the only side without natural defences. Excavation would be necessary to determine when this took place.

[1] *JADD*, iv. 162–212.

[2] *Anabasis*, II. iv to III. v. There is some confusion in Xenophon's account of this part of the journey, for he mentions the crossing of only one of the two Zabs; it may be that the identity of the name was responsible for the omission. The river he calls Zapatas is usually thought to be the Greater Zab. This would place the villages belonging to Parysatis near the junction of the Lesser Zab with the Tigris, and it has been suggested that the large and prosperous city, Caenae, which the Greeks saw on the west bank during their first day's march north of these villages, was Aššur (W. Andrae, *Das Wiedererstandene Assur*, p. 169). Although the city itself was largely, if not entirely, deserted at this time, it probably still looked imposing from a distance, and the valley below would have been cultivated. If Xenophon's account from this point onwards is substantially correct, there was little settled occupation between the two Zabs, for he describes this part of the route as 'desert stages', the term applied to the country between the Adhaim and the Lesser Zab. The Greeks must have forded the Greater Zab some distance upstream from its junction with the Tigris, perhaps at Quwair or Tell Abu Sheetha, for they did not regain the Tigris at Kalḥu until late on the following day.

Clearly the great cities had disappeared and the only town he saw, Mespila, owed its existence to the importance of the Tigris crossing which had been the original *raison d'être* of Nineveh and accounts for the rise of later Mosul. The villages which dotted the countryside must have been in a moderately prosperous condition. On the three occasions when he describes the stopping-places of the army between Nineveh and the upper Tigris in the region of Jazirat ibn Omar he always comments on the plentiful supplies that were available. Since the Greeks must still have numbered close on 10,000 men, this argues a considerable production of grain, and it is interesting once again to notice that he was passing through precisely those areas where a comparatively large modern population demonstrates their resilience in the face of periods of insecurity.

Alexander too passed through Assyria, and the battle named after the city of Arbela, in which he finally defeated the last Achaemenid, Darius III, was actually fought on the plain of Keramlais, 23 km. east of Nineveh.[1] But the contemporary records of Alexander's campaigns are lost, and later descriptions tell us nothing of the country. For the Hellenistic period we have isolated pieces of archaeological evidence. Nineveh at some time acquired at least the superficial forms of Hellenistic city organization. An inscription found there during the excavation of the Nabu Temple in 1904 records a dedication by one Apollophanes, the son of Asklepiades, on behalf of Apollonios who is described as *strategos* and *epistates* of the city, to the *theoi epēkooi*.[2] The reading of the date is uncertain but appears to point to the first century A.D., and the script certainly cannot be earlier than the second century B.C. The offices mentioned, although characteristic of Greek cities in the Parthian period, indicate a Seleucid origin for the municipal organization. Whether the citadel itself was continuously occupied is difficult to say, for the strata and architectural remains associated with Hellenistic pottery are too confused to permit analysis. It seems probable that the greater part of the town lay in the plain below, where a small shrine of Hermes, the travellers' patron peculiarly appropriate to a bridge-head site, was recently identified.[3] Again no direct evidence of its date was forthcoming, for the cult statue was a provincial Hellenistic product which might have been made at almost any time in the Seleucid or Parthian periods, but it is interesting to note that the cella in which the statue was found, a raised platform approached by steps from the ante-cella and with a door leading into a small lateral chamber, is very reminiscent of Assyrian prototypes.

Two other sites afford isolated but significant additions to the general pattern, although in the first case the evidence is negative. At Aššur no traces of Seleucid occupation were identified, and very little that can be confidently assigned to the Achaemenid period. Although we cannot assume from the absence of occupation on the citadel that the site was deserted, there is not nearly as much room for settlement outside the citadel at Aššur as at Nineveh and Kalḫu, and it had virtually no 'outer city' in the sense in which the term has been applied to the other capitals. It is noticeable, too, that the published pottery from Aššur does not include even those Hellenistic types which have been found at Kalḫu,

[1] Sir A. Stein, *Geog. Jl.* c (1942), 155.
[2] R. C. Thompson and R. W. Hutchinson, *Archaeologia*, lxxix. 140-2.
[3] Mohammad Ali Mustafa, *Sumer*, x (1954), 280-3 and pls. 1-3 (in Arabic).

where they date from a period of insecurity when the citadel was reoccupied on a small scale. Andrae remarks that the period from the fall of Aššur in 614 B.C. to the appearance of Parthian buildings, which he dates to the first century B.C., has no history.[1] It is plausible that this should be so on two counts. The local agricultural economy of Aššur had been founded on irrigation canals constructed and maintained by the Assyrian kings, and could hardly have survived their disappearance; and Aššur lies, as we have seen, on the very boundary of the rainfall zone, open to the steppe, and would be the first site to show the effect of any breakdown in the authority of the settled peoples over their nomad neighbours. It seems possible, on the evidence of the fifth-century letter of Aršam referred to above, that Aššur was temporarily replaced as a local centre of administration and perhaps as a road-station by Ubaše, 15 km. to the north.

The apparent decline of Aššur is complemented by another significant event which must be assigned to the period under consideration, the foundation of Hatra on the Wadi Tharthar about 55 km. to the north-west.[2] Recent excavations there have shown that the great Parthian shrines were preceded by temples of purely Hellenistic aspect. The smaller temples of distinctively Hatrene plan which surround the main precinct also seem in some cases to antedate the Parthian monumental complex. A sounding beneath one of these smaller buildings revealed a succession of trodden surfaces with traces of ash, but no structural remains, and the excavators have suggested that Hatra was a camping ground before it became a permanent settlement. On the very slight evidence we at present possess it would thus seem that the site was first used for seasonal occupation by nomads from the Jazira who were attracted to it by the presence of perennial though brackish springs in the Wadi Tharthar near by. It may or may not have been discovered at this stage that wells within the area of the later city produce sweet water; this seems to be drawn from a permeable layer, which is here found close to the surface, sandwiched between two sloping strata of impermeable rock, and thus acts as a natural cistern drawing supplies of water from a wide area. To judge from modern analogy, this encampment would be an obvious choice as the site of more permanent quarters for the tribal leaders and for their gods when they first began to adopt a more sedentary mode of life, although settlement would have been, then as now, a gradual process, and it seems likely that a part of the population of Hatra was always semi-nomadic. This would help to explain the religious prestige of the site, and perhaps also the simultaneous existence of a monumental temple complex and of large numbers of smaller shrines of a more specifically local character which may have belonged to families or subsections of the tribe.

Although admittedly hypothetical, such a reconstruction of the early history of the city gains some support from its name, of which the Arabic version is *al-Hadhr*. The root has in the vocabulary of the nomad a specialized meaning, 'settled land', as opposed to *al-badīya*, the 'steppe' which affords transient pasture only in the spring months.[3]

---

[1] W. Andrae, *Das Wiedererstandene Assur*, p. 169.

[2] I am indebted for my information about the excavations at Hatra, and for hospitality there on many occasions, to the Directorate-General of Antiquities, Government of Iraq, and especially, for many profitable discussions, to Sayyid Fuad Safar, Inspector-General of Excavations, and Sayyid Mohammed Ali Mustafa.

[3] E. W. Lane, *Arabic–English Lexicon*, London and Edinburgh, 1863–93, i. 2. 589.

From this is derived the sense 'permanent residence' in which *al-hadhāra* is used to describe the mansions of the Umayyad caliphs, of whom many retained the predilection of their forebears for a semi-nomadic existence.[1] There is an obvious parallel with modern sheikhs who have built themselves country houses on the fringe of the settled lands, in which they spend an increasing proportion of their time, while their tribesmen still pursue the seasonal pattern of migration, in search of pasture, imposed on them by their herding economy. If the name may be explained in this way, then its application to the city that grew out of the original encampment can be compared with the derivation of *al-Hīra*, 'the camp', which became at a later date the capital of the Lakhmid princes in southern Iraq. The later province of which Hatra became the capital was known as *'Arbaye*, Arabia, and the original settlers at Hatra were almost certainly Arabs although their inscriptions, of which the earliest yet found date from the first century A.D., are in Aramaic, the Semitic *koine* of the Near East. They represent in fact one of a ring of Arab principalities around the fringe of the steppe, at Petra, Palmyra, Chalcis, and Edessa, each of which originated in a successful incursion by nomads and rose to autonomy and often striking prosperity in the third and second centuries B.C.[2] In the case of Petra and later of Palmyra their prosperity was founded on the control of important trade routes, but whether this was true also of Hatra is not yet clear. It is safe to assume that her rulers would have exacted tolls from caravans passing along the great highway which ran north-westwards from the Tigris valley to Nisibin and the Khabur, but there is no evidence, such as we find in the inscriptions of caravan leaders from Palmyra, that the Hatrenes played a more active part in the organization of commerce.

A HELLENISTIC VILLAGE AT KALHU

From the middle of the third century the Seleucid Empire was also under pressure from the Parthians of Iran, and despite a temporary restoration of authority in the eastern provinces by Antiochus III (223–187 B.C.) the struggle ended in complete Parthian control of Mesopotamia by 130 B.C. The effect of these political uncertainties on the countryside of Northern Iraq can be seen in the foundation of a small village on the south-east corner of the citadel mound of Kalhu.[3] The sequence of post-Assyrian occupation was much disturbed by nineteenth-century excavations and, since the pottery of this period was virtually unknown before the investigation of this site, there remains an element of uncertainty about the date of some earlier material found outside the limits of the village. It seems, however, that there was a very small settlement of perhaps one or two houses on this part of the mound in the late Achaemenid or early Hellenistic period, and that the village was founded about the middle of the third century B.C. It lasted for rather more than a hundred years, and we identified a series of six building levels. These are to some extent arbitrarily defined, since the extension, repair, and replacement of small

---

[1] H. Lammens, *La Badia et la Hīra sous les Omayyades*, 1910, p. 100 and n. 3. See above p. 12.

[2] R. Dussaud, *Les Arabes en Syrie avant l'Islam*, 1907, pp. 1–23.

[3] D. and J. Oates, 'Nimrud 1957: The Hellenistic Settlement', *Iraq*, xx (1958), 114–57. For the coins used to date the occupation levels, see G. K. Jenkins, 'Hellenistic Coins from Nimrud', *Iraq*, xx. 158–68.

mud-brick structures is a continuous process of which the individual stages are historically significant only when they reflect deliberate destruction of a large part of the settlement. But the levels can be approximately dated by a small number of coins found in them and serve as a convenient framework of reference for the chronology of other finds, notably the pottery. They may be summarized as follows:

Level 6: Beginning uncertain, perhaps 250–240 B.C. One house was destroyed by fire; the destruction may have been accidental, but failure to recover a hoard of six tetradrachms found in the ruins suggests that the owner may have been killed. A *terminus post quem* for the destruction is given by a coin of Seleucus III (226–223 B.C.).

Level 5: Begins *c.* 220–210 B.C. The latest coin was an issue of Antiochus III minted 206–203 B.C., but a Rhodian jar handle, dated 190–180 B.C., was found in a rubbish deposit with pottery types of the Level 5 range.

Level 4: Begins *c.* 180–170 B.C. Coins of Aradus, 170–169 B.C., and Alexander Bala, 150–145 B.C.

Level 3: A late phase of Level 4, not always present. A coin of Alexander Bala stratified between floors of Levels 4 and 3 indicates that 3 began after 150 B.C. at this point.

Level 2: Probably begins *c.* 145 B.C.; a coin of Demetrius II Nicator, first reign, 146–140 B.C. Ended in a violent destruction at an unknown date.

Level 1: After 140 B.C., probably not of long duration. No legible coins.

This settlement differed little in character or, as far as we can estimate, in size from any one of the smaller villages that today dot the plain below the mound. The houses seem to have been irregular agglomerations of two, three, or four rooms, ranged about small courtyards in which were bread ovens of the type still used for baking flaps of unleavened bread, and brick-covered drainage pits that probably served as a secondary source of water after the rains, since the river had by now changed its course to the western side of the valley and the deep Assyrian wells in the citadel had long gone out of use. The material equipment of the inhabitants was simple, to judge from the surviving objects, and reflects in almost equal measure the survival of traditional Mesopotamian types and the introduction of new fashions as a result of the conquest of Alexander and the domination of his Seleucid successors. The external connexions of the area at this time can be seen to some extent in the coinage, with a great predominance of coins from the mints of Syria and Asiatic Greece.[1]

The pottery provides our largest body of evidence, and a valid example of the type of western influence that existed.[2] Side by side with some recognizable Assyrian types, we have a number of new wares and decorative motifs that clearly derive from the

[1] G. K. Jenkins, op. cit., pp. 166–7, points out that the bronze coins, which did not have such a wide international currency as the silver, are a good index of economic connexions. Here it is very noticeable that among fifteen pieces there is none from the important mint of Seleucia on the Tigris, and only one was minted east of the Euphrates, at Ecbatana.

[2] For a description and discussion of the pottery, see Appendix A, pls. XIV–XV, and figs. 15–20.

Hellenistic pottery of Syria and Anatolia, although the number of actual imported pieces is very small. The Mesopotamian ceramic tradition was a strong one, and there are indications that some, at least, of the coarse pottery was still being made by the traditionally conservative women potters—the finger impressions behind the stamps used to decorate large jars are too small to have been made by a man's hand. Some wares, for instance the better types of painted bowl with a local version of the palmette stamped in the base, and the palmette-handled lamps, which are not found further west, were probably produced in the provincial towns. Whatever the size of the pottery trade in the larger centres, there would in any case have been little money to spare for imported luxuries in a village of this size. The prosperity of the settlement, as far as we can judge, varied considerably over the period of its life. At no time do we find any quantity of coinage, which was obviously too scarce to lose, but the hoard of six silver tetradrachms, lost in the burning of a Level 6 house, shows that in the early years the villagers made an occasional profit; and the well-built houses of Levels 5 and 6 confirm this impression of modest prosperity, which is regained, after an interval, in Level 2. The graves, too, reflect the varying fortunes of the village, and Level 5 produced two collections of jewellery which imply considerable wealth. It is interesting to note, among the grave furniture, the occurrence of charming miniature animal figurines, and small antiquities in the form of cylinder seals and amulets, for which the villagers, or at least their wives, had a considerable affection, probably joined with a regard for their magical properties. The only standard feature of the burials is the practice of flexed inhumation; the graves, with a few possible exceptions early in the period, were sited outside the houses but within the limits of the village, and this lack of a defined cemetery area perhaps continues the Assyrian tradition. They consisted in many cases of simple cists of burnt or mud brick, sometimes covered with capstones, but occasionally either filled directly with earth or provided with a wooden lid. Earthenware 'bath-tub' coffins are also found, usually with rounded ends, although one example is square at one end; the two types appear to be contemporary.

In view of the very recent identification of the Hellenistic pottery series in Northern Mesopotamia, which differs radically from that in the south, it is too early to attempt to define the distribution of settlement at this period. A certain amount of evidence has, however, been collected from our own observations and soundings, and the reports of other excavators. A brief sounding was made at Tell Abu Sheetha, on the south bank of the Upper Zab some 10 km. north-east of Quwair, in 1955. This large mound lies at the point where the old road from Mosul and Nineveh to Altun Köprü and Kirkuk crosses the Upper Zab. Surface finds promised an interesting range of occupation through most of the major periods, but unfortunately our sounding demonstrated that the surface was entirely covered with Islamic graves, which made excavation impossible. At one point, however, in a gully on the west side of the mound, we exposed a few courses of mud brick of the same dimensions as that in use at Kalḫu in the Hellenistic buildings, associated with two grain silos which produced a number of sherds of painted and grooved bowls, one bearing the potter's mark XP roughly incised on the base. Two similar sherds from Nineveh also bore Greek potters' marks. This type does not appear to be a western import and may have been produced in some local town, perhaps Nineveh itself. Another group, including a palmette-handled lamp, has been found during recent excavations at Balawat, the Assyrian Imgur-Enlil, 15 km. north-east of Kalḫu, and sherds of the painted ware occur on the surface of a small mound 1 km. north-west of the village of Khidhr Basatliyah, 7 km. north-east of Kalḫu. Campbell Thompson found several examples of the palmette-handled lamp, and a number of sherds of painted and moulded bowls, in the excavation of the Nabu Temple at Nineveh. Finally, we have two interesting pieces of evidence from sites far to the north-west of Kalḫu. Baron von Oppenheim mentions a collection of late pottery from the upper levels at Tell Halaf in which we can confidently identify the principal wares of the Kalḫu series, and Seton Lloyd records similar material from Sultantepe in which a number of our dated types can be recognized. This suggests that, at any rate within the chronological limits of our evidence, the ceramic repertoire is the same for the whole North Mesopotamian province, although we naturally cannot claim to describe the full range on the basis of a single village site, and it is probable that in wealthier and more important centres a greater variety of local and imported types would be found. The only change in the character of the pottery, other than the normal evolutionary process, occurs after the destruction of Level 2, which appears to mark a general disaster involving the whole village, and is succeeded by the impoverished settlement of Level 1. Glazed wares become noticeably more common, and include new types such as the large bottle with an impressed panel motif for which there is no Hellenistic precedent; other decorative techniques, such as the use of impressed concentric circles, the 'falling leaf' zigzag and wavy comb incisions, now appear for the first time and are common on the later Parthian pottery found at Dura, Seleucia and, in the north, at the Roman site of Ain Sinu. In general, the range of types assumes a more Parthian aspect.

Our dates thus give us a period of occupation from about the middle of the third century B.C. for the beginning of Level 6 to some time after 146 B.C. for the destruction of Level 2, followed by a brief reoccupation in Level 1. We cannot eliminate entirely the possibility of settlement elsewhere on the mound outside these limits but, apart from the possibly Achaemenid phase, we have no material that suggests a radically different date, and it seems probable that this period of about a century of occupation does in fact represent the life of a single village. It would be unreasonable to expect to trace the detailed history of the country in its fortunes, but we must note the apparent prosperity of Level 5, co-inciding with the long reign and military successes of Antiochus III. At what stage the Parthians conquered the northern plain we do not yet know, but it seems reasonable to suggest that their advent in the area is reflected at Kalḫu in the destruction of the Level 2 village and the appearance of their distinctive pottery in the short-lived upper level some time after 146 B.C. The area was for some time in dispute between the kingdoms of Parthia and Armenia, but the final establishment of Parthian authority presumably brought with it the conditions of peace and order in which villages could once more exist in safety on the plain.

IV

EAST AGAINST WEST: 1. ROME AND PARTHIA

FRONTIER STRATEGY

BY the beginning of the Christian era the political inheritance of the Seleucid kingdom had been divided between Rome and Parthia, and from this time until the coming of Islam the northern plain of Mesopotamia was intermittently a battleground, always a frontier region, between these powers or their respective successors, the Byzantine Empire on the west and Sassanid Persia on the east. Such formal history as we possess is incidental to the narrative of their wars and is far from complete; only in the latter half of the period do we gain an insight into social and economic conditions from the literature of the Eastern Church. The only episode in the history of Northern Iraq during the first three centuries A.D. that can yet be documented in any detail is the Roman occupation which took place about A.D. 200. Although the Roman frontier in the territory of modern Syria has been the subject of extensive study by historians and archaeologists,[1] its topography and consequently its strategic development are still obscure in some particulars, because many of the sites were discovered from the air and their span of occupation has not subsequently been defined by work on the ground. Excavation alone can provide the information necessary for a historical analysis of this material, and until this has been carried out there is no profit in attempting a detailed synthesis of the studies that have already been published. On the other hand, the extension of Roman control to the Tigris, over an area which appears naturally to lie within the Parthian orbit, can only be explained in terms of the overall strategy of Rome's eastern frontier and in particular of the geographical factors which dictated it.

Strategy was not, of course, dictated by geography alone. There were certainly military considerations which limited the range of action open to either of the protagonists. The Parthian army was largely composed of contingents levied for the occasion from the various provinces of the empire, or provided, equipped, and led by individual nobles. The cavalry, consisting of mail-clad cataphracts armed with the lance as well as lightly equipped archers, was the principal arm. Its main advantage was mobility, its defects the

---

[1] See especially Chapot, *La Frontière de l'Euphrate*; Dussaud, *Topographie historique*; Poidebard, *Trace de Rome*. These works embody most of the information that can be gained from examination of the documentary evidence and superficial survey. I have refrained from discussing archaeological or topographical problems outside the territory of Northern Iraq, of which I have personal knowledge, since I feel that these can only be elucidated by a more precise dating of the individual sites. Although I have the greatest respect for Poidebard's unique achievement, my own experience leads me to suspect that his map is in places a palimpsest of earlier and later material. For the history of the wars between Rome and Parthia, see N. C. Debevoise, *A Political History of Parthia*, 1938, and D. Magie, *Roman Rule in Asia Minor*, 1950, both of which are very fully annotated with references to ancient sources and modern literature; also *CAH*, ix, ch. xiv; x, chs. ix, xxii; xi, chs. iii, vi, ix; xii, chs. i, iv.

natural reluctance of levies to engage in a protracted campaign, however successful, and an incapacity for siege operations. When it was employed in an offensive capacity it was, under an able commander, a formidable and elusive raiding force, but its efforts were directed to pillage rather than to the occupation of territory. Its tactics in defence were to intercept the enemy, if possible, in open country which afforded freedom of movement to the cavalry, and there to wear down resistance by a shower of arrows.

The Roman army of some 300,000 men, divided in approximately equal proportions between legionary troops and a variegated assemblage of light-armed auxiliary units, was only adequate to its extensive military commitments as long as it adhered to a well-defined strategic pattern. The essence of this strategy was defence by punitive expedition, which ideally anticipated any nascent political opposition or military threat beyond the frontiers. Thus the provinces were insulated from the unpredictable barbarian world by a series of buffer states in which régimes favourable to Rome were maintained by a constant threat and an occasional parade of force. The legionary infantry formed the core of the field armies which put this policy into effect and, at least in theory, the deterrent effect of their invincibility in pitched battle was complemented by their skill in siege operations. The auxiliaries served as a mobile screen to an expeditionary force in time of war, and undertook patrol and police duties in time of peace; the type of unit employed on a particular frontier was chosen with an eye to its suitability for local conditions.

This approach to the problems of defence can be discerned on the Parthian as on the other frontiers of the Roman empire. The object of the traditional expedition into Mesopotamia was to capture the royal city of Ctesiphon, and thus to inflict material damage which would be a lesson for the future and might also undermine the prestige of the existing Parthian king, whose power of offensive action was limited by the degree of loyalty he could expect from his nobility. The execution of this strategy was, however, rendered more difficult by the existence of a much more powerful opposition than the barbarian neighbours with whom Rome was accustomed to deal, and the vastly greater size of the theatre of war; larger forces had to be employed and they had to operate over much longer distances. The first difficulty was met by the temporary reinforcement of the Syrian garrison with detachments from other frontiers, a serviceable though never entirely satisfactory expedient, rendered inevitable by the overall shortage of troops and also the potential danger which a larger permanent concentration in any one province represented to the authority of the emperor. The second problem is closely linked with the extension of Roman control over the northern plain of Mesopotamia.

The logic of this departure from the principle of restraint in territorial expansion laid down by Augustus must be seen against the background of Mesopotamian geography. The Euphrates as a frontier line suffered from one important defect, that the great westerly bend of the river at the point where it emerges from the Anatolian highlands outlined a salient of Parthian territory pointed at the heart of Syria, at the great city of Antioch and the routes leading to the Mediterranean coast and the plain of Cilicia, thus giving the Parthians an advantage which had been exploited with destructive effect by Pacorus in the middle of the first century B.C. Moreover, a Roman army based behind this line was 800 km. from Ctesiphon. To reach the Parthian capital it had an effective choice of two routes, either down the Euphrates or along the foothills of Anatolia and down the Tigris valley. Both afforded the protection of broken country against the attacks of Parthian cavalry, and the memory of the battle of Carrhae, where they wiped out the army of Crassus, eliminated any intermediate route across the open plain of northern Mesopotamia. On the return journey the Euphrates was rarely if ever employed, since the river could not be used for transport in this direction, locally available supplies had been consumed by the army in its outward passage, and the heat of late summer impelled the Roman troops to move northward by the shortest possible route. Even the Tigris valley road caused them intense discomfort at this season. The control of Northern Mesopotamia was thus essential for two reasons: it covered the left flank of the army's advance and subsequently its line of communication along the Euphrates, and it afforded a haven to which the weary troops could retire after the campaign. But the principal highway in the northern plain, linking Syria with the Tigris valley through Nisibin, was controlled at its western end by the Arab princes of Osrhoene, and dominated in the east by the much larger and more powerful kingdom of Armenia. The maintenance of Roman control in Osrhoene was a comparatively simple matter, though not so simple that the necessity could be ignored, and we find that its formal reaffirmation was a prelude to every major campaign, for the defection of its ruler could have consequences disproportionate to his military power. Armenia was a problem on a far greater scale, and here again Rome found herself at a military disadvantage as long as her army operated from remote Syrian bases.

In the face of this situation there were two Roman policies. The first was a constant, empirical process of adjustment by diplomatic manœuvre and by military action when it was necessary to redress the balance of power or of prestige, an important factor in determining the allegiance of the smaller kingdoms. It envisaged the maintenance of the Euphrates frontier with, at most, the affirmation of control over neighbouring client states such as took place under the Flavian emperors. It had the advantage of observing the logic of Augustus's dictum, which was that any further territorial expansion might overstrain the resources of the empire. Its disadvantage has been summarized above: successful military action against Parthia, which was the ultimate diplomatic argument, depended on the control of distant Armenia. The second policy was the permanent conquest of the north Mesopotamian plain, creating a forward base from which Armenia could be controlled and Ctesiphon threatened. The military advantage of this course is obvious, but it had the disadvantage that Augustus had foreseen, for it could hardly be maintained without an expensive increase in the size of the legionary armies unless other frontiers were to be permanently deprived of troops that they could ill spare. It was by its nature a solution calculated to appeal to emperors who were themselves soldiers and who saw frontier problems and the balance of power in clearcut military terms, and it is no surprise to find that it was first outlined by Trajan, deliberately abandoned by Hadrian, probably revived under Marcus Aurelius, and finally put into execution by Septimius Severus.

THE SECOND CENTURY A.D.

The immediate occasion of Trajan's attack on Parthia was the seizure of the throne of Armenia, without Roman consent and in defiance of the negotiated convention, by Partha-masiris, son of Pacorus II of Parthia, who was supported by Pacorus's successor Osroes. Trajan's first move in the following year,[1] A.D. 114, was the invasion and subjugation of Armenia, which was placed under Roman provincial administration; the homage of neighbouring kings was received and their position confirmed. From Armenia Trajan turned south, probably in the autumn of 114, captured Nisibis and accepted the sub-mission of Abgar VII of Osrhoene, who had previously awaited the outcome of events. Then followed the conquest of the northern plain, the occupation of Singara, and the creation of a province of Mesopotamia with its southern boundary on the line of the road running east and west through Singara at the foot of Jebel Sinjar. Individual thrusts at either end of this line captured Dura Europos on the Euphrates, and perhaps also pene-trated south-eastwards to the region of Hatra,[2] which at first submitted to Trajan. These operations probably occupied the winter of 114 and the summer of 115, after which the emperor retired to Antioch for the following winter.

[1] I have here followed the chronology suggested in F. A. Lepper's detailed and scholarly analysis of these campaigns, *Trajan's Parthian War*, 1948; summary, pp. 205 ff.

[2] The results of recent excavations seem to show that Hatra had greatly increased in importance in the first half of the first century A.D. During this time the earlier temples of Hellenistic type in the centre of the city had been incorporated in a much larger complex of buildings in the Parthian style, with the open-ended *iwan* as the basic architectural unit. The names of two successive princes, Urud and Nasru, appear as builders' marks on the masonry. After Nasru the rulers of Hatra bore the title *Malka*, 'King', and the change seems to have taken place about the middle of the first century (information based on unpublished inscriptions, generously communicated by Sayyid Fuad Safar). This architectural development and the enhanced dignity of the rulers denote an increase in the wealth and prestige of Hatra both as a religious and a political centre. It must be related to the decline in the central power of Parthia during the first half of the first century when the Parthian nobility exploited rival claimants to the throne as a means of weakening the royal authority to their own advantage (Debevoise, *Political History of Parthia*, pp. 155–76 and refs.). At this time many parts of Mesopotamia achieved virtual independence for varying periods. Two Jewish brothers who, as robber barons in northern Babylonia, had defeated the Parthian satrap, were officially recognized by Artabanus III as rulers of the satrapy from about A.D. 20 to 35. Seleucia was in revolt from A.D. 35 to 42. Izates II of Adiabene was granted an extension of territory, including Nisibis, and advanced in rank for supporting Artabanus against a pretender. The weakness of Parthia also contributed to the preservation of peace with Rome, from which trade and the prosperity of Mesopotamian communities would have benefited. The greatest of the early kings of Hatra, Sanatruq I, was, however, a contemporary of Vologases I of Parthia (A.D. 51/52–79/80), who was a strong and able king. It may be that Vologases deliber-ately fostered the rise of Hatra in the face of renewed Roman activity under Corbulo, as a frontier fortress and a means of exercising control over the tribes of the Jazira, whose religious centre it was. Perhaps it was also a counterpoise to the excessive pretensions of Adiabene, which Vologases attempted to reduce to its former status.

Archaeological evidence shows that Aššur was also a considerable city in the Parthian period, probably as a result of its position on important trade-routes from the north and north-west (W. Andrae, *Das Wieder-erstandene Assur*, pp. 171–89). It is interesting to notice that, despite a long period of apparent neglect, the site of the original temple of Aššur retained its sanctity and was re-used for the Parthian shrine. There was also a temple of Aššur-Bel at Hatra, with a cult statue which is a most significant blend of Oriental and Western tradition (*ILN*, 18 December 1954, pp. 1115 and 1116, figs. 5, 6). The full square beard, the horizontally extended forearms, and the feathered cloak hark back to the Assyrian original, while the Tyche at the god's feet is no less obviously Hellenistic. The presence of the cult in Hatra is a powerful reminder that, although her rulers may have been Arabs, the population must have included a considerable indigen-ous element.

In spring 116 he made a rapid thrust across the Tigris into Adiabene, and then led the main division of his army down the Euphrates, sacked Ctesiphon, and embarked on a leisurely expedition to the Persian Gulf, from which he was recalled by widespread revolts in his rear, encouraged by Parthian counter-strokes at Mesopotamia and possibly also at Armenia. The revolts were suppressed, but the emperor was forced to abandon whatever ambitions he may have entertained in the south. A puppet, Parthamaspates, was crowned king of Parthia in Ctesiphon, and Trajan retired up the Tigris, attempting unsuccessfully *en route* to reduce Hatra, which had joined the rebellion against him. The motives of his apparently irrelevant journey to the Persian Gulf are not now clear, but his strategic intentions up to that time seem obvious: to establish direct Roman control over Armenia and northern Mesopotamia as a position from which it was possible to threaten Adiabene, and perhaps also Media, on the east and Ctesiphon in the south, thus swinging the military balance decisively in favour of Rome. It must be emphasized that his original purpose may have been the defence of Syria and Asia Minor even though this greatly extended frontier constituted an offensive base and not, in the simple sense, a defensive line. The Tigris was no more an ideal frontier for linear defence than the Euphrates had been, but we have seen that linear defence was a concept incompatible with the character of the Roman military system at this time. The position was not, however, maintained. The Jewish revolts in other parts of the empire forced the withdrawal of troops from the east, and after Trajan's death in 117 the prudence of Hadrian dictated the abandonment of all the newly acquired territory and a return to the earlier system.

Such a brief occupation could hardly be expected to leave much trace on the ground, and in fact no remains of military installations of this period have been found, nor any inscriptions that might throw light on Trajan's intentions for the garrisoning of the new province. One milestone was, however, reported in 1927, when it was seen built into a house in the small village of Karsi 15 km. north-west of the modern town of Beled Sinjar, Roman Singara.[1] The text included *Parthicus* among the emperor's titles and should therefore be dated at the earliest to A.D. 116. The stone has since disappeared, but its location is significant, for it is unlikely to have been transported very far in a country plentifully supplied with building stone. Karsi lies at the mouth of a narrow gorge which pierces the northern escarpment of Jebel Sinjar, giving access to a broader valley descending from the east within the confines of the mountain (pl. v). A mule track now winds upwards along the north flank of the valley, crosses its head and gains the crest of the Jebel; then it drops into another valley which runs south-eastwards to emerge on the south side of the range at Beled Sinjar. On the slopes above Karsi this track shows traces of terracing which suggest that its easy gradients are the result of deliberate and skilful engineering. The road surface itself has been largely obliterated by the deposition of eroded material from the mountainside, but it is difficult to resist the conclusion that the present track follows a line laid down by Trajan's engineers. From the mouth of the gorge near Karsi an old road-bed, now a slight depression in the plough-land or a streak of greener vegetation, can be seen running in a straight line north-westwards in the direction

[1] R. Cagnat, *Syria*, viii (1927), 53 ff.

of Nisibin. Although the physical traces of this road cannot be dated and its use in the medieval period is attested by the existence of a fortified *khan* at the village of Khan as-Sur near the Iraqi frontier,[1] it probably followed a more ancient alignment. Clearly the milestone at Karsi recorded the completion of a direct road linking Nisibis, the military headquarters of the province, with Singara which would have been one of its more important frontier posts. It is worthy of note that this was probably one of the few roads in the province that required any major engineering work to render it suitable for Roman military use; elsewhere the existing caravan tracks had served the needs of civilized communities for more than 2,000 years, and we should not expect to find the network of new highways that enmeshed a province in the barbarian west.

The events of the Parthian war in the reign of Marcus Aurelius are very ill documented, but the main outline has been reconstructed.[2] On this occasion the immediate cause of the outbreak was more serious. In A.D. 161 Vologases III wiped out a Roman legion in Armenia, captured Edessa where he installed a Parthian vassal, Wa'el, on the throne, and thence invaded Syria; an object lesson, if one were needed, in the dangers of the Euphrates frontier. Lucius Verus, colleague of Marcus Aurelius in the imperial power, was given charge of the operations, although the effective command seems to have been exercised by three experienced generals, Avidius Cassius, Statius Priscus, and Martius Verus. In 163 Priscus advanced into Armenia and installed a Roman protégé, Sohaemus, on the throne, leaving a legionary garrison in a new fortress city near his capital. In 164, or perhaps 165, Cassius advanced down the Euphrates, capturing Dura Europos which thereafter remained in Roman hands; Ctesiphon was taken late in 165. At this point the Roman army was forced to withdraw by the outbreak of a severe epidemic, and the Parthians quickly seized the opportunity to expel Sohaemus from Armenia. In a new Roman offensive in 166 across the northern plain Edessa was taken and the former ruler Ma'nu VIII restored to his throne,[3] Nisibis was besieged and captured, and the army may have penetrated well to the east of the Tigris. The absence of any connected historical narrative makes it difficult to say what permanent arrangements were made as a result of these operations. But from this time the coinage of Edessa bears Roman imperial portraits and titles, sometimes to the exclusion of the local ruler, whose name when it appears is often accompanied by the epithet *Philoromaios*. Similarly the coins of a new mint at Carrhae describe the citizens as *Philoromaioi*, and the city may have become a Roman *colonia* at this time, although this is not certain.[4] Further to the east, Nisibis would appear to have remained in Roman hands, since it had a Roman garrison in 193, and Singara later bore the title *Aurelia*, which indicates that it may have become a *colonia*

---

[1] This site provides a good example of the drawbacks of superficial survey. On my first visit in 1955 I examined the building, then a low mound on the bank of a *wadi* some 500 m. north of the modern village; its plan seemed to confirm the identification as a small Roman post proposed by Sir Aurel Stein. On a second visit in 1957 I found that the villagers were in course of rebuilding their houses on the site of the ancient mound which had been partially excavated, exposing rubble and mortar walls of medieval aspect.

[2] Campaigns of Lucius Verus, N. C. Debevoise, *Political History of Parthia*, pp. 247 ff.; D. Magie, *Roman Rule in Asia Minor*, ii. 1529–32.

[3] Hill, *BMC Arabia*, xcvii ff. There is no evidence for a king Abgar VIII sometimes inserted between Wa'el and Ma'nu VIII.

[4] Hill, *BMC Arabia*, xc.

under the Antonines.[1] These isolated pieces of evidence suggest a return to Trajan's concept of a forward base, at least in modified form, but it is impossible to say precisely what its limits were or how consistently it was maintained.

THE SEVERAN FRONTIER
(Fig. 5)

During the civil wars of A.D. 193 the rulers of Osrhoene, Adiabene, and Hatra had furnished troops to Pescennius Niger, governor of Syria, in his bid for the imperial throne, and Vologases IV of Parthia offered support which was prudently never sent. Forces from Adiabene and Osrhoene also took advantage of the general confusion to besiege and capture Nisibis. The first task of Septimius Severus, after his defeat of Pescennius Niger, was to bring order to the eastern frontier.[2] Setting out from Syria in the spring of 195 he received the submission of Abgar VII of Osrhoene, who assumed the name of Septimius and gave his sons as hostages for his good behaviour; the greater part of his kingdom was constituted the province of Osrhoene, but Edessa and its immediate territory apparently remained under Abgar's rule. The emperor then established his headquarters at Nisibis, from which he dispatched forces to complete the subjugation of the northern plain. The details of these operations are lacking, but they were recognized by his assumption of the titles Parthicus Adiabenicus as well as Parthicus Arabicus, indicating that Adiabene as well as Arab vassals of Parthia had formally acknowledged his supremacy. In 196 Severus was forced to quit the East to suppress a rival, Clodius Albinus, in Gaul, and Vologases took advantage of his absence to invade Mesopotamia, where Nisibis was saved only by a desperate defence; Armenia may have passed under Parthian control. In the following year the emperor returned to prosecute the war, for which he raised three new legions, *I–III Parthicae*. Nisibis was relieved and the Parthians expelled from northern Mesopotamia, and the army then advanced down the Euphrates and sacked Ctesiphon in 198. On the return march up the Tigris Hatra was unsuccessfully besieged, and a renewal of the attack in the next year, after extensive preparations, also failed in the face of a stout defence and intolerable climatic conditions.

The next military episode on the frontier was the abortive attack on Parthia by Caracalla in A.D. 215–17. The pretext for it was slight, its motives are obscure and seem to have arisen in part from a megalomaniac desire for military glory; Caracalla apparently identified himself with Alexander, and even formed and trained a phalanx on the Macedonian pattern. The preliminary moves, however, were a distorted repetition of the standard formula. Probably in 215 Abgar IX, who had succeeded his father in the previous year and had displayed both an ambitious and a tyrannical temper, was arrested by trickery and his kingdom was added to the province of Osrhoene. The king of Armenia was similarly invited to present himself before the emperor and he and his family were imprisoned, whereupon his kingdom revolted and a Roman army sent to suppress the revolt was

[1] Hill, *BMC Arabia*, xcii.

[2] Campaigns of Septimius Severus and Caracalla, N. C. Debevoise, *Political History of Parthia*, pp. 256– 67; D. Magie, *Roman Rule in Asia Minor*, ii. 1540–4, 1553–4.

defeated. Caracalla himself in 216 advanced across the Tigris into Adiabene and sacked Arbela, but before he could undertake the final stage of the war, the march on Ctesiphon, he was assassinated between Edessa and Carrhae in April 217 by his praetorian prefect Macrinus, who succeeded him. Artabanus V simultaneously attacked Roman territory, and Macrinus, after an abortive request for peace, met him in battle near Nisibis. The Parthians seem to have had the better of the three days' engagement, although victory was officially claimed by Macrinus. Neither side, however, was anxious to continue the war, and peace was concluded with the payment of a large indemnity by the Romans, who none the less retained their Mesopotamian territory.

Parthia had undoubtedly been seriously weakened by her wars with Rome, and the existence of two claimants to the royal title at this time was both a symptom and an aggravation of her weakness. The combination of external pressure and internal division led to the breakdown of discipline in this always heterogeneous and loosely-knit state, and a revolt which began about A.D. 220 in Persis under the leadership of the Sassanid family, hereditary priests of Istakhr, rapidly brought about its final downfall.[1] Vologases V, who seems to have controlled Babylonia, ceased to issue coinage after 223, and Artabanus V, his rival in the north who had come into conflict with Rome, was defeated and killed by the Sassanid Ardashir about 227. Even before his final victory Ardashir had allied himself with the ruler of Kirkuk and Shahrat, king of Adiabene, in an expedition which took him up the Tigris into Armenia, and it may have been at this time that he made his first unsuccessful assault on Hatra. In 230 he returned to the attack, invading the Roman province of Mesopotamia and threatening Syria.

The Roman army retaliated in 232, under the leadership of the young emperor Severus Alexander.[2] It advanced in three divisions which were to execute simultaneously the operations that had been successive features of the earlier pattern of campaign. One division entered Armenia, another marched down the Euphrates, and the main body, under the emperor himself, advanced across the northern plain. Alexander visited Palmyra *en route* to the front, and it seems probable that he then crossed the Euphrates and marched up the Khabur valley to modern Fadghami, and thence north-east to Singara. A Roman road leading from Fadghami in the direction of Singara was reported by Poidebard, and a milestone of Severus Alexander recently discovered 5 km. south-west of Beled Sinjar,[3] which clearly belongs to this road, show that it was constructed or more probably repaired at this time; at Singara it joined the road leading eastwards to the Tigris. Herodian reports that the campaign was a failure, that the defeat of the Euphrates division demoralized the emperor's own force, and that he was compelled to order a general withdrawal.[4] This verdict should probably be qualified, for Ardashir did not immediately follow up his alleged success, and Alexander seems to have achieved at least a limited gain in bringing the important fortress of Hatra under Roman control. Three Latin inscriptions have been

[1] T. Nöldeke, *Geschichte der Perser und Araber zur Zeit der Sasaniden aus der arabischen Chronik des Tabari*, 1879, pp. 1–8 and 409 ff.; A. Christensen, *L'Iran sous les Sassanides*, 1944, pp. 86–90.

[2] Campaigns of Severus Alexander and Gordian III

D. Magie, *Roman Rule in Asia Minor*, ii. 1560–3.

[3] Poidebard, *Trace de Rome*, pp. 156–7; milestone, Fr. J. Fiey, *Sumer*, viii (1952), 229. I located the find-spot in 1954 but could see no trace of a road.

[4] Herodian, vi. 2–6.

found there, on the earliest of which only a consular date corresponding with A.D. 235 survives.[1] The other two record dedications by Quintus Petronius Quintianus of Nicomedia, a tribune of the *I Parthica* in command of the *Cohors IX Maurorum*, which bore the title *Gordiana*; these must be dated to the reign of Gordian III. It seems that the Arab king of Hatra, who had already shown his opposition to Ardashir, had been encouraged by Alexander's show of force to accept the presence of a Roman unit within his walls, the first ever to set foot there.

The situation was, however, only temporarily restored. In 237 Ardashir once more swept through Mesopotamia, and the absence of coinage from the Mesopotamian mints until the reign of Gordian III suggests that they remained under Sassanid control. In 241 Ardashir was succeeded by his son Shapur, who launched a further attack. In the face of this new threat to Syria a Roman army was assembled and advanced into Mesopotamia, under the nominal leadership of Gordian III but the actual direction of his able praetorian prefect and father-in-law, Timesitheus. The client kingdom of Osrhoene was restored and Abgar X placed on the throne. Carrhae was recaptured and, after a victorious engagement at Resaina, Nisibis fell once more into Roman hands, followed by Singara. The army turned south-west to the Euphrates, but Timesitheus fell ill, and his death was quickly followed by the murder of Gordian, instigated by the new praetorian prefect, Philip the Arab, who usurped his throne. The necessity to assert his position in the west without loss of time led Philip to come to terms with Shapur. It is not clear what the terms were, although they do not appear to have been grossly unfavourable to Rome. Armenia was still under a Roman client king in 250, and the province of Mesopotamia was certainly retained, though probably diminished in size. The coinage of Carrhae comes to an end with Gordian III, but Nisibis continued to mint under Philip, and Resaina and Edessa resumed under his successor Trajan Decius (A.D. 249–51).[2] The single issue of coins bearing the name of Singara ceased with Gordian III, but these coins were not minted at Singara,[3] and in any case the closure of a mint cannot be taken as certain evidence that it had passed out of Roman hands; the production of bronze coinage appears to be directly correlated with demand stimulated by periods of military activity. It is clear that Roman control was maintained as far east as Nisibis, and Singara may have remained in Roman hands as an outpost beyond the Khabur–Nisibis line, as it was to be in the fourth century. It is unlikely, for reasons set out below, that the posts east of Singara towards the Tigris were ever reorganized by Gordian III and their surrender may have been agreed by Philip. If so, the withdrawal of the cohort of Moorish cavalry from Hatra would seem an inevitable corollary. The situation was soon thrown into confusion once more by the great series of campaigns after 250, in which Shapur overran first Armenia and Mesopotamia and then Syria, and finally captured the emperor Valerian. But from this time the nature of the conflict underwent a fundamental change, and it is an appropriate moment to review such archaeological evidence as we have for the

---

[1] D. Oates, *Sumer*, xi (1955), 39–43. For an improved restoration of one of the texts, see A. Maricq, *Syria*, xxxiv (1957).

[2] *BMC Arabia*, cvi, cx.

[3] Bellinger, *Dura, Coins*, p. 208.

organization of the Severan frontier, the logical conclusion of the phase of Roman offensive strategy.

The possibility of identifying Roman sites on the ground varies inversely with the density of more recent, and particularly of medieval, settlement in the areas where they

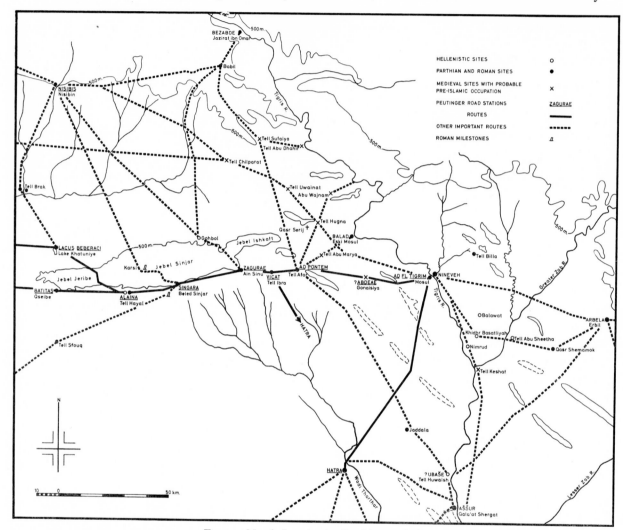

FIG. 5. North Iraq in the Parthian period

may be expected to occur. The eleventh to the thirteenth centuries A.D., when Northern Iraq was under the control of an independent Seljuk dynasty, the Atabegs of Mosul, was a period of great prosperity when most naturally favoured sites were extensively occupied. In consequence, many which we may reasonably suspect to have been Roman stations are so thickly covered with the rubble of medieval buildings that the remains of a comparatively brief earlier occupation, if it existed, have been obliterated. This is particularly true of the eastern frontier of Roman Mesopotamia on the Tigris, which must have been organized, at the least, with posts dominating the main river crossings.

The points which would have been occupied are obvious, since the ridges of hills running from west to east down to the right bank of the river define a series of natural corridors leading to the major crossings. Four of these are accessible from the plain north of Jebel Sinjar which formed the eastern part of the Roman province. The most important is, and probably always has been, the crossing at Nineveh. Here the modern town of Mosul has effectively obliterated any trace of an earlier site. There was a pre-Islamic town here, of which the name Budh-Ardashir[1] given by Arab writers suggests that it was founded or refounded by Ardashir I, perhaps as a deliberate rival to Nineveh, which seems to have retained in the Parthian period a Hellenistic character which would have been much more obnoxious to the Sassanid dynasty than to the philhellene Arsacids.[2] There would in all probability have been an earlier suburb of Nineveh on the west bank, but the fact that it is never mentioned, except perhaps as 'ad flumen Tigrim' of the *Tabula Peutingeriana*, suggests that it was of minor importance. The next ford to the north of Mosul was occupied in the Sassanid period by the town of Balad, a descendant of the Assyrian Balata, now Eski Mosul[3]; here there is an extensive ruinfield around the Assyrian *tell*, enclosed by a medieval city wall. The survival of the name from Assyrian to medieval times suggests continuity of occupation. It was certainly a considerable community in the sixth century A.D., but no material trace of Roman occupation remains.

About 25 km. north of Eski Mosul, between the ridges of Jebel Butmah and Jebel Ain Zala, a wide valley gives easy access to the Tigris, and we again find the remains of a large medieval village or small town, now called Abu Wajnam. A ruinfield some 800 m. in extent on the south side of the valley runs up to a *tell* with a Muslim tomb and cemetery on its summit. The pottery found here was all of medieval or modern date, but it has often been observed on these sites that the debris of medieval masonry acts as a seal which prevents earlier material from coming to the surface; the *tell* must certainly be of earlier origin. The site does not lie on any of the routes described in medieval route-books and we have consequently no information about its history. The last crossing south of the modern Turkish frontier is also marked by a *tell* on the river bank, surrounded by the modern village of Tell Abu Dhahir, but here too there is no documentary evidence to throw light on its history and the pottery was of no assistance. It seems likely, however, that some if not all of these strategic points would have had *castella* in their neighbourhood. A chance remark of Ammianus Marcellinus suggests that the site known to the Romans as Castra Maurorum lay between Nisibis and the Tigris valley in the region of Abu Wajnam or Tell Abu Dhahir,[4] so it may well be that the task of patrolling this sector of the frontier was in the hands of units of the Moorish auxiliary cavalry of whom a detachment was also stationed in Hatra for a brief period.

[1] G. Le Strange, *Lands of the Eastern Caliphate*, p. 87.

[2] See above, p. 61 n. 2. Another Greek inscription bearing a list of Macedonian months is dated to the third century A.D. (*CIG* 4672). It is also worthy of note that the Boswell who accompanied Apollonius of Tyana on his eastern travels in the middle of the first century, and whose record in Greek was used by

Philostratus, was Damis of Nineveh (Philostratus, *Life of Apollonius of Tyana*, i. 19).

[3] G. Le Strange, *Lands of the Eastern Caliphate*, p. 99. See above, p. 54 and n. 2.

[4] Ammianus Marcellinus, xviii. 6, 9. Strategic considerations would suggest a location on the road from Nisibis to Nineveh, perhaps in the region of Tell Hugna or Tell al Hawa.

The military dispositions on the southern frontier are somewhat easier to reconstruct, since the frontier road features on the *Tabula Peutingeriana*, and some of its sites, lying outside the area of intensive settlement near the Tigris, can be more positively identified. In north-east Syria the frontier was studied by Poidebard.[1] In the territory of modern Iraq it followed the more ancient highway along the southern foot of the Sinjar range. As a military alignment this had considerable advantages. Posts could be sited on high ground which gave excellent visibility over the steppe to the south, and could also take advantage of perennial springs on the lower slopes of the range. Garrisons could rely to some extent on local supplies of grain and fodder, since they were within the rainfall zone; at the same time they were sufficiently close to the boundary of agriculture, especially in troubled times such as these, that there would have been very little settled population outside their immediate control. The only sector in which this line did not follow the boundary of agriculture lay between Tell Afar and the Tigris, where a triangle of settled land extended southwards along the west bank of the river, and an important highway led past the Parthian fortress of Hatra; the great efforts which were made by Septimius Severus to take Hatra may represent in part a desire to eliminate this potential threat to the security of the frontier.

Sections of this road appear on two routes of the *Tabula Peutingeriana*, one from the Khabur to Hatra through Singara, the other from Nisibis by way of Singara to the Tigris, and thence to Hatra.[2] Where the two overlap, from Singara eastwards, the names and distances on the first route are corrupt, but they are readily corrected from the second which appears to be surprisingly accurate. By combining the available data we obtain the following list of road-stations and intervening distances, in Roman miles, from the modern Syrian frontier to the Tigris:

Batitas XXIII Alaina XXI Singara XXI Zagurae X Vicat VIII ad Pontem XVIII Abdeae XX ad flumen Tigrim XX unnamed station XXXV Hatris.

At Alaina the road is joined by another coming from *Lacus Beberaci* (Lake Khatuniye), at Singara by the road from Nisibis:

Nisibis XXXIII Thebeta XVIIII Baba XXXIII Singara.

From Vicat a branch leads to Hatra, evidently the most direct route, with three intervening unnamed stations and no distances marked, with the exception of the last stage which was XXIV M.P.

Batitas is identified by Poidebard with Qseibe, south of the gap between Jebel Chembe and Jebel Jeribe, the two hill-chains which continue Jebel Sinjar towards the Khabur. Alaina may now be firmly identified with Tell Hayal, 32 km. east of Qseibe and just to the south-east of the pass of Bara between Jebel Jeribe and the western end of Jebel Sinjar. Tell Hayal itself is a high mound situated on the south side of the modern village of Majnuniye (pl. VI, *a*); the pottery shows evidence of occupation from the prehistoric

---

[1] Poidebard, *Trace de Rome*, pp. 152–8.
[2] K. Miller, *Weltkarte des Castorius*, Ravensburg, 1888, Segmentum, xi. 4–5.

to the Late Assyrian periods. The Roman site lies about 500 m. east of the *tell*, where a partly effaced ditch and the debris of a massive stone wall can be traced from east to west for a distance of over 100 m. This was probably the exterior wall of a *castellum*, for among the piles of stones collected by ploughmen near the site was found, in 1956, a brick bearing the stamped inscription COH[ORS] VI. I[TVRAEORVM].[1]

A distance of little over 30 km., corresponding with the XXI M.P. of the *Tabula*, brings the road to Singara, Beled Sinjar. Little is known of Singara in the Severan period. It may have been garrisoned by the *I Parthica*, which was certainly stationed there in the fourth century.[2] The existing Roman remains are entirely of the fourth century, and are described in the next chapter. It is not clear whether the road marked by the *Tabula*, linking Nisibis with Singara by way of Thebeta and Baba, was Trajan's road through Karsi or a less direct route over the Bara pass. The latter course would have taken it through Alaina, which is not mentioned, but this is not an important consideration since the *Tabula* is a compilation of separate route-books, each marking the night-stops appropriate to a particular journey, and not a complete and homogeneous description of the road-system; it does not, for instance, recognize the identity of the two routes which it records leading east from Singara. It seems unlikely that Poidebard is right in making this road cross the eastern end of Jebel Sinjar, since it was a route from Nisibis to the Tigris, which would in this case have had to make a considerable detour to touch Singara at all. Either of the other possible alternatives would require emendation of the distances given by the *Tabula*, which can only be guesswork in the absence of any definite identification for Thebeta and Baba. Baba may be Bara of the Ravenna Geographer,[3] which would suggest the Bara pass. Thebeta was a sufficiently large site in the second century for its capture by Trajan to be recorded by Arrian.[4] It is probably identical with Tabite, where Tukulti-Ninurta II of Assyria spent the night, two days' march out of Nisibis on the way from the Khabur,[5] and might then be expected to lie south-west or south of Nisibis rather than south-east, where Poidebard places it. The distance given by the *Tabula* would locate it on the Wadi al-Radd, perhaps in the neighbourhood of Tell Brak, where there was a considerable group of Roman and Byzantine posts marking a strategic point of some importance.[6]

The next road-station east of Singara, Zagurae, has been located near the modern village of Ain Sinu, below the pass of Gaulat at the eastern end of Jebel Sinjar. The results of a sounding carried out here in 1957 are described in the next section. Beyond Zagurae we have placed Vicat at Tell Ibra, a mound 14 km. east of Ain Sinu and just south of the modern road from Sinjar to Tell Afar. Here occupation during the Severan period is attested by surface pottery, but the site had a long history; it was of prehistoric origin, and an Aramaic inscription now in the Iraq Museum records that it was fortified in 116

---

[1] Information from Sayyid Fuad Safar and Sayyid Kadhim al-Jenabi.

[2] Dessau, 9477. Ammianus Marcellinus, xx. 6, 8.

[3] *Ravennatis Anonymi Cosmographia*, ed. M. Pinder and G. Parthey (1860), lxxxi. 14; Dussaud, *Topographie historique*, p. 496.

[4] Arrian, *Parthica*, ed. A. G. Roos, 1928, frag. 11; F. A. Lepper, *Trajan's Parthian War*, pp. 127–8.

[5] *LAR*, i. 132.

[6] Poidebard, *Trace de Rome*, pp. 143–5; M. E. L. Mallowan, 'Excavations at Brak and Chagar Bazar', *Iraq*, ix (1947), 48–49.

B.C.[1] Ad Pontem must represent Tell Afar, where a deep perennial watercourse east of the Assyrian citadel is the only obstacle on the road that would have required a bridge for its crossing (pl. VI, b).

Between Tell Afar and the Tigris, where the road strikes across the cultivated lands, we are in some doubt, for the sites here are heavily overlaid by later occupation. The shortest and the most obvious alignment would have lain through Tell Abu Marya to Eski Mosul, but the acceptance of this line involves the emendation of all the distances in the *Tabula*. It seems more likely that the road followed a medieval track which is plainly visible over long distances as a deep trough running almost due east from Tell Afar and over a rocky but still negotiable pass through Jebel Atshan to Mosul; at the point where it emerges from Jebel Atshan there is a ruined khan known as Khan al-Juma'a. Ad flumen Tigrim would then be Mosul itself, and the purpose of this line would be to hold the important crossing at Nineveh, which afforded the easiest and most direct access to Adiabene. The intermediate station of Abdeae coincides with a large medieval ruin-field, just south of the modern village of Gonaisiya, which as a military post would have controlled the head of the valley between Jebel Sheikh Ibrahim and Jebel Atshan. From Mosul the actual distance by a direct track to Hatra is some 90 km. or LX M.P. against a total of LV on the *Tabula*, an inconsiderable discrepancy.

When this survey was first undertaken, it was clear from historical sources that Singara and presumably also the country to the north and west remained in Roman hands, except for comparatively brief intervals, until the middle of the fourth century A.D. The historical problem was the fate of the easternmost extension of the frontier beyond Singara, first attempted by Trajan and then established by Septimius Severus. Of the sites listed above the road-station of Zagurae near Ain Sinu seemed to offer the best prospect of an answer to this question, and also an opportunity to obtain a dated series of pottery, the absence of which had previously made the precise identification of sites of this period virtually impossible.

AIN SINU—ZAGURAE

(i) *The Site*

The site is situated some 30 km. east of Beled Sinjar, 3 km. east of the modern village of Ain Sinu, and 800 m. north of the modern road from Tell Afar to Beled Sinjar.[2] It lies on the upper, southern slopes of an outlying ridge of the Jebel Sinjar–Jebel Ishkaft hill chain and has a commanding view of the flat country to the south and east. The pass of Gaulat, between Jebel Sinjar and Jebel Ishkaft, is some 5 km. away to the north-west; the caravan track to the pass from Tell Afar and the south-east passes 1 km. from the

---

[1] Salem al-Alousi, *Sumer*, x (1954), 145 (in Arabic).
[2] The site was visited by F. Sarre and E. Herzfeld, who published a sketch plan under the name of Ain al-Shahid, now unknown locally (*Archaeologische Reise im Euphrat und Tigris Gebiet*, ii (1911), fig. 283). They suggested the identification with Zagurae on the evidence of the *Tabula Peutingeriana*; although no evidence of the ancient name was found during the recent excavations, there seems no doubt that this is correct.

site on the north side of the ridge, and the track from Beled Sinjar to Gaulat lies 6 km. to the west. The old caravan route from Beled Sinjar to Tell Afar and Mosul runs through the middle of the site. Militarily the position is a good one for three reasons: it is an excellent observation point, it controls both the east–west route and the roads to Nisibin and the north over the Gaulat pass, and it has a good water-supply from perennial springs originating on the southern slopes of the ridge.

The principal modern sources of water are two abundant springs known as Ain al-Sharqi of Ain Sinu, about 600 m. apart at the western end of the site. Other smaller and less reliable sources are scattered over a distance of a kilometre to the east. Traces of underground tunnels indicate that the two main springs had been channelled in antiquity to their present outlets.[1] The water, in common with other springs in the Tell Afar area, is bitter to the taste, but drinkable, and is now used for seasonal irrigation of small patches of cultivation lower down the slope, and for watering the flocks of the Beduin who migrate north from the Jazira in summer. Traces of other underground channels indicate that it may have been more abundant in antiquity, and it is possible that it was also sweeter, since it was apparently not until the thirteenth century A.D. that the half-way road station between Tell Afar and Beled Sinjar was transferred to al-Khan, the modern eastern limit of the sweet waters of Jebel Sinjar. This cannot, however, be regarded as conclusive, since the choice of a military site, as Ain Sinu originally was, involves considerations other than those of a simple caravan halting place.[2]

The superficial remains consist of a scatter of low mounds, some with traces of stone or mortared rubble walls, outlining buildings ranged over a distance of $1\frac{1}{2}$ km. to the east of the western spring. Surface finds indicate occupation during the first millennium A.D. and the Atabeg period down to the twelfth century, but a few worked flints and earlier sherds suggest that the springs had previously attracted at least occasional settlers. The earliest building so far discovered, AS I on the plan (fig. 6), lies at the western end of the site between the two principal springs, where a series of low mounds of debris outline a large fortified barracks some 340 m. square. Gates are recognizable in the middle of the north, west, and south walls, but much of the east wall has been lost through erosion. The gates were connected by internal roads on the axes of the camp. The outlines of fourteen blocks of quarters can be discerned, ranged seven on each side of the axial

[1] These underground channels (Arabic *qanāt*) are constructed by linking the bottoms of a series of vertical shafts sunk from the surface of the ground; the line of disused *qanāt* can often be detected by the depressions which mark the blocked shafts. They are most widely used at the present day in Iran, where the systems are of high antiquity, but in their nature difficult to date precisely. They occur in Northern Iraq in the districts of Kirkuk and Erbil east of the Tigris, at Eski Mosul on the river, and in the Sinjar region, and are reported by Poidebard (*Trace de Rome*, p. 181 and pl. cxlv) from Jebel Chembe just across the Syrian frontier, where they are said to be associated with a Roman camp, al-Ḥan. It has been suggested by J. Laessøe (*JCS*, v. 21–32) that the technique was introduced into Assyria by

Sargon, and certainly it was used by Sargon's successors, Sennacherib and Esarhaddon, when they had occasion to carry the water-supplies of Nineveh, Kalḫu, and Erbil through subterranean channels (see above, p. 47 and n. 4). At all events it was known in Northern Mesopotamia long before the Roman period, but we cannot be sure whether its adoption in the Sinjar region was due to Assyrian or later Roman precedents.

[2] The khan at al-Khan, about 25 km. east of Beled Sinjar on the caravan track, has a remarkable sculptured gateway with reliefs depicting St. George slaying the dragon, and an inscription recording its erection by Badr-ad-Din Lulu, A.D. 1234–58 (G. Reitlinger, 'Medieval Antiquities West of Mosul', *Iraq*, v (1938), 150–1 and pl. xxiii, figs. 9–11).

east–west roadway at intervals of about 30 m., each block being upwards of 100 m. long from north to south. Adjoining the barracks on the east, and enclosing the eastern spring, are the remains of a second building, also of Roman date (AS II). Traces of a stone wall indicate a less regular enclosure with sides of about 200 m., and higher mounds mark the position of small towers. The irregularity of the outline and the internal layout seem to indicate that more advantage was taken of natural mounds for the siting of buildings, and this in turn makes the plan more difficult to reconstruct from superficial observation.

To the east and south-east of AS II at least five more buildings can be identified, smaller but still of impressive size, and each containing one or more internal courtyards. Sherds of Roman date are found scattered all over the site, but the predominance of Islamic sherds in the eastern buildings suggests that in most cases the surviving structures represent a later extension of the original settlement, sometimes re-using materials from the Roman buildings. On the south side of one building pottery water-pipes and traces of carefully cemented tanks indicate a small bath-house; a fragment of a Roman lamp was found embedded in the mortar, which is largely of the dark grey colour typical of medieval and modern masonry.[1] In addition to these large buildings, outlines of smaller rubble houses can be seen all over the site.

Soundings were carried out in the two buildings at the western end of the site, AS I and AS II. Our purpose was not to undertake large-scale clearance, for which our resources were insufficient, but to recover as much as possible of the plan, together with evidence of the chronology of the Roman occupation and a type series of pottery.

(ii) AS I—The Barracks

(Fig. 6)

In AS I we cleared the west and north gates, and traced the outer wall for some distance on either side of the north-west corner; elsewhere its line was determined by trial trenches. The entrances were of a simple, standard pattern without projecting towers, and consisted of outer and inner gates about 2 m. wide, separated by a guard-chamber just over 5 m. square. A range of long rooms, probably magazines, lined the inner face of the outer wall, but their walls had been eroded to below floor level and it was difficult to ascertain their extent. Inside the camp the plan of the north-west barrack block was recovered in its entirety, and proved to consist of a single row of twenty-two long rooms, each 8·10 by 3·60 m., arranged in pairs with interconnecting doors. Each room had a doorway opening to the east, and each pair of rooms was flanked by short walls projecting from the east face of the buildings; these had been eroded and it was nowhere possible to determine the exact length of the projection, but they probably served to support an extension of the roof which would have shielded the rooms from the full heat of the sun. A limited investigation of the next barrack block to the east revealed a similar arrangement of the quarters, with the addition of a range of smaller square rooms on the west side, back to back with the large chambers, and opening westwards. The position and

---

[1] The mortar employed in the Roman buildings at Ain Sinu and Beled Sinjar, and in the sixth-century basilica at Qasr Serij is white.

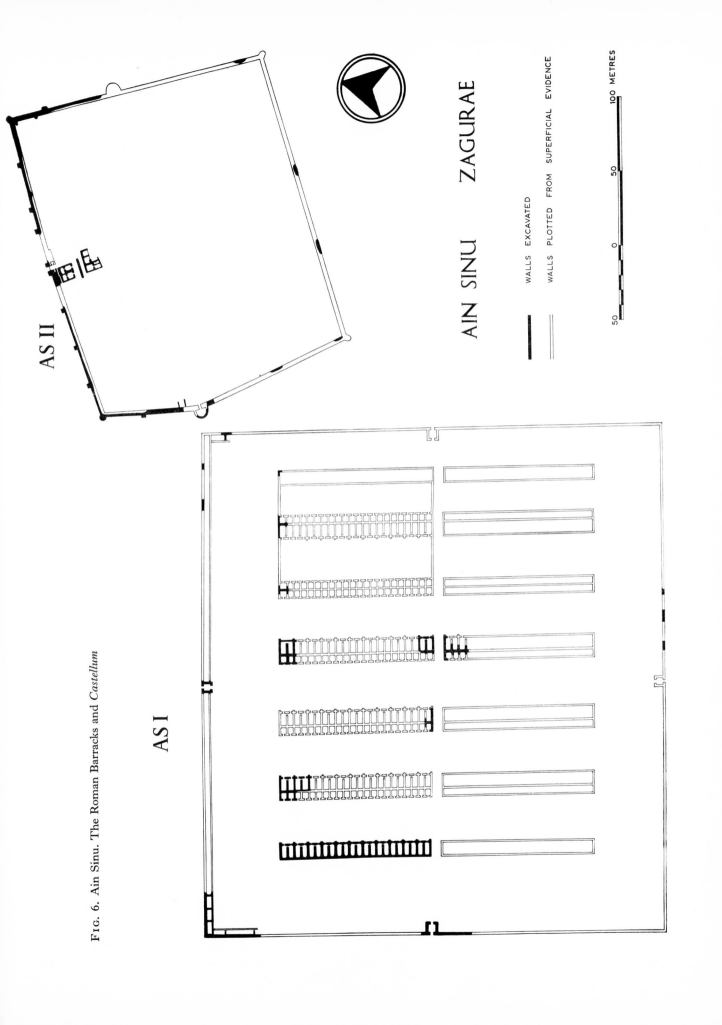

AIN SINU   ZAGURAE

WALLS EXCAVATED

WALLS PLOTTED FROM SUPERFICIAL EVIDENCE

50   0   50   100 METRES

AS II

AS I

FIG. 6. Ain Sinu. The Roman Barracks and *Castellum*

general layout of the other barrack blocks were also ascertained in a series of soundings, and this information, taken in conjunction with the striking regularity of the superficial remains, has enabled us to reconstruct the plan of the camp with a fair measure of probability. The water supply seems to have been provided by an underground channel, which approached the north gate from the north-west; its course can be followed as a line of greener vegetation, with a patch marking what appears to have been a well-head, on a direct line between the north and south gates, and it has a modern outlet, now dry, a short distance below the south gate.

The construction of the barracks and of the outer wall was of mud-bricks, averaging 43 cm. square with a course height of 9 cm. The coursing was somewhat irregular, with wide joints, and our workmen, who are accustomed to build in the same material, were contemptuous of the quality of the bricks, which contained very little straw; this may be due to hasty manufacture, or to an insufficiency of supplies in the neighbouring country-side, a difficulty which we have ourselves encountered after a poor harvest. The absence of straw made the brickwork unusually difficult to distinguish from the surrounding debris, and in the face of this problem the men were much impressed by the Roman surveyors, whose rigid planning made it possible to predict the size of a room or the thickness of a wall to within half a foot's length, a degree of accuracy unknown to the Assyrian archi-tects to whose work they are accustomed. The walls were usually founded directly on the hard ground surface, but in low-lying parts of the site a rubble foundation was used, and in some areas only the stones remain to mark the line of the wall. They are, for instance, our only evidence for the walls which enclose the spaces between the three eastern barrack blocks in the northern half of the camp, and it is possible that similar walls connecting the other buildings have been completely eroded. Rubble packing was also employed to provide a firm roadway in the north, and probably in the west, gate although in the latter case it appears to have been removed while the walls were still standing.

The existence of the courtyard walls in the north-east quarter of the camp, whether or not they were an invariable feature, helps to emphasize one important characteristic of the plan, the basic element of which is not the individual building, but the range of eleven pairs of barrack rooms, facing a row of small square rooms across a rectangular space which was, at least in some cases, enclosed.[1] This suggests that the camp was designed to

---

[1] The rows of barrack rooms correspond approxi-mately in size and arrangements with the barrack blocks in the northern half of the fort at Chesters on Hadrian's Wall (Collingwood Bruce, *Handbook to the Roman Wall*, ed. I. A. Richmond, 1947, p. 90, and plan, 83). At Chesters each block consisted of ten rooms, opening on to a portico, with a more complex suite of officers' quarters at one end, and each accommodated two squadrons of auxiliary cavalry. This suggests the possibility that of the eleven pairs of barrack rooms in each block at Ain Sinu, ten served as *contubernia* or messes for other ranks, while the end pair, although superficially identical, housed the officers of the unit. It must be admitted, however, that we know of no parallel for such an arrangement, and can find no plausible explanation for the pairs of intercommunicat-ing rooms; it is possible that one room of each pair served as a stable, but we found no material evidence to support this, or any other, hypothesis. It is strange, too, to find the barrack rooms separated so widely from the smaller store-rooms or armouries which were obviously designed to complete the accommodation of each unit, but we must conclude that the intervening space was an important feature in the layout, perhaps intended for the picketing of horses or as an exercise ground. The question of the purpose for which the camp was built is discussed more fully below, p. 89.

accommodate fourteen units of considerable size, each requiring basically similar quarters; there is no sign whatsoever of any irregularity which might suggest the presence of a headquarters building, or of the many ancillary services which were housed in the normal Roman legionary camp. Unfortunately the excavated areas produced virtually no evidence of occupation to explain this unusual layout. Only in one room, at the south end of the north-west barrack block, did we find any trace of furniture, in the form of a low mud-brick pedestal, with two sockets for wooden posts, just inside the doorway;[1] the depth of occupation debris on the beaten earth floors of the rooms, and in the gate-chambers, was only a few centimetres and almost barren of objects. Moreover, the collapsed mud-brick of the walls lay directly on the floors with no intervening trace of organic material such as usually marks the fallen roof of a mud-brick building that has been destroyed, and nowhere did we find the stone door-sockets or sills that might have been expected in an area where stone is plentiful. The general aspect of the camp suggested, in fact, either that it had never been finished, or that it was occupied for a very brief period and then abandoned or relegated to minor use as a storehouse, most of the re-usable building material being removed. Enough sherds were, however, found on the floors and embedded in the mud brick to enable us to identify types of some distinctive wares, including thin dark-red ribbed cooking pots and jugs, and jars decorated with patterns of diamond-shaped stamps, similar to those found in the occupation levels at Hatra, where they are dated to the first half of the third century A.D. (pl. XVI). Two coins were found inside the camp in debris just above the floor or ground level, both from the mint of Resaina, the first dated to A.D. 216 and the second to the reign of Elagabalus, A.D. 218–22. Two further coins came from the topsoil outside the north gate and north wall, both issues of Severus Alexander, A.D. 222–35, from the mints of Nisibis and Edessa respectively.

(iii) *AS II—The Castellum*

(Figs. 6–7)

The smaller building, AS II, which overlooks the camp from the north-east was easily recognizable as a *castellum* of the type commonly occupied by auxiliary units engaged in frontier patrol or defence. The irregularity of the plan prevents us from making any reconstruction of the internal layout, but our trenches yielded extremely interesting historical evidence, which to some extent complements our negative findings in AS I. In addition to the soundings made to determine the limits of the building and the nature of its defences, we excavated an area some 15 by 40 m. in the middle of the north side, exposing one side of the north gate and parts of adjacent buildings. The inner and outer faces of the north wall were constructed of large roughly dressed limestone blocks, laid

---

[1] During a visit to the local police post we observed an exactly similar mud-brick pedestal on the right of the guardroom doorway, with two posts set in its upper surface which formed the ends of an arms rack. We did not find any pedestals of this sort in the other excavated chambers, and it is possible that this pair of rooms near the west gate did in fact house the guard.

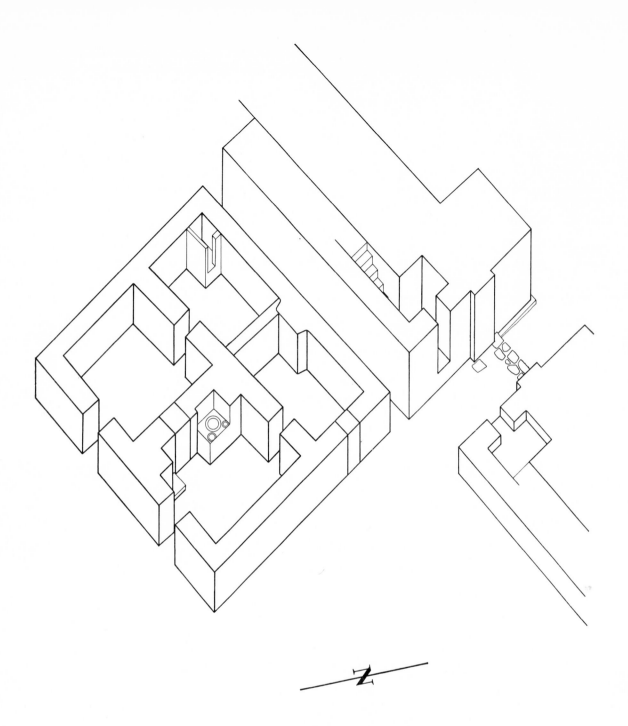

AIN SINU

Quarters adjoining the North Gate of the Castellum

1   0   5   10 metres

FIG. 7. Ain Sinu. Quarters adjoining the North Gate of the *Castellum*

in courses of *c.* 40 cm. and set in a strong white mortar; the core of the wall was composed of loosely mortared rubble and earth, and its overall thickness was almost 3 m. The north gate, 2·5 m. wide and paved with large, irregular stone slabs, was flanked by towers 3 m. wide with a projection of 2 m.; simple, tapering, stone corbels found among the fallen debris outside the towers suggest machicolation on the top of the wall above the gate. Similar towers were set along the outer face of the wall at irregular intervals, with larger, oval towers at the corners. The inner face of the wall on the west side of the gate was thickened for a distance of 10 m. by the addition of a mud-brick abutment 2 m. wide, and a small guardroom was set in the thickness of the wall behind the west tower, with its doorway opening on to the roadway; there was probably a similar arrangement on the east side of the gate, but this has not been excavated (fig. 7). The floor of the guardroom was covered with a double thickness of hard gypsum plaster, suggesting that it had been resurfaced at least once, and in the plaster was embedded a coin of Caracalla, issued in A.D. 216 from the mint of Resaina. The roadway was spanned by a brick vault of which large fragments lay among the fallen debris. It was of somewhat unusual construction, with the rings of bricks set at right angles to the axis of the vault, as in the ancient Mesopotamian 'pitched-brick' technique of which the Arch of Ctesiphon is perhaps the best-known example.[1] After recording their position, the fragments of the vault were dismantled in a search for stamped bricks which would have given us the name of the unit responsible for the erection of the *castellum*, but without success.

A narrow passage separated the north wall from a small, four-roomed house inside the gate. Its walls, 70–80 cm. thick, were of mud brick on a foundation of roughly laid, undressed blocks laid in mud mortar, and were coated with mud plaster.[2] This building had originally been divided from east to west, with a single long chamber on the north and a suite of two smaller rooms on the south; at the east end of either half two steps and a door gave access to the beaten earth roadway leading to the gate. This arrangement was, however, found unsatisfactory, perhaps owing to a rise in the level of the road surface, and the doors were blocked; at the same time the long north chamber was subdivided by a transverse wall, the door between the two southern rooms was also blocked and new

---

[1] The Mesopotamian origin of pitched-brick vaulting has recently been discussed by J. B. Ward Perkins in *The Great Palace of the Byzantine Emperors, Second Report*, ed. D. Talbot Rice, Edinburgh, 1958, pp. 93–95. It was essentially a mud-brick technique; examples in this material date from the second millennium B.C. to the present day, and are found in the Parthian period at Seleucia, Aššur, and Hatra. Hatra has also produced a mortared stone vault built on the same principle, but the use of baked brick in vaulting of this type appears to be an innovation due to Roman influence; there are two instances in buildings of the Roman period at Dura, which must be approximately contemporary with the *castellum* at Ain Sinu (*Dura-Europos, Preliminary Report, Sixth Season*, 1936, pp. 84 and 266). The standard brick employed at Ain Sinu

was 28 by 23 cm. and 3 cm. thick, smoothed with a straight edge 7–9 cm. wide; some bore two finger grooves on one diagonal, and many showed the fortuitous impressions of bare feet or of domed shoe nails of which a number were found on the site. A small number of bricks were trapezoidal in shape, of the standard length but tapering from 24 cm. at one end to 21 cm. at the other. These resembled Assyrian well bricks and may have been made for the same purpose; they served no obvious function in the gate arch.

[2] The flimsy construction and irregular layout of the buildings exposed in the comparatively small excavated area of the *castellum* are in striking contrast to the massive walls and regular plan of the barracks, and would not in themselves be out of place in any ancient or modern village in the countryside.

doorways were cut to transform the building into two suites of two rooms, aligned from north to south and now opening on to a cobbled yard on the south side. In the north-west corner of the house we found the remains of a cupboard or grain bin set on a plinth of mud-brick, and in the south-east room, beside the blocked doorway in the west wall, a curious shelf with a large raised ring of mud plaster in the middle and a similar smaller ring at each of the outer corners. The whole shelf was covered with a liberal coat of gypsum plaster, and on it was a broken lamp, but its purpose was difficult to determine, although it is possible that the rings served as stands for the round-based jars which we found shattered on the floor. The floors of all these rooms were covered with an extraordinary quantity of sherds,[1] which were also scattered over the cobbles outside, as if the building had been sacked and its contents violently dispersed. Among the pottery were also a number of iron weapons and tools, and three coins, two issues of Caracalla from the mint of Resaina dated to A.D. 216, the third of Severus Alexander from the same mint.[2]

The same evidence of sudden destruction was observed in the other rooms across the cobbled courtyard to the south. It was unfortunate that much of the building of which these rooms formed part was buried beneath the ruins of a medieval house, since it appeared to be of considerably greater size and importance than the quarters immediately adjoining the gate. In the rooms were found a scatter of broken pottery, and a few metal objects as well as a number of fragments of plastered mud-brick corbels on which the ends of roof beams must have rested; stone blocks with a hollow, cylindrical projection on the upper surface were presumably the sockets for wooden pillars supporting the beams. One coin of Severus Alexander from the mint of Edessa was found on the floor; three others from the fill of the rooms were all dated between A.D. 211 and 222.

The third area which we examined briefly in AS II was the site of the great round tower on the west wall, which stands on a knoll overlooking the modern caravan track, and must originally have dominated the ancient road from Singara. The masonry of this bastion had been robbed down to the foundation course, and the interior gutted to make way for a medieval house, for which an approximate date was given by two unidentified, but certainly Atabeg, coins. Just to the north of the tower, on the ancient ground level, was found a coin of Elagabalus, from the mint of Edessa; and among its fallen masonry there came to light the only piece of sculpture discovered on the site, a crude and battered, but vigorous, lion's head with gaping mouth and swirling mane, projecting from the outer face of a block which must have been set high up in the tower wall above the road, to the discomfiture of potential enemies. There was probably a corresponding tower on the east side; we can reconstruct little but the outline of the defences south of the ridge connecting these two points, since the southern half of the *castellum* was built on low-lying ground and the masonry has been almost completely destroyed.

---

[1] For the pottery see Appendix B. One of the sherds bore three letters, roughly incised and underlined, which appear to be the Greek CEΠ, perhaps the beginning of a personal name such as Septimius.

[2] For a selection of the metal objects see Appendix B, p. 159 and fig. 24. A complete catalogue of the small finds and of the coins appears in *Iraq*, xxi (1959), 235–42.

(iv) *Conclusions*

The principal problems that remain in the interpretation of this evidence are the historical implications of the apparently brief occupation of the site, and the purpose for which the large barracks was built in such close proximity to the *castellum*. The range of coins from both buildings and from surface finds in the neighbourhood gives, with the exception of an obviously intrusive fifth-century specimen, a close series of dates from Septimius Severus to Severus Alexander, with the great majority falling between A.D. 216 and 235, although this numerical distribution may reflect the increased activity of the mints of Carrhae, Edessa, Resaina, and Nisibis, from which all except one of them derive. This confirms our belief that the *castellum* formed part of the defensive system of the new frontier, inaugurated by Septimius's Mesopotamian campaigns of A.D. 197–9, for which he raised the new legions *I–III Parthicae*. Two of these legions, *I* and *III*, remained in garrison in the enlarged province, and the plentiful issues of bronze from the Mesopotamian cities under Caracalla and his successors were obviously designed to meet their needs and those of the newly conquered population; many of the Resaina coins bear the *vexillum* and number of the *Legio III Parthica*.[1] It is significant, however, that our comparatively small number of coins includes five examples from the reign of Severus Alexander, but none of Gordian III, who also issued bronze in considerable quantity after A.D. 242, including a number of coins purporting to come from a new mint at Singara.[2] It seems likely that we must look for a date between A.D. 235 and 242 when the *castellum* at Ain Sinu might have fallen to a Persian attack, and for this the most obvious occasion is the offensive of Ardashir I in A.D. 237, in the course of which he overran Mesopotamia and captured Nisibis and Carrhae. The counter-attack by Gordian III in A.D. 242 regained some of the lost territory, but the evidence on this site suggests that the area east of Singara was surrendered once more by the usurper Philip the Arab two years later, as the price of a hasty peace. There is no sign, in the excavated area of the *castellum*, of any attempt at reoccupation; and Diocletian's acceptance of the Singara–Nisibis line in his frontier settlement, when he held the Sassanid royal family captive and could dictate his terms, implies that the frontier through Ain Sinu to the Tigris had long been abandoned.

For the second problem, the purpose of the barracks, we can unfortunately suggest no such tidy solution. It is somewhat uncertain, in view of the very small amount of occupation debris, whether it was ever finished; if it was, the period of occupation was brief and the buildings were dismantled before the loss of the *castellum*, but in either case this does not materially affect the question of its intended function. If our reconstruction of

---

[1] The coinage of the Resaina mint has been definitively studied by K. O. Castelin, *Numismatic Notes and Monographs*, no. 108 (1946), whose dating I have followed. The *vexillum* issues clearly indicate that this was the base of the *III Parthica* at least as early as Caracalla, and Castelin rightly remarks that it was probably stationed here to watch Rome's somewhat unreliable allies in Osrhoene as well as the eastern frontier; Osrhoene was in fact annexed under Caracalla. A city wall of Resaina has recently been published (McEwan and others, *Soundings at Tell Fakhariyah*, *OIP*, lxxix (1958), 14–17, pls. 10–12, 24–27), but its close resemblance to the enceintes of Diyarbekr and Sinjar must date it to the fourth century A.D.

[2] See above, p. 75 and n. 3.

the plan is correct, it contained fourteen principal units, each consisting of eleven pairs of barrack rooms facing a row of twenty-two smaller rooms across a wide open space, as well as a number of other chambers of indeterminate size and function ranged around the outer wall. If we accept the normal figure of eight men to each of the barrack rooms, and assume that one pair of rooms in each block served as junior officers' quarters, we arrive at a total capacity of 2,240 men; even supposing that the interconnecting pairs of rooms represent adjoining quarters for men and horses—a supposition for which we found no evidence and know of no parallel—there would still be accommodation for over 1,100 men. There is no sign of the staff quarters which form an essential and easily recognizable part of the typical Roman fort of this size. It is possible that at Ain Sinu the administration of the barracks was housed in the *castellum* close by, but on the other two sites in the province which appear from superficial evidence to follow a similar plan, there is no adjoining *castellum*.

These two sites are known only from air photographs and the brief accounts of Poidebard. The first,[1] 5 km. east of Tell Brak on the east bank of the Wadi Jaghjagh (*Saocoras* or *Mygdonius flumen*) which flows south from Nisibin, is approximately 200 m. square and contains four parallel mounds running from east to west; each mound presumably represents two barrack blocks, separated by the north–south axial roadway, although only faint traces of this can be detected. Some 300 m. west of the camp is a small mound on the river bank, described as a 'tell observatoire', although there is no evidence that it was in use in the Roman period. Poidebard conducted a hurried sounding in the camp, where he found 'on the site of the *praetorium* clearly defined by the *strigae* and the internal roads' bricks identical with those found in a *castellum* close to Tell Brak itself. These bricks are not described in connexion with either site, but the *castellum* was more completely excavated and is said to be Byzantine. It does not seem that there is any real evidence of the date of the camp, and it is perhaps permissible to doubt whether it did, in fact, have a *praetorium*, since no remains of such a building are described and the air photograph shows no irregularity in the plan. The second camp is situated at Tell Bati,[2] some 28 km. west of Tell Brak, at the junction of two roads leading from the Khabur valley north to Mardin. It is poorly preserved, and only the outline and five barrack blocks in the south-east quarter are visible; its overall dimensions are given as 250 by 235 metres. The north-west corner lay close under a rough circle of high mounds some 250 m. in diameter, the enceinte of a small town, probably of the second millennium B.C. No sounding was made on this site. Both camps have features, apart from their distinctive plan, in common with the barracks at Ain Sinu. All three are on important highways and well supplied with water, as might indeed be expected of Roman military sites, and all are placed on the fringes of areas which were, to judge from the distribution of *tells*, populous agricultural regions; but they also have access to the open plains where the sparser population is now, and probably was in the Roman period, semi-nomadic. Moreover, the line of the Khabur

[1] Poidebard, *Trace de Rome*, p. 144 and pl. cxxii; *Syria*, ix (1928), 219.

[2] Poidebard, *Trace de Rome*, p. 150 and pl. cxxxix.

The location of these two sites is shown on Poidebard's map of the Khabur region, pl. cxl.

and the Jaghjagh was, for a period before the campaigns of Septimius and again after A.D. 364, the Roman frontier, but this is not necessarily a relevant consideration, since we cannot date the camps at Tell Brak and Tell Bati.

It is clear, at all events, that we must explain the camp at Ain Sinu in terms of an establishment the staff of which differed from the ordinary military command either because it was less complex or because it was, from choice or necessity, remote from the rank and file who occupied the barracks. Three suggestions may be put forward, but for various reasons none seems entirely satisfactory. Firstly, we must consider the possibility that this was intended as a temporary base for troops, reinforcements, or supplies during one of the actual or projected Parthian campaigns of Caracalla or his successors, and that the accommodation was laid out on a simplified pattern because it was only to be used for a brief period. We have suggested that one purpose of this Severan extension of the frontier to the Tigris at Mosul was to provide an effective base against Parthia, and to shorten the exhausting retreat in late summer which usually detracted from the success of campaigns against Ctesiphon. We know from Ammianus Marcellinus that in his time the retreating army of Jovian was met by the *dux Mesopotamiae* with supplies at some point on or near the Sinjar–Mosul line, which was by then within Persian territory;[1] and Caracalla or Severus Alexander might reasonably have provided for such an eventuality by establishing a forward base. Against this it must be objected, however, that the layout of even a temporary camp was defined within fairly rigid limits, and it is difficult to accept any explanation involving a unique departure from Roman military tradition. We must then consider circumstances in which the barracks might have been designed for a large body of men without the usual military organization, administered by officials who were housed in the *castellum*. This might have been a local labour force of considerable size, engaged on the construction of roads and frontier defences; but there is no sign that any such works, with the exception of the *castellum* itself, were ever undertaken in the locality, and the existing system of highways had been adequate for the needs of previous imperial administrations from the Assyrian period onwards. The last possibility, which is undeniably speculative, but is perhaps the most plausible in the political circumstances of the time, is that the barracks were intended to house recruits for the Roman auxiliary forces, drawn from the surrounding countryside and more particularly from the desert country to the south, the Parthian province of 'Arbaye of which the capital was Hatra. Such recruitment was a normal feature of Severan policy as a method of pacifying newly conquered territories, and it is by no means improbable that the drafts would have been concentrated in a place of safety away from the more settled areas of the Roman province and under the supervision of a unit of the frontier garrison, until their preliminary training and organization were completed. This hypothesis would help to explain the provision of a large open space as part of the quarters of each unit, since local troops would almost certainly have been light cavalry who brought their horses with them. There is, unfortunately, no epigraphic evidence for auxiliary units recruited in this area during the Severan period,[2] but if this was in fact the purpose of the barracks at Ain Sinu,

[1] Ammianus Marcellinus xxv. 8. 7.   [2] The *Cohors I Augusta Parthorum*, stationed in

such recruitment would have been politically possible only for a very few years. Until A.D. 226 the country to the south formed part of the hostile Parthian client kingdom of Hatra, and it need hardly be emphasized that the recruitment of Beduin would have been difficult in friendly, and impossible in hostile, territory. After the overthrow of the Parthian dynasty by the Sassanids, however, the Hatrenes held out against the new rulers and accepted alliance with Rome, and in this new situation the Romans might well have conceived the possibility of recruitment among the tribes who acknowledged the supremacy of Hatra. Herodian in fact states that Severus Alexander on his German campaign of A.D. 234–5 was accompanied by a great number of archers from Osrhoene, the kingdom of Edessa west of the Khabur, and also by such Parthians as had been enlisted, voluntarily or by force, in the Roman army.[1] This enlistment, although it may not have met with much success during Alexander's brief stay in Mesopotamia, would have required the construction of training barracks, and the other two sites at Tell Brak and Tell Bati might similarly have served for recruits gathered from the western part of the province towards Osrhoene; but we cannot regard this as more than a very tentative explanation of a puzzling building.[2]

Mauretania, seems to have been in existence for at least a century before this date, and the other known eastern units come from Palestine, Syria, or Osrhoene (Pauly–Wissowa, *Real-Encyclopädie*, iii, s.v. *Cohors*).

[1] Herodian, vi. 7, 8.

[2] I am indebted to the late Professor Sir Ian Richmond for a very helpful discussion of this problem, and especially for the suggestion that the barracks may have been a training ground for recruits.

V

EAST AGAINST WEST:
2. THE BYZANTINE EMPIRE AND SASSANID PERSIA

THE last chapter was concerned with the military history of Northern Iraq as a frontier zone between Rome and Parthia. We do not know what effect the constant military movements, and the insecurity that must have resulted from them, had on the population or the economy, yet the question is an important one, for it is often in such turbulent conditions that the new elements of later social and economic patterns first emerge. Much more evidence on these matters during the next three centuries can be gained from the early Christian writers who often have, for all their shortcomings, an advantage denied to most of the professional historians of the time, a personal acquaintance with and interest in the country and its people.[1] So, while the military theme remains important, it can at least be relieved by a more human insight into civilian life, although these sources provide a series of vignettes rather than a coherent picture of the situation; the archaeological study of the period is in its infancy and cannot yet contribute the general information that is needed. In the circumstances it seems best to give a brief outline of the contemporary scene as it is revealed by the texts, and then to discuss the two sites in Northern Iraq which can be definitely dated to this period and which contribute to our understanding of it.

THE FRONTIER AND THE PEOPLE

The disastrous incursions of Shapur I into Roman territory mark a change in the military scene. Henceforward Roman dominance was broken. The balance sometimes swung dramatically in favour of the Sassanids, while Roman retaliation, on the rare occasions when it followed the old pattern, even more rarely achieved its former striking though impermanent victories. In general a state of rough equilibrium was maintained, and this is expressed on the Roman side in the transition from a frontier which had been an offensive base to a less ambitious defensive line. The Sassanid monarchy, like the Arsacid, was a feudal system in the broad sense and its strength at any moment was dependent, as the strength of Parthia had been, on the personality of the monarch.[2] The army remained in large part a levy, with cavalry dominant in prestige if not in numbers, and was still an instrument suited to the destructive raid rather than to the permanent occupation of territory. Even under a great commander such as Shapur it lost cohesion if kept too long in the field; after he had captured the emperor Valerian and invaded Cilicia and

---

[1] A selection of the evidence for social life in Northern Mesopotamia, largely derived from Syriac sources, has been set out in an excellent study by J. B. Segal, 'Mesopotamian Communities from Julian to

the Rise of Islam', *PBA*, xli (1955), 109–39.

[2] A. Christensen, *L'Iran sous les Sassanides*, pp. 206 ff.

Cappadocia in A.D. 260, his forces spread out to pillage Cilicia, and individual units were defeated piecemeal by the remnants of Valerian's army. On his homeward march it is said that he was obliged to surrender a part of his booty to the city of Edessa as the price of unmolested passage, and Odenathus of Palmyra was subsequently able to inflict on him a serious reverse. Odenathus was rewarded for his achievement by appointment as Roman supreme commander in the east, and after his death his wife Zenobia even claimed the imperial titles for herself and her son.[1] This led to the reduction of Palmyra by Aurelian, but the unsupported actions of Edessa and Palmyra at this time afford a foretaste of the significance that the frontier cities and principalities were to acquire. Hatra on the Parthian side had provided an early example of the hedgehog fortress which passing armies ignored only at great risk to their communications, but Hatra had been defended as much by its geographical position as by its walls. The cities which now came to play an increasing part in Roman frontier defence had not this unique advantage, for they lay well within the boundaries of the cultivated land. At the same time there was an important change in the Sassanid military machine, which learnt from the Romans the technique of siegecraft, including the design of siege engines, which the Parthians had never employed. As a result the Romans were obliged to develop more elaborate systems of fortification, and the account of their wars so vividly presented in the fourth century by Ammianus Marcellinus, himself an officer on the eastern front, is the story of one disastrous expedition to Ctesiphon under the emperor Julian, and for the rest a tale of the siege and defence of cities conducted with extraordinary ferocity on both sides.

From this time, too, Roman military dispositions changed. The legions stationed on the frontier were, after the third century, smaller units which served as garrisons for the new fortresses, and the field army was now provided from a strategic reserve. The task of manning the outposts, of policing and patrolling the frontier zone, remained in the hands of auxiliary units, but of these an increasing proportion were of local origin, probably little more than a peasant militia or yeomanry.[2] Local troops and even the civilian population joined in the defence of the cities when they were attacked. Bezabde, Singara, and Amida had numbers of local auxiliaries among their garrisons in the fourth century, and the citizens of Nisibis preferred to undertake their own defence rather than be handed over to the Persians by Jovian.[3] Villagers from the country around Edessa, who had taken shelter in the city during a Persian invasion in 502, made a successful sally which forced the Persian army to raise the siege.[4] In consequence local authorities, and particularly the bishops as the religious heads of their communities, played an important role in military affairs which must have enhanced their political prestige.

The inhabitants of the towns were tradesmen, artisans, and labourers with an upper stratum of small landowners and officials, as they are at the present day. In the countryside there was a threefold division of the population. The villagers were farmers and peasants, on their borders were the semi-nomadic tribesmen known as the 'Arab or

---

[1] D. Magie, *Roman Rule in Asia Minor*, ii. 1568–1570.

[2] V. Chapot, *La Frontière de l'Euphrate*, pp. 110 ff.

[3] Ammianus Marcellinus, xx. 7. 1; xx. 6. 8; xviii. 9. 3; xxv. 9. 2.

[4] Segal, 'Mesopotamian Communities', pp. 118–19.

'Arbaye,[1] and in the steppe ranged the true Beduin, usually described collectively as Tayyaye, from the name of the great tribe of Tayy, to which many of them belonged. Many of the villagers were serfs tied to the land, who were bought and sold with the estates on which they worked. This system existed throughout the Roman Empire from the early fourth century, but it was not a Roman innovation in the east, for it was common in Asia Minor in Hellenistic times and is well attested in Northern Mesopotamia by Late Assyrian charters.[2] There seems no reason to suppose that the organization of agriculture had undergone any marked change in the last thousand years. The boundaries of cultivation, on the other hand, seem to have receded considerably, and this would have been a natural result of the devastation wrought by passing armies and the insecurity which permitted the encroachment of nomads. Certainly a large part of the population of the northern plain was semi-nomadic by the fourth century, for in the reign of the emperor Julian an attempt was made to reinforce its discipline by settling the 'Arab, together with people from Bezabde and from Arzanene on the borders of Armenia.[3] The mention in this context of groups from the north and north-east is of particular interest, for it calls to mind the modern conjunction of Kurds and Arabs in the same area. It seems likely that the Roman government was not creating an artificial mixture of peoples but simply stabilizing an existing situation by the encouragement of village life, very much as the Syrian government has done in the Khabur basin in recent times. It is impossible to say whether the measure had any degree of success. Ammianus Marcellinus, referring to the middle of the fourth century, comments that the country between Nisibis and Singara was desiccated and waterless,[4] and when the monastery of St. Sergius was founded here in the sixth century it was specifically intended as a centre for the Beduin.[5]

The background of the true Beduin tribes in the northern plain is a complex subject, full of uncertainties, which cannot be discussed in detail here. They were known to Syriac writers under the collective name of Tayyaye but, even if the authors intended the term in any precise sense, it does not follow that they were all members by origin of the tribe of Tayy, for a common feature of Bedu organization is the assimilation to a powerful tribe of weaker elements which first seek its protection and eventually become identified with it.[6] The Tayy, in common with the tribes of the Ghassanid and Lakhmid confederations of Syria and Southern Mesopotamia, were of Yemenite ancestry and ascribed their departure from South Arabia to the breaking of the Ma'rib dam. This tradition clearly assimilated to one memorable event a continuing process of migration, probably linked with the slow decay of settled life in South Arabia, which extended over several centuries. The Tayy spent some time in the north of the Arabian peninsula before moving to the Euphrates and the Northern Jazira, and it is impossible to date their arrival in the border

---

[1] Segal, op. cit., p. 119. For a discussion of the meaning of 'Arab, see Segal, *AS*, iii (1953), 106–7, and *BSOAS*, xvi (1954), 25.

[2] M. Rostovtzeff, *Social and Economic History of the Hellenistic World*, iii (1941), 1515; *JADD*, iii. 378.

[3] G. Hoffmann, *Auszüge*, p. 23, quoting the life of Mar Sabha.

[4] Ammianus Marcellinus, xx. 6. 9.

[5] See below, p. 116.

[6] The Syrian Tayy now number ten fractions, of which only three are Tayy by origin. *Tribus nomades*, pp. 144–5.

region between Persia and Roman Syria with any accuracy, particularly as western writers refer to all Beduin as Scenite Arabs or Saracens without distinction of tribe. The political confusion of the third century A.D. provides a plausible setting for the first appearance as nomads of the tribes which were later united under the control of the Ghassanids and Lakhmids, and other groups such as the Tayy, and the Taghlib who are later found in Southern Mesopotamia, probably followed not long after them; a parallel for the movement, although not necessarily for its timing, can be found in the successive migrations of the Jubūr, the Shammar, and the Anaiza in the seventeenth and eighteenth centuries A.D.[1] An early sign of unrest on the northern fringe of Arabia has been read into a Nabataean inscription from Sinai, dated to the year A.D. 189, which mentions the devastation of the country by the Arabs.[2] The causes of the movement can only be guessed. The general breakdown of prosperity in the third century A.D. would have caused a serious decline in the caravan trade on which the economy of many settled Arabian communities depended and from which the nomads also profited as the leaders and 'protectors' of the caravans. This has been adduced as a reason for increasing nomadization in Arabia, where in default of external sources of income the inhabitants came increasingly to adopt the pastoral economy which afforded the only possible way of life over much of the country. This brought growing pressure on grazing and water supplies and the resultant tribal rivalries which were often the immediate cause of further migration.[3]

We are better informed about the impact of these people on the settled lands of Northern Mesopotamia. Like their recent successors they took advantage of the breakdown of discipline in the countryside to rob travellers and raid settlements. A letter of Barsauma, bishop of Nisibis, written in A.D. 484 to the Nestorian patriarch Acacius paints a vivid picture of the situation.[4] Two years of drought had brought famine to his people, and their distress was aggravated by a concentration of the 'tribes of the south' with their flocks, which had devastated the villages of the plain and of the hill-country on both sides of the frontier. A Byzantine protest to the Persian authorities, whose subjects they were, was backed by the massing of troops, together with nomads under Byzantine rule, on the frontier. A conference was held during which the Persian governor of Nisibis promised the return of property looted from Byzantine territory if the Byzantines would restore the proceeds of raids which had been carried out by their Beduin subjects in the region of Nineveh and into Adiabene. The conference broke up on the news that a further raid on Byzantine villages had taken place. This incident affords a good example of the disruptive capacity of the Beduin and of the way in which they took advantage of the political situation. It would be wrong, however, to regard them as a completely anarchic element. Their attitude to their nominal overlords was often one of suspicious reserve, once summarized by a member of the Taghlib tribe who, after complaining of the fiscal exactions of the Lakhmids, said: 'Obey kings? Certainly, as long as they treat us with justice. But we

[1] See above, p. 10.

[2] W. Caskel, 'The Beduinization of Arabia', *American Anthropological Memoirs*, 76 (1954), 40.

[3] On conditions in Arabia during this time see G. Levi Della Vida, 'Pre-Islamic Arabia', in *The Arab Heritage*, 1944, pp. 25–57.

[4] Quoted by F. Nau, *Les Arabes chrétiens de Mésopotamie et de Syrie du VIIᵉ au VIIIᵉ siècle*, 1933, pp. 13–15.

think it no crime to kill them.'[1] We must also remember that the raids of which Barsauma complained occurred during a two-year drought, and it is a matter of common observation that the failure of the rains and consequent shortage of pasture in their accustomed grazing grounds is a prime cause of the concentration of nomads on the borders of cultivation,[2] and their own poverty one of the motives for their depredations. The tribes responsible for this incursion are not named, but the leaders of the Tayy at least maintained a semblance of deference to Sassanid authority, to their own advantage. When the Sassanid government resolved on the suppression of the Lakhmid dynasty, the Tayy refused to grant asylum to the last king al-Nu'man IV although they were connected by marriage with his family, and a member of the tribe subsequently became governor of al-Hira and even led a Persian and Arab army against another nomad tribe, the Rabi'a.[3]

It is against this background that we must consider the two sites described in the following pages. They do not provide the representative cross-section of the material remains of a society at which the archaeologist should aim, and the description of the characteristic local community in its physical setting remains to be done. But in each case we can supplement archaeological observation with some literary evidence bearing on their individual fortunes, and each has a wider relevance to the history of the time which is emphasized by its architectural connexions. Singara is a fortified city of a type that appears to have been developed on the Mesopotamian frontier in the fourth century in response to specific local requirements and later became the standard pattern of military architecture employed on a much grander scale for the walls of Constantinople itself. The church of St. Sergius in Beth 'Arbaye, on the other hand, is a unique example in Northern Iraq of a peculiarly Syrian form of Christian basilica, and its sudden appearance so far from its native land throws an interesting light on the great significance of Christianity, and particularly of its heresies, to the population and to the rulers who were competing for their allegiance.

SINGARA AND ITS FORTIFICATIONS
(Pl. VII, *a*, fig. 8)

Beled Sinjar, ancient Singara, lies at the southern foot of Jebel Sinjar, at the point where a valley and watercourse issuing from the heart of the mountain cut through an eroded outlying ridge parallel with the main range. The nucleus of the modern town is situated on the slopes of the ridge east of the valley, with extensions across the watercourse to the west and on to the plain to the south. In the valley are abundant springs of sweet water which serve the needs of the population and, except in a very dry year, feed a perennial stream which is used to irrigate orchards in the plain for a distance of about 1 km. south of the town. Late Assyrian land records name estates in the country of Singara,[4]

[1] H. Lammens, *L'Arabie occidentale avant l'Hégire*, 1928, p. 217.

[2] The *Report to the Council of the League of Nations on the Administration of Iraq, 1928* (London, H.M.S.O., 1929) records that drought caused the Shammar from the Northern Jazira to move south into the alluvial plain as far as Kut, Hilla, and Diwaniya in 1923, 1925, and 1928, and that measures had to be taken for their control.

[3] *Encyclopaedia of Islam*, s.v. *Taiy*.

[4] *JADD*, iv. 31, 82, 202.

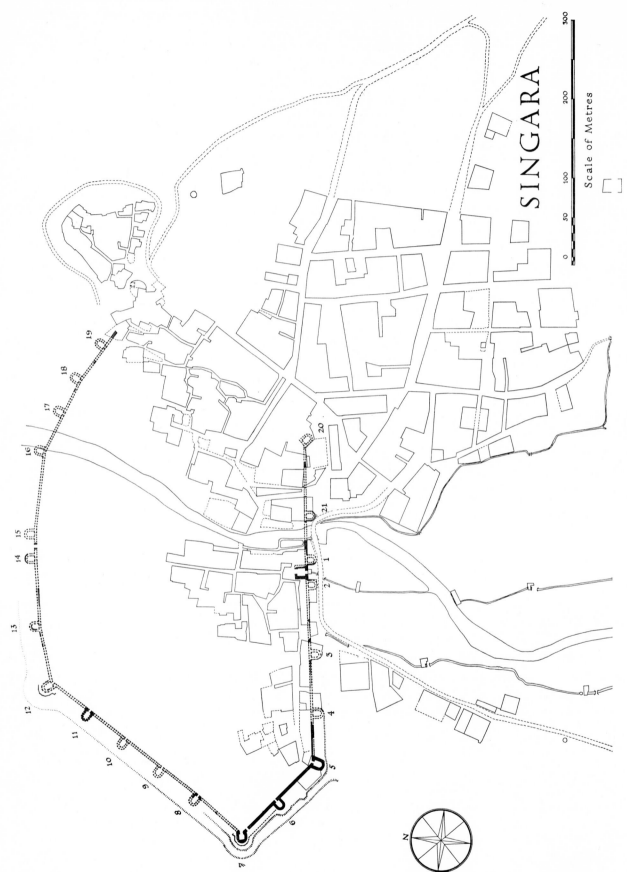

SINGARA

Scale of Metres

0   50   100   200   300

Fig. 8. Beled Sinjar. Town Plan showing the Roman Walls

but there is no reference to the town as such and no sign of an important *tell* on the site; it seems to have lain within the administrative province of Rasappa, which is to be looked for further to the south.[1] Any early settlement that existed is almost certainly covered by a group of houses on the crest of the eastern ridge, now unfortified but still referred to as the Burj, or citadel. In common with much of the country on the borders of the steppe it came under the control of people of nomad origin during the centuries after the fall of Assyria. Pliny refers to it as the capital of an Arab tribe, whom he calls the Praetavi;[2] nothing is otherwise known of this people, but their appearance in the area is probably to be compared with that of the Hatrenes and the Arab dynasties of Batnae (Anthemusia) and Edessa.

Singara first came under Roman control when it was captured by Lucius Quietus, the general of Trajan, in A.D. 114–15, and the road linking it directly with Nisibis was built soon afterwards. Together with the rest of Trajan's eastern conquests it was surrendered by Hadrian, and there is no further reference to it in the second century. The use of the title Aurelia in the third century suggests that it may have become a *colonia* after the campaigns of Lucius Verus, but if so it seems unlikely that it was retained for long. It was, as we have seen, incorporated in the Severan frontier line from the Khabur to the Tigris, and may have been garrisoned by the *I Parthica*.[3] Its communications with the lower Khabur were improved at the time of Severus Alexander's campaign in A.D. 232 when it lay on the line of march followed by the main body of the army under the emperor's command. We do not know whether it survived Ardashir's counter-attack in 237 when apparently Zagurae was captured, but it was certainly in Roman hands in the reign of Gordian III when coins were struck bearing its name. It presumably passed under Persian control between 250 and 260 when Shapur I carried all before him, but may have been regained in 283 under Carus, who made a successful attack on Ctesiphon; the power of the Sassanids had greatly declined under the successors of Shapur, and Vahram was ready to cede Northern Mesopotamia as the price of peace.[4] During the fourth century it was an outlying fortress, difficult to reinforce in case of attack by reason of its distance from Nisibis and the barren nature of the intervening country, and Ammianus Marcellinus says that it was taken on a number of occasions with the loss of its whole garrison. When it fell to Shapur II in 360 the *I Parthica* and *I Flavia* were taken into captivity, together with a number of local troops and a detachment of cavalry which had been caught in the city by the unexpected attack. It was finally ceded by Jovian, with Nisibis and Castra Maurorum, after the death of Julian in 363.[5]

The date of the existing walls is not given by any literary reference or surviving inscription and must be determined, within the limits laid down by the historical framework set out above, by comparison with similar systems elsewhere. The enceinte enclosed an area appreciably larger than that of the present town, for the walls were carried across the valley and along the crest of the ridge on the other side, so as to enclose the perennial

[1] See p. 55, n. 1, above.
[2] Pliny, *Natural History*, v. 21.
[3] See p. 79, n. 2, above.

[4] A. Christensen, *L'Iran sous les Sassanides*, p. 227.
[5] Ammianus Marcellinus, xx. 6. 9 and xxv. 7. 9.

springs in the low-lying ground west of the watercourse (pl. VII, b). In the period of the town's greatest prosperity, under the Atabeg princes of Mosul in the twelfth and thirteenth centuries A.D., even this area was exceeded; the wall was built over and settlement extended some 500 m. to the south-west. In consequence any buildings of the Roman period that may have stood within the walls are buried under mounds of medieval rubble or modern houses, and only the line of the main north–south street can be detected. In the older part of the town east of the watercourse the wall is completely lost among the existing buildings, but the ancient road and modern caravan track coming in from the east suggests an original gate at the head of the present market street, and from here north-eastwards to the Burj another street seems to preserve the line of the ditch. In the western, largely deserted, quarter the course of the wall and the position of the towers can be traced, but very little of the masonry has escaped the limekilns. There are, however, enough features to show that the defences consisted of a ditch about 15 m. wide and still, in places, up to 3 m. deep in solid rock; its inner face was retained by a scarp built of drafted masonry, with the main wall, over 3 m. thick, about 8 m. behind it. The towers, which were U-shaped in plan, projected from this wall at intervals of some 80 m., with a pair guarding each main gate. They were at least two storeys high, but the means of access to the upper storey is not visible. The facing of the inner wall and towers is of dressed limestone blocks, set in courses of approximately 40 cm. on a projecting footing; the core is of rubble and white mortar, poured and levelled course by course.

The north and south walls are now completely destroyed in the vicinity of the watercourse, but it is said that in the last century there still survived the remains of arches which originally carried the wall across the stream at these points. The arch of the south gate, through which would have passed the roads from the Khabur valley, can still be seen just to the west of the watercourse (pl. VIII, b, fig. 9). It is blocked, and its gate-chamber has been incorporated in the substructures of a comparatively recent house, now abandoned and in ruins. The stonework on the outside above the arch is a refacing on the earlier concrete core, but the voussoirs and the lower courses of the wall on either side are original. Water emerging from a conduit on the axis of the Roman road now feeds a bathing pool immediately outside the gate. The conduit is tapped by well-heads within the town, and its original purpose was probably to spread the outflow from the springs, which would otherwise have required a dangerously large passage through the wall. The interior of the gateway is filled to a height of some 3 m. with the debris of later buildings, but the visible Roman masonry outlines a gate-chamber some 10 m. square, with its axis set at a slight angle, obviously to conform with the alignment of the street leading to the north gate. The road itself is not visible, but a sounding on the site of the north gate revealed it at that point, and incidentally cast a gloomy light on the prospects of more general excavation. The area within the gate-chamber had been paved with limestone slabs about 40 cm. square, continued on the outside by a causeway, surfaced with large pebbles set in mortar, which led across the ditch to the northern road over the crest of Jebel Sinjar (pl. XII, a). The whole structure had been cleared in medieval times, and the paving stones and walls coated with bitumen, presumably to serve as the substructures of a house; but

SINGARA
The South Gate

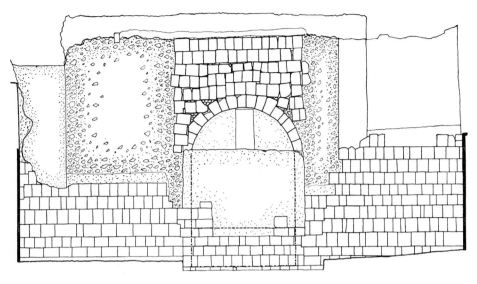

Elevation

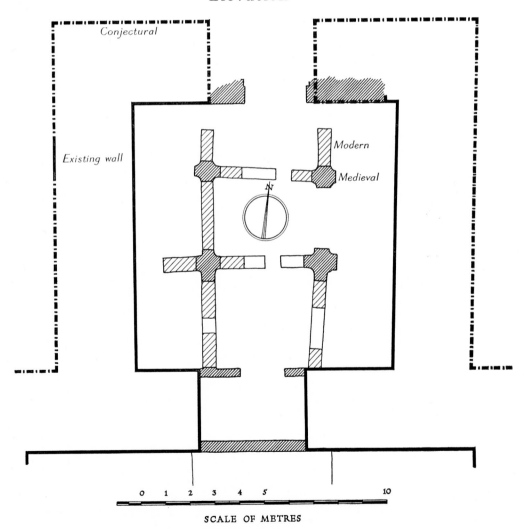

FIG. 9. Beled Sinjar. The Roman South Gate

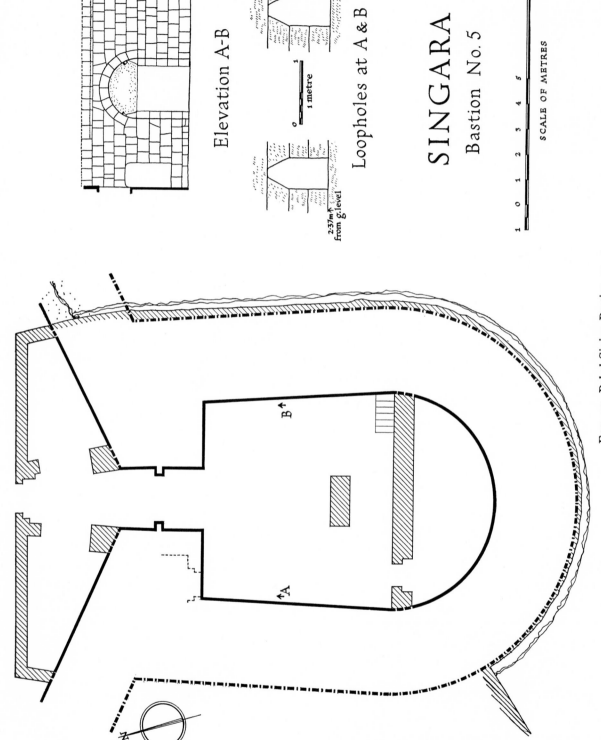

Elevation A-B

Loopholes at A & B

2·15
from g.level

2·37m
from g.level

1 metre

SINGARA
Bastion No. 5

SCALE OF METRES

FIG. 10. Beled Sinjar. Bastion no. 5

the debris of this reoccupation had been lately dug over and the limestone blocks removed to a kiln on the site of the adjacent gate-tower. We found two surviving blocks bearing segments of the moulding of a large *tabella ansata*, but the building inscription which they probably enclosed had completely disappeared.

The best surviving stretch of the wall runs along the crest of the western ridge (pl. IX). Bastion no. 5, at the south-west corner, has been incorporated in the lower storey of a modern house, and its interior, preserved up to first-floor level as the courtyard of the present building, gives us our most complete example of Roman masonry (pl. X, fig. 10). But it is to the more ruined bastions, nos. 6 and 7 (fig. 11), that we must look for the distinctive details they reveal of the original layout of the defensive system. The ditch is clearly marked, with the drafted masonry of the scarp standing to a height of over 2 m. on the north side of bastion no. 7 (pl. XI, *b*). Its masonry has been removed elsewhere, but the line of the robber trench can be traced around the tower on the west and south-west, and running parallel with the inner wall, on the lip of the ditch, as far as bastion no. 6, which it skirts in the same way; the seating for one of its blocks, cut in the rock outcrop on which the tower is founded, gives its exact line. Access to the platform between the scarp and the main wall was gained by a postern gate under the protection of the corner bastion no. 7; it was blocked by medieval revetments, but one of its jambs can be seen just to the south of the ruined tower. This gate would have been of little use unless masked from the outside, and we may assume that the wall or parapet which crowned the scarp was originally carried up to a considerable height. Bastion no. 6, which also owes its preservation in part to re-use in the medieval period, gives us a complete ground plan, with the position of the radial slit windows in the lower storey (pls. XI, *a*, XII, *b*, fig. 12); their inaccessibility, at a height of 3 m. above the floor, and their small field of view make it probable that their purpose was lighting rather than defence. The medieval repairs and additions, here and elsewhere, are clearly distinguished from the Roman masonry by the darker colour of the mortar, containing a high proportion of ash, and the dating criterion afforded by this marked difference has often proved useful on other sites, where medieval *khans* often reproduce very closely the plan, as in part they served the purpose, of Roman *castella*.

Ammianus Marcellinus gives an account of the last siege of Singara in 360, when a large battering ram eventually caused the collapse of a recently repaired round tower.[1] This implies that the walls were built, at the latest, in the first half of the fourth century. The system, as described above, has a close, though larger and more elaborate, parallel in the city of Amida, modern Diyarbekr, some 240 km. to the north-west.[2] The date of the walls of Amida has been the subject of a controversy in which it is dangerous to intervene without first-hand knowledge of the site, but it may be useful to recapitulate the evidence here. An Arabic inscription, *in situ*, dates the walls in their final form to A.D. 1068, but this can hardly be taken as a record of their original construction, since there is good authority for the erection or re-erection of parts of the circuit on three earlier occasions.

[1] Ammianus Marcellinus, xx. 6. 3–7.
[2] A. Gabriel, *Voyages archéologiques dans la Turquie orientale*, 1940, pp. 85 ff.

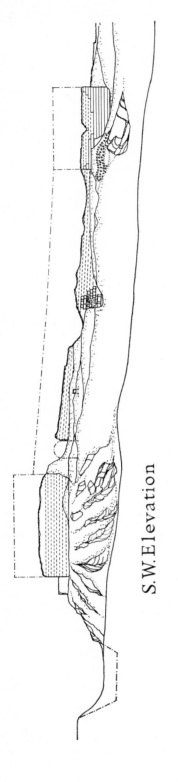

S.W. Elevation

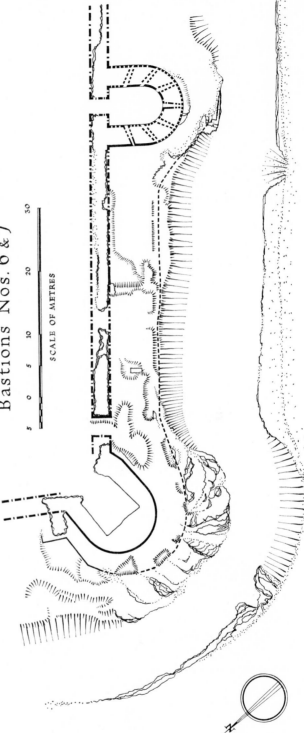

SINGARA

Bastions Nos. 6 & 7

SCALE OF METRES

5   0   5   10   20   30

FIG. 11. Beled Sinjar. Bastions nos. 6 and 7

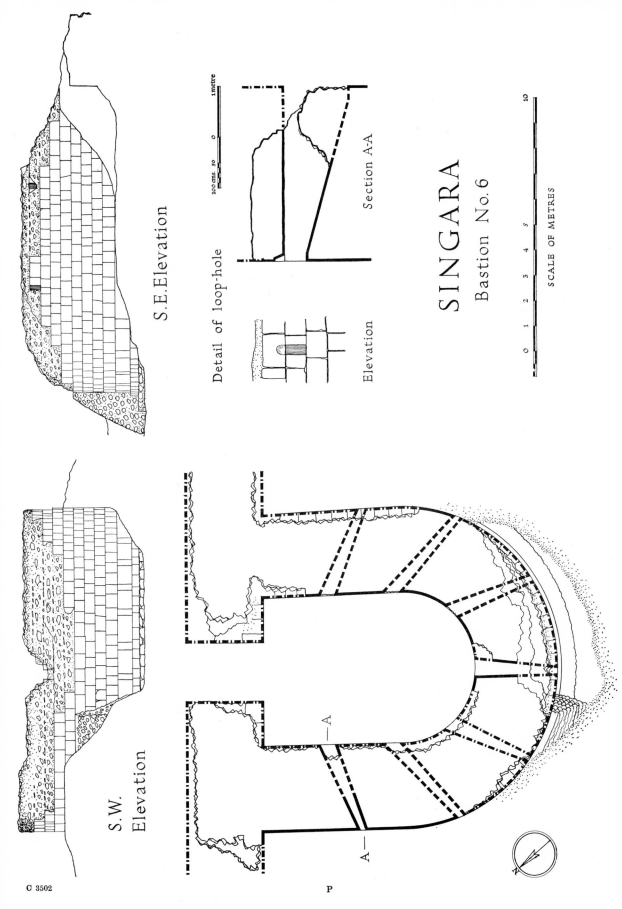

S.E. Elevation

S.W. Elevation

Detail of loop-hole

Section A-A

Elevation

100 cms. 50 0 1 metre

SINGARA

Bastion No. 6

SCALE OF METRES

0 1 2 3 4 5 10

A

A

N

FIG. 12. Beled Sinjar. Bastion no. 6

C 3502

P

Ammianus Marcellinus, who had personal knowledge of the place since he survived its capture by Shapur II, states that it was quite a small town when it was fortified by Constantius II while he was still Caesar, that is between A.D. 324 and 337.[1] A Latin inscription, re-used in the Islamic masonry, records a building 'a fundamentis' under Valentinian, Valens, and Gratian which must be dated about 370,[2] and probably represents the extension of the city after the surrender of Nisibis and the resettlement of its evacuated population at Amida. Finally, Procopius claims that the walls were built by Justinian,[3] and Byzantine activity is attested by inscriptions bearing the name of an official responsible for fortifications.[4] Only one circuit of walls survives. Apart from obvious Islamic repairs no changes in structural technique have been identified, and the variations that occur in the plan and disposition of the walls and towers cannot easily be interpreted in terms of a chronological sequence of major reconstructions and additions.

From this two opposite conclusions have been drawn, firstly that the essentials of the existing layout go back to the fourth century,[5] secondly that they should be ascribed to Justinian two hundred years later.[6] The latter argument is founded on the impossibility of distinguishing, on architectural grounds, between the work of Constantius and the extension added under Valentinian, Valens, and Gratian. But it involves the assumption that the fourth-century walls were so completely dismantled by Justinian's architects as to leave no present trace, which seems improbable. It is surely easier to conclude that the pattern employed in the extension about 370 was copied from the work of Constantius which can hardly have been more than forty years earlier, and that later builders repaired or reconstructed according to this established plan. The hypothesis of a sixth-century date rested also on the belief that the essential elements of Byzantine military architecture, the ditch, the outer wall and the inner wall with salient towers, were first combined in the Theodosian walls of Constantinople in the early fifth century, and that this great work was the first practical expression of the current Byzantine theory of defensive tactics. To this Singara provides an answer, for it combines all these elements in a rudimentary form which must be dated before the middle of the fourth century. It seems reasonable to suggest that Singara and Amida together represent early steps in the development of the type in response to special conditions of warfare on the Mesopotamian frontier, that later theory embodied the results of this experience, and that the walls of Constantinople are its most grandiose product.

QASR SERĪJ—THE CHURCH OF ST. SERGIUS

(i) Description of the Building

Qasr Serīj lies 5 km. south-west of Tell Hugna, and some 60 km. north-west of Mosul, on gently undulating ground at the southern foot of Jebel Qusair.[7] It is watered by a small

---

[1] Ammianus Marcellinus, xviii. 9. 1.
[2] CIL, 6730; A. Gabriel, op. cit., p. 181.
[3] Procopius, Buildings, ii. 3, 27.
[4] A. Gabriel, op. cit., p. 161.
[5] Ibid., pp. 175–82.

[6] D. van Berchem, 'Recherches sur la chronologie de Syrie et de Mésopotamie', Syria, xxxi (1954), 265–7.
[7] The site was recorded in the course of a survey by Seton Lloyd and G. Reitlinger, sponsored by the Neilson Expedition to the Near East, and briefly

perennial stream, now used to irrigate the fields of the modern village of Qusair just to the north of the ancient site.

The church stands in the middle of a ruinfield extending half a kilometre to the east of the watercourse. The other buildings, although some at least may be contemporary, were built apparently of mortared rubble in the common medieval tradition of the region, and are so far buried in their own debris that no coherent plan can be recovered. The church, on the other hand, was constructed of carefully dressed limestone blocks, and parts of the structure stand to nearly their original height. The plan (fig. 13), which is unique among the existing monuments of Iraq, is that of a small basilica of North Syrian type, of which many well-preserved examples exist further to the west. It is an approximate rectangle c. 23 by 14 m., with a central nave flanked by aisles and terminating in an inscribed semicircular apse. On either side of the apse were small rooms projecting some distance to north and south of the external walls of the church. These may be identified as the *diakonikon* or sacristy on the north, and on the south the *martyrion*, which replaced in North Syrian basilicas the *prothesis* of the standard Byzantine plan, and housed such relics of the martyrs as the community possessed.[1] The lateral projection of these chambers is unusual, but probably reflects the integration of the church with the surrounding monastic buildings.[2] The surviving remains are buried to a depth of over 3 m. in accumulated earth and debris, and some features of the reconstruction (fig. 14) must necessarily be conjectural, since no excavation can be undertaken without incurring the expense of conserving the existing structure.

The west wall (pl. XIII, *a*) stands to a height of 5 m. above present ground level, and nearly 9 m. above the estimated level of the original floor. The upper part of the arch which surmounted the central doorway is exposed. It was decorated externally with a moulding, now badly weathered, which apparently resembled that employed on the voussoirs of the nave arcade. The lintel and jambs of the door itself are not visible, nor can we say whether it was flanked by subsidiary entrances leading into the north and south aisles.[3] Above the arch is a flat relieving arch, and above this again a line of beam sockets along the surviving length of the façade. These must have housed the rafters of the narthex, which was a simple portico extraneous to the main structure of the church. The outer edge of the roof probably rested on an architrave supported by piers or columns. In comparable Syrian buildings the ends of the narthex were usually closed,[4] but at Qasr

described by Reitlinger, *Iraq*, v (1938), 148–9. I am greatly indebted to Fr. John Fiey, of the Dominican Community in Mosul, who called my attention to documentary evidence for the foundation of a monastery and church of St. Sergius in this region and suggested the identification with Qasr Serīj (*Sumer*, xiv (1958), 125–7).

[1] J. Lassus, *Sanctuaires chrétiens de Syrie*, 1947, pp. 162 ff., first pointed out the significance of this architectural variation, the origin of which he dates to the early fifth century (p. 177).

[2] Better preserved Syrian examples show that the church was only the most prominent feature of the architectural ensemble of the monastery, and cannot fully be understood in isolation from it.

[3] The siting of doorways in churches of this type seems to have been governed largely by practical considerations of access from adjacent parts of the monastery, and they do not conform to any standard pattern; in the North Church at Brad (G. Tchalenko, *Villages antiques de la Syrie du Nord*, 1953, pl. xi, 4) there was no west door, and many churches of comparable size had only one. I have suggested three on the reconstruction of Qasr Serīj, since it was a copy of the larger basilica of St. Sergius at Resafa (see below, p. 115).

[4] H. C. Butler, *Early Churches of Syria*, 1929,

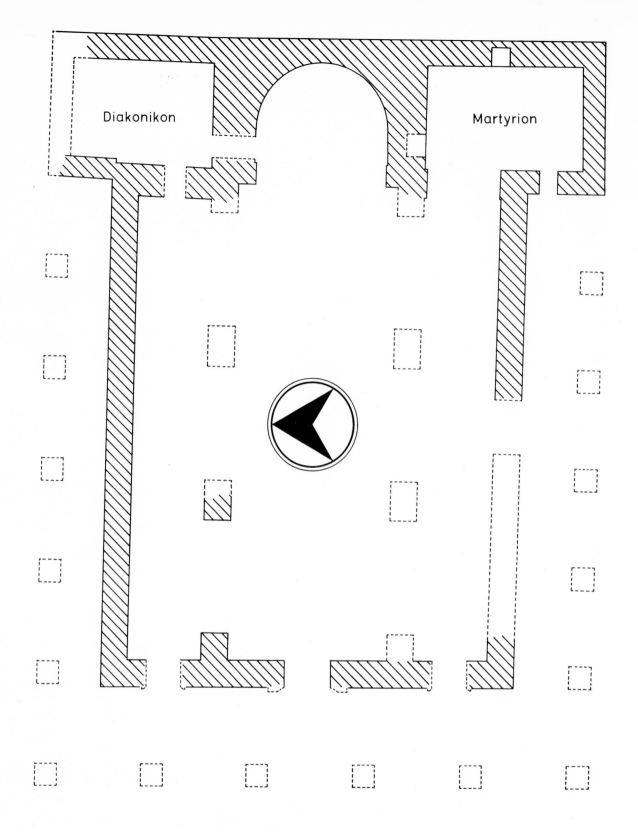

Diakonikon

Martyrion

QASR SERĪJ

Plan at 1.50 metres above estimated floor level

Hatching indicates masonry surviving above present ground level

1 0   5   10 metres

Fᴵɢ. 13. Qasr Serīj. Plan at 1·50 m. above estimated floor level

Serīj there is no trace of walls abutting on the corners of the façade, and it seems possible from other evidence that the portico continued along the north and south sides of the church. Above the narthex roof the wall was pierced by three windows. The largest of these, over the central doorway, survives intact with its lintel. The smaller side-windows which lit the north and south aisles from just below the apex of the roof on either side, were of the same width internally, but narrowed towards the outer face of the wall. Only the outline of the bottom of the north window now remains, as a shallow, tapering trough cut into the upper surface of a block; but its original height was limited by the aisle roof and can be estimated with reasonable accuracy, since the height and slope of the roof are preserved in the profile of a single block on the inner face of the west wall.

Very little of the south wall stands above present ground level. The top of the surviving masonry is visible at the south-west corner of the church, and again from its junction with the west wall of the *martyrion* to a point 7·10 m. to the west, which may mark the jamb of a south door (pl. XIII, *b*). A door at this point seems plausible, since it would have been on the same axis as the middle arch of the nave arcade. The north wall of the building survives virtually intact, but only the upper four courses below cornice level are exposed, and we cannot say whether there are any doors or windows on this side. The cornice has entirely disappeared, but would have been an essential element in the original structure, to mask the outer ends of the trusses supporting the aisle roof. At a height of approximately 1·70 m. below cornice level the outer face of the wall is set back along its whole length, forming a ledge 15 cm. deep. The purpose of this ledge was probably to support the inner ends of beams or trusses which carried the roof of an external portico, as suggested above. Although such a portico has been shown on the reconstruction, its existence cannot be confirmed without excavation and its dimensions are of course hypothetical.

The method of roofing the aisles can be determined with more certainty, since the masonry at the west end of the north aisle is preserved almost to its original height, and the system of supports is clearly visible (pl. XIII, *c*). Mention has already been made of the surviving block in the west wall which preserves the profile of the roof. In addition to this there is a line of beam sockets cut at intervals of 80 cm. in the face of the wall above the arcade which separated the aisle from the nave. The lower ends of the rafters which were set in these sockets rested on the inner face of the north wall. The top of the inner face of the west wall, as represented by the single surviving block, was aligned with the upper surface of the rafters so as to carry the ends of the purlins, which would have been masked on the outer face by a sloping continuation of the north wall cornice. Projecting from the face of the wall above the arcade was a line of corbelled brackets of which two survive, one on either side of the crown of the only standing arch. Their purpose was evidently to support a longitudinal beam of which the end was housed in a socket in the west wall. This socket is concealed, in the north aisle, under a fragment of later mortared rubble vaulting which adheres to the masonry, but it is plainly visible in the corresponding

pp. 198–9. The internal narthex is comparatively rare in Syrian and Palestinian churches. In hotter climates its function, as a place to which the unbaptized withdrew during the Eucharist, could readily be served by an open portico (J. W. Crowfoot, *Early Churches in Palestine*, 1941, p. 54).

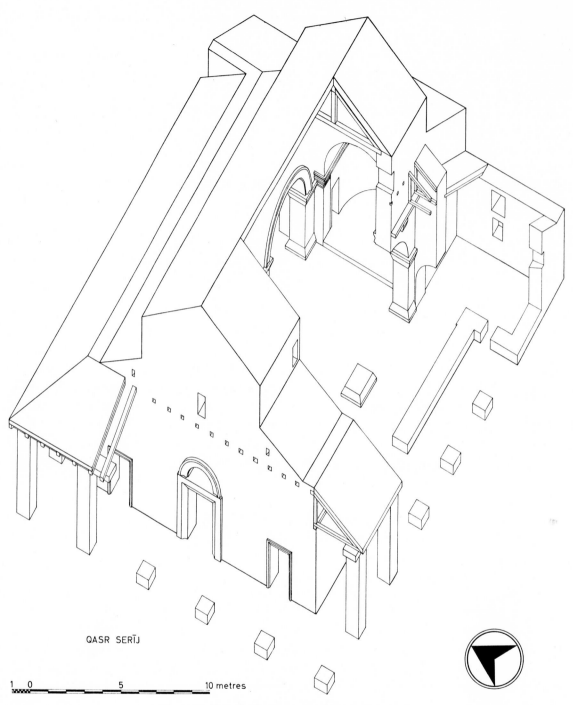

QASR SERĪJ

1 0   5   10 metres

FIG. 14. Qasr Serīj. Axonometric reconstruction

angle of the south aisle (pl. XIII, b). The purpose of this beam was clearly to support the horizontal tie-beams which spanned the aisle beneath the rafters. Of the roofing material employed there is no evidence. No fragments of tile were found, but this does not prove that they were not originally used. The timbered roof was eventually replaced, at least in the north aisle, by a system of mortared rubble vaults, but this development cannot be dated by the constructional technique alone, which has persisted throughout medieval into modern times. The crown of the vaulting was at a considerably lower level than the original roof, and its profile, with surviving fragments of the material, can be seen on the west wall of the north aisle. It rested on the inner face of the north wall, which was reduced in height by one course, and on a ledge cut into the face of the wall above the arcade, at a level intermediate between the original beam sockets and the corbelled brackets.

This unusually well-preserved portion of the church also provides the evidence for the reconstruction of the nave. The surviving arch had a span of c. 3·85 m., and from this it may be calculated that there were three arches on either side of the nave, with intermediate piers approximately 1·40 m. long by 98 cm. wide. Such a system of piers, rather than columns, supporting arches of relatively wide span is characteristic of a particular group of North Syrian basilicas, and appears to be a development native to that region.[1] The height of the piers, the proportions of impost blocks and bases, and the use of the mouldings suggested on the reconstruction are based on parallels from sixth-century churches of this group. The evidence at Qasr Serīj awaits excavation, but the simplicity of the moulding employed on the voussoirs of the arcade does not lead us to expect elaborate ornament elsewhere. Above the existing arch the wall is pierced by a flat relieving arch, and above this again can be seen the only remaining clerestory window (pl. XIII, b). Comparable buildings of this period usually had a large number of windows in the clerestory, sited without particular reference to the arcade below. In this case, however, the architect clearly intended a symmetrical relationship, and we may assume that there were originally five, one over the crown of each arch and two over the intervening piers. We do not know the original height of the nave, but analogy suggests that the walls rose one, or at most two, courses above the lintels of the clerestory windows, and the roof trusses were carried either on corbels like those in the aisles, or in slots in the masonry.

At the east end of the church the apse is intact, with the exception of a large hole in the east side of the semi-dome. This has at some time been repaired with mortared rubble, but the repair has in turn collapsed. The exterior of the semi-dome has been faced with the same material, and the whole operation may have been contemporary with the vaulting of the north aisle. The curve of the semi-dome was probably never visible from the outside, since the semicircle of the apse is inscribed within a rectangular block of masonry which would customarily have been covered with a sloping roof. The interior of the apse is buried to just below the level of the moulded cornice (pl. XIII, d), and it is impossible to say whether there were any windows. Analogies elsewhere suggest that there were at most two, set close together on the east–west axis, and it may have been

[1] G. Tchalenko, *Villages antiques de la Syrie du Nord*, p. 17.

the structural weakness caused by an opening at this point which brought about the collapse of the overlying masonry of the semi-dome. A second moulding immediately below the cornice on the outer angle of the chancel arch suggests the presence of a shallow pilaster on each side. The responding piers of the arcade at the north-east and south-east corners of the nave are not visible at present ground level, and it is impossible to determine how their ornament was related to that of the apse, or how the problem presented by their apparent asymmetry was resolved.

Little can be seen of the *diakonikon*, on the north side of the apse. Its north wall is completely buried, but it may be presumed to have been approximately the same length as the *martyrion*. A slight change in the line of the inner face of the west wall, opposite its junction with the north wall of the church, probably reflects an adjustment to conform with the dimensions of an adjacent building on the north. No entrance is visible, but there were usually two small doorways communicating respectively with the north aisle and with the apse. Such windows as existed were presumably above the level of the surviving masonry; in most churches they were few and inaccessible, since the *diakonikon* served as both vestry and treasury. The entrance to the *martyrion* was, by contrast, an archway spanning almost the full width of the south aisle. This uncharacteristic asymmetry must reflect the importance which was attached in North Syrian churches to relics of the martyrs and the ceremonies associated with them. There were rectangular niches in the east and north walls of the room, and tapering windows at a higher level, one above the east niche and one in the middle of the south wall. A further aperture in the west wall, 65 cm. wide, appears to penetrate the full thickness of the masonry, although the outer face and the bottom of the opening are concealed by debris. Its lintel is *c.* 2·00 m. above the original floor, and it may have been a third window or a narrow door giving on to the south portico; an entrance to the *martyrion* from outside the church is not uncommon. Relics may have been housed in the niches, but were more probably enshrined in reliquaries set against the east wall of the room. Many such reliquaries, with orifices through which oil could be poured, have been found in Syria, and it is known that the oil which had thus been brought into contact with the martyr's bones was greatly prized for its beneficent qualities.[1]

This superficial survey of Qasr Serīj has enabled us to reconstruct a basilical church of a type which appears to have developed in North Syria. It incorporates the *martyrion* on the south side of the apse which is itself a characteristic feature of churches in that area from the early fifth century onwards; but its architectural antecedents are even more closely defined by the form of the nave arcade, consisting of wide arches springing from a small number of rectangular piers. Basilicas of this pattern are common in the basalt region of North-east Syria from the fifth century,[2] and it is probable that the system there reflected in part the intractability of the local building material, which greatly restricted the use of columns. But its adoption and diffusion in the massif east of Antioch, where the excellent local limestone imposed no such limitations, must represent a deliberate choice by the architects, who appreciated the unifying effect of the larger openings on the

---

[1] J. Lassus, *Sanctuaires chrétiens de Syrie*, pp. 163–7.
[2] G. Tchalenko, op. cit., p. 297, n. 1; H. C. Butler, *Early Churches of Syria*, p. 201.

interior of their buildings. This plan was adopted, in the first half of the sixth century, for the 'cathedrals' of the great centres of pilgrimage, Cyrrhus and Resafa-Sergiopolis,[1] and our literary evidence shows that its unexpected appearance in the northern plain of Mesopotamia, more than 200 miles to the east, is a direct outcome of this development.

(ii) *The Foundation of the Monastery*

In the first half of the sixth century the tribes on the Persian side of the frontier were under the leadership of the pagan Lakhmid dynasty of al-Hira, ruled at this time by al-Mundhir III (c. 508–54). Their traditional enemies on the Syrian fringe of the desert were the banu-Ghassan, a group of tribes like the Lakhmids of South Arabian origin,[2] who had been Syrianized and converted to Christianity during the fourth century. They were unruly subjects, not averse to raiding Byzantine as well as Persian territory, and in 529 Justinian sought to discipline their aggressive spirit by recognizing a Ghassanid confederacy under the greatest of their leaders, al-Harith II, to whom he granted the title of *patricius*, the highest rank in the Byzantine nobility.[3] Al-Harith thus succeeded to the control of the Syrian desert once exercised by Zenobia of Palmyra, and earlier by the kings of Petra. He had distinguished himself by defeating the Lakhmids in 528, and subsequently served under Belisarius at the battle of Callinicum in 531; his adversary al-Mundhir was simultaneously assisting the invading Sassanid forces. With the accession of Khusrō I to the throne of Persia later in the same year negotiations began, and the so-called Endless Peace between the two empires was signed in 532. Khusrō had not, however, foreseen the grandiose schemes of conquest which Justinian, freed from the threat to his eastern frontier, proceeded to undertake in the west, and it is probable that fear for the safety of his own dominions combined with personal ambition to dictate his next move. A dispute between the Lakhmids and the Ghassanids over grazing rights in the desert of Palmyra, encouraged, if not instigated, by the Persian government, was made the pretext in 540 for an attack on Syria in which Antioch was captured and burnt. Despite a truce in Mesopotamia in 545, the war dragged on in Armenia for another twelve years, and it was not until 562 that a peace treaty was signed. Among the terms of this treaty was a stipulation that it should be binding on the Arab frontier states, and a further clause guaranteed freedom of worship, including the right to build churches, to Christian subjects of the Persian Empire, on condition that they did not attempt to proselytize among the followers of Zoroaster.[4]

Religious issues were closely interwoven in the politics of the day. The greatest issue of Justinian's time was the monophysite heresy, which had enjoyed imperial support under Zeno, and suffered rigorous repression under Justin I. Justinian found himself on the horns of a dilemma, since his ambitions for the reconquest of orthodox Italy would have

---

[1] G. Tchalenko, loc. cit.

[2] F. Nau, *Les Arabes chrétiens de Mésopotamie et de Syrie du VIIe au VIIIe siècle*, pp. 36–49. P. K. Hitti, *History of the Arabs*, 1953, pp. 78–84.

[3] Procopius, *Wars*, i. xvii. 47 ff.; Theophanes, *Chronographia*, ed. de Boor, 240, 14.

[4] Menander, *Fragmenta*, Teubner ed., 24, ll. 16–28, translated, P. N. Ure, *Justinian and his Age*, 1951, p. 99.

been seriously compromised by the taint of heresy, yet in the east he relied on the loyalty of Syria, which was largely monophysite. Like many of his countrymen he was an enthusiastic amateur theologian, but it is difficult to decide how far his religious policy was founded on personal conviction. It was at the least politically convenient that the Empress Theodora's heretical leanings counterbalanced the orthodoxy of her husband, and enabled her to maintain under her protection in Constantinople the monophysite clergy, including the patriarch Theodosius of Alexandria, whom Justinian had publicly condemned.[1] Thus it was that al-Harith obtained, in 543, at a time when the importance of his loyalty had been emphasized by the disastrous Persian invasion of Syria, the ordination by Theodosius of two monophysite bishops, one to his own diocese in the Hauran, the other, Jacob Baradai, to the see of Edessa. Even after the death of Theodora in 548 Theodosius seems to have retained the esteem of Justinian and continued to administer the affairs of his followers; when al-Harith paid a state visit to Constantinople in 563 to discuss the succession to his kingdom, he brought letters from Jacob Baradai to Theodosius.[2]

Jacob Baradai was an indefatigable traveller, and devoted his life to his appointed task, the ordination of clergy to replace those arrested or banished in the recent persecutions. In the newly reorganized community there was little sympathy for the orthodoxy of Constantinople, too often represented by the imperial police, and the liturgical use of Syriac, combined with ignorance of Greek, accelerated a tendency to separatism; it may have entered the mind of the astute and ambitious al-Harith that a Syrian national Church under his patronage would powerfully enhance his own position.[3] Certainly Justinian's attempts to restore uniformity, whether by coercion or compromise, met with no response, and it is relevant to note that at a Council held in 554 the Church of Armenia, which was also predominantly monophysite, formally declared its independence of Constantinople.

Issues which aroused such strong feeling could hardly fail to be, as Justinian saw, of political importance, particularly in the vital frontier areas of Syria and Armenia, and it is not surprising to find Khusrō taking an active interest in the welfare of the monophysites. The Christians of Persia were for the most part Nestorians, headed by a patriarch who was often a prominent figure at the court of the King of Kings, but in Mesopotamia they included monophysites who were steadily increasing in numbers, both by conversion and by the accession of transplanted populations from Syria.[4] Ahudemmeh, the founder of the monastery at Qasr Serīj, was born in Balad of Nestorian parents, and was ordained in the Nestorian Church, probably becoming bishop of Nineveh.[5] He was involved, together with a number of other bishops and priests, in a dispute with the Nestorian patriarch

[1] Procopius, *Anecdota*, x. 13 ff.; L. Duchesne, 'Les protégés de Theodora', *Mélanges d'archéologie et d'histoire*, xxxv (1915), 57–79.
[2] F. Nau, op. cit., pp. 52–56; R. Devréesse, *Le Patriarchat d'Antioche*, 1945, pp. 75 and 78, n. 6.
[3] Devréesse, op. cit., pp. 96 and 281, n. 3; Segal, 'Mesopotamian Communities', pp. 121–2.

[4] J. Labourt, *Le Christianisme dans l'Empire perse*, 1904, p. 199. A growing number of monophysites had taken refuge in al-Hira of their own accord, to escape Byzantine persecution (F. Nau, *Les Arabes chrétiens*, p. 40).
[5] 'History of Mar Ahudemmeh', ed. and trans. F. Nau, *Patrologia Orientalis*, iii. 8. 10.

Joseph, whose behaviour was not such as to endear him to his clergy.[1] It is not clear whether the dispute originated from theological differences or personal antipathy, but it culminated in a formal debate between the patriarch and the rebels, led by Ahudemmeh, in which the latter expounded the monophysite doctrine. Khusrō acted as arbiter and adjudged the victory to Ahudemmeh, to whom he then granted freedom of worship and permission to build churches.[2] The date of this pronouncement is unknown, but in 559 Ahudemmeh was consecrated by Jacob Baradai as bishop of Beth ʿArbaye and metropolitan of the monophysite Church in Persia.[3] He showed great vigour in proselytizing among the Beduin tribes, to whom the asceticism of the monophysites seems to have made a particular appeal, and so far succeeded in his mission that he is said by his biographer to have ordained a priest and a deacon for every encampment.[4] When the first part of his missionary work was completed,

he built a great and beautiful house of dressed stone in the middle of Beth ʿArbaye, in a place called ʿAin Qenoye (Barhebraeus, ʿAin Qena). He placed in it an altar and some holy relics, and called the house by the name of Mar Sergīs, the famous martyr, because these Arab peoples bore great devotion to his name and had recourse to him more than to all other men. The saint (Ahudemmeh) attempted by means of this house which he had built in the name of Mar Sergīs, to keep them away from the shrine of Mar Sergīs of Beth Resafa, since it was far distant from them. He made it, as far as he was able, resemble the other, so that its beauty might hold them back from going to the other. Near this shrine which he had built, he further constructed the great and famous monastery of ʿAin Qenoye . . .[5]

This can be no other than Qasr Serīj, and the modern name embodies a corruption of its original dedication to St. Sergius. The exact date of the foundation is uncertain, but it is further recorded in the *Life* that the monastery was burnt by jealous Nestorians, and was subsequently restored with its contents by order of Khusrō, reinforced by the prayers of Ahudemmeh, who then renewed his charge to the brethren. Ahudemmeh fell from favour with Khusrō in 573 when he baptized a prince of the royal house, who subsequently fled to Syria, and he was imprisoned until his death in 575. If the sequence of events described in his *Life* has any meaning, the foundation of St. Sergius in Beth ʿArbaye must have come some time after his consecration by Jacob Baradai; 565 seems a reasonable approximation, and would agree well enough with dated parallels from North Syria, such as the North Church at Brad which was built in 561.[6]

Two points in the description are worthy of especial notice. The provision of relics is mentioned immediately after the erection of the altar, and bears out the importance of the

[1] Joseph was patriarch from 552 to 565, having attained this dignity through his influence with Khusrō, whose physician he was. According to the monophysite Barhebraeus (*Chronicon Ecclesiasticum*, ed. Abbeloos and Lamy, iii (1877), 96–98), he tyrannized over his clergy, and would order a visitor of humble station to be tethered to a manger in his stables. He was eventually deposed.

[2] John of Ephesus, *Ecclesiastical History*, trans. R. Payne Smith, 1860, pp. 418–19. John, after a formal apology for eulogizing a Zoroastrian and an enemy of his country, praises Khusrō's wisdom and beneficence.

[3] Barhebraeus, *Chronicon Ecclesiasticum*, cols. 100–2. Beth ʿArbaye at this time was the northern plain of Mesopotamia between Nisibis and Jebel Sinjar, bounded on the west by the Khabur and on the east by the Tigris.

[4] F. Nau, 'History of Mar Ahudemmeh', p. 27.

[5] F. Nau, ibid., pp. 29–30.

[6] *Publications of the Princeton Archaeological Expedition to Syria*, ii, B, *Architecture* (1920), iii. 340. Corrected plan in Tchalenko, *Villages antiques de la Syrie du Nord*, pl. xi, 4.

martyrion, already illustrated by its architectural prominence. Secondly, the statement that the new church was, as nearly as possible, a copy of the great church of St. Sergius at Resafa explains the adoption of the peculiarly North Syrian form of basilica which, as we have seen, was employed at Resafa.[1] St. Sergius in Beth ʿArbaye is on a smaller scale and simpler in design and decoration, reflecting no doubt the more limited resources in men and money available to Ahudemmeh, but internally it must have been a convincing reminder of its famous original.

The motive for this architectural emulation of a Syrian model is intriguing, and it is here that the political and religious circumstances of the time become relevant. It was designed particularly as a place of pilgrimage for the Beduin who were Ahudemmeh's chief concern, but the statement of his biographer that Resafa was too far away can hardly be the whole truth, since the tribes of the Jazira habitually, until the establishment of modern frontiers, ranged from the Middle Euphrates to the Upper Tigris. Nor is it likely that the support of Khusrō, both for Ahudemmeh's mission and for the protection of his new monastery against his Nestorian rivals, stemmed entirely from a benevolent desire to save his Beduin subjects unnecessary exertion. It is more comprehensible as an act of policy. Khusrō, as well as Justinian, probably desired a period of peace after the long, inconclusive wars of the last half century, particularly when the peace treaty provided for an annual payment of 30,000 pieces of Byzantine gold to his treasury. One of the pre-requisites of a stable peace was the control of the frontier tribes, and important clauses of the treaty regulate the movement of travellers and merchandise and the control of smuggling, and the settlement of disputes between the people on either side of the frontier.[2] The establishment of a religious centre on the Persian side would, as in the case of Hatra 500 years before, tend to reinforce secular control over the tribesmen who worshipped there, and as a deliberate substitute for Resafa it would prevent them from contracting undesirable loyalties or liaisons in Byzantine territory.[3] Moreover, an advertised policy of tolerance might have wider repercussions. The cessation of open warfare did not inhibit Khusrō from using diplomatic means to increase his influence in Syria and Armenia, and the growing estrangement between the monophysite populations of these regions and the Byzantine government must have seemed a heaven-sent opportunity.[4] It is curious to see how both monarchs attempt to gain the political credit for ensuring freedom of Christian worship, Justinian by the clause appended to the treaty of 562, Khusrō in

[1] For the basilica of St. Sergius at Resafa, see H. Spanner and S. Guyer, *Rusafa*, 1926, pp. 22 ff. and 56 ff.

[2] Menander, *Fragmenta*, Teubner ed., pp. 21–22, trans. P. N. Ure, *Justinian and his Age*, pp. 97–99.

[3] The same motive led al-Nuʿman of al-Hira, in the early fifth century, to tolerate Christian worship and the building of churches among his subjects, who were flocking to the pillar of St. Simeon the Stylite in Northern Syria. Our authority, Cosmas, had this story from a Syrian official, Antiochus, who in time of peace had been invited to dine with al-Nuʿman in his encampment near Damascus; in conversation al-Nuʿman

displayed great curiosity about St. Simeon, and finally revealed the reason for his questions (Assemanus, *Bibliotheca Orientalis*, i (1719), 247). The students of Nisibis university were forbidden by statute to enter Byzantine territory, although the regulation could hardly be enforced (Segal, 'Mesopotamian Communities', p. 127).

[4] We may recall that one of the pretexts for the outbreak of war in 540 had been the complaints of an Armenian embassy to Khusrō about Byzantine oppression (J. B. Bury, *History of the Later Roman Empire*, ii (1923), 92–93).

virtually identical terms in his pronouncement to Ahudemmeh; and in view of the constant persecution to which Jacob Baradai and his followers were subject, the tolerance of a Zoroastrian may well have seemed preferable to the orthodoxy of a Christian sovereign.

It is true that al-Harith the Ghassanid had, despite his monophysite convictions, been a loyal subject of Justinian. Although he was undoubtedly ambitious, and on occasion not above suspicion, his allegiance was probably assured by his own ultimate interest and his hatred of the Lakhmids; for in 544 al-Mundhir III had sacrificed to al-Uzza, his patron goddess, a son of al-Harith whom he had captured, and was himself killed in battle by al-Harith in 554. After the death of al-Harith in 569, however, Byzantine suspicions of the Ghassanids revived, and an abortive attempt was made to execute his son al-Mundhir, who emulated his father's military exploits and his enthusiasm for the monophysite cause;[1] despite a temporary reconciliation, the dynasty was suppressed in 584. Of the tribes which composed the Ghassanid federation many henceforward supported Persia, and it may not be too fanciful to see in this some reflection of Khusrō's policy of tolerance towards their co-religionists, which continued under his successors despite a brief period of persecution after the imprisonment and death of Ahudemmeh. Of this policy Qasr Serīj remains a visible monument.

[1] This incident is a pleasing example of muddle in Byzantine bureaucracy. Justin II, who had succeeded Justinian, wrote a letter to the governor of Syria, with instructions to invite al-Mundhir to visit him and then have him executed; the emperor also drafted the invitation. Unfortunately the letter ordering his execution was addressed to al-Mundhir, and the invitation to the governor. It was a very long time before al-Mundhir could be persuaded to speak to any Byzantine official (John of Ephesus, *Ecclesiastical History*, trans. R. Payne Smith, pp. 372–3). The motive for this piece of treachery may not have been entirely logical, for the moronic Justin apparently retained fearsome memories of the majestic appearance of al-Harith on his visits to Constantinople. In his moments of insane frenzy, his chamberlains used to quiet him with the threat 'Al-Harith will come!' (John of Ephesus, op. cit., p. 168).

EPILOGUE

A SMALL state in Northern Iraq, with a nucleus of territory nowhere more than 150 km. in extent, became for a period of over 200 years the paramount power in the Near East. The impetus of this expansion must have come from the resources of land and population within its borders. Yet the city which had been its capital for more than a millennium before this time and housed the shrine of its divine patron, lay on the very border of the cultivable land, an obvious site for the first settlement of a nomadic tribe or, by virtue of its special position on a great highway, for a trading community. The Assyrians believed that their early rulers were of nomadic origin, and they themselves first appear in history as merchants. The creation of their empire was accompanied by the transfer of the administration first to one, then to another, of a series of three great cities, each constructed on a more monumental scale than its predecessor. Then, within fifty years of the time when the empire was at its greatest extent, the country was overrun, the cities destroyed and Assyria ceased to exist as a political entity. From this moment until the coming of Islam the people have no formal history. The little we learn about them from contemporary sources is largely concerned with the struggle between eastern and western empires for the control of their territory, which cannot have justified by its intrinsic value such an expenditure of men and money.

This is an oversimplified account, but it is sufficient to emphasize the historical anomalies that have been discussed in this book. Some of the questions that have been raised cannot yet be answered, others might be answered differently by specialists in the fields on which I have trespassed. My object has been to define the problems more closely rather than to solve them, and to do so by assessing one particular factor, the influence of the geographical environment on different historical situations. Geography does not dictate human action. It imposes the limitations and creates the opportunities of economic, and hence of political, development. Its general relevance to the history of the area is too obvious to require further comment, although it deserves more detailed and cautious consideration than it has often received. But a considerable part of our evidence, both documentary and archaeological, is derived from, and largely relevant to, individual sites. In order to determine the relationship of this material to the over-all picture, we have to consider the circumstances of each site, its agricultural potential, its communications and possible commercial or military importance, and its susceptibility to external influences. Thus the specific examination of topography and climate, and of their effect on the habits and distribution of the modern population, suggests a possible explanation of the character of early Assyrian settlement, and certainly leads us to expect a great difference between the earliest history of Aššur and that of Nineveh, which is borne out by the archaeological evidence. It also illuminates the practical considerations which led to the eventual choice of Nineveh as the imperial capital. It does not explain why Nineveh was so large, and for that we must look to the ambition of its founder; but it does suggest that it was too large, and that such material expressions of ambition were an intolerable burden on the resources of the country. This is, however, in common with most of the conclusions in this book, a suggestion and not a proven statement. The statistics do not yet exist by which a true assessment of Assyrian resources can be made, and a similar lack of comprehensive evidence afflicts many of the basic problems even in comparatively well-documented situations.

For the post-Assyrian period, when written history fails us and very little excavation has yet been carried out, we are only just beginning to collect the evidence for such observations, but even at this stage a knowledge of the patterns of settlement under varying conditions sometimes suggests an explanation for isolated facts. The appearance of a short-lived Hellenistic village inaccessibly situated on the ruins of Kalḫu hints at the breakdown of security in the countryside, a condition which favours the intrusion of the nomad. When we look at the border of the steppe, it can be no coincidence that the earliest evidence from Hatra suggests an origin in the Hellenistic period for this Arab principality. It is hardly necessary to emphasize that Roman and Parthian frontier strategy was largely influenced by geographical considerations; but again, when we find documentary evidence for the condition of the local population, it is interesting to see the recession of agriculture and the increasing importance of the nomad element, whose particular version of Christianity received official encouragement for political ends.

The expression 'pattern of settlement' has frequently been employed in this book. The identification of such a pattern is not an end in itself. It is a convenient way of assessing the range of different types of settlement that may reasonably be expected to occur under specific geographical, climatic, and political conditions. As such it is of use in the interpretation of existing evidence, perhaps even more in identifying its deficiencies; a comparison of the ancient and modern maps shows only too clearly that in Assyrian times we have located the towns but not the villages; during the brief Roman occupation we know something of the military, nothing of the non-military sites. It may also lead to the more effective investigation of outstanding problems, now that the pioneer work of our predecessors has created a framework of historical knowledge that makes the definition of these problems possible. I have earlier remarked that few societies leave records of their weakness, and that such periods of obscurity are none the less important because they mask the emergence of new elements in the historical situation. In such circumstances the archaeologist is often called upon to supplement the deficiencies of history, and must select a site that will prove an effective barometer of the political or economic climate. Obviously this purpose will best be served by a settlement exposed to any dangers that insecurity may bring. In the case of Assyria, the power of the state to protect its subjects will be more clearly reflected by a site on the borders of the steppe than in the Tigris valley, and a road-station on an important highway will record the vagaries of long-distance trade better than a palace.

In conclusion it may be useful to consider briefly some of the problems that remain. In the course of this book I have deliberately omitted to discuss two major topics, the composition of the population of the northern plain which was incorporated into the early Assyrian kingdom, and the history of the country during the long and obscure period of the second millennium after the collapse of Šamši-Addu's short-lived empire. An important part of the evidence for the first question depends on the linguistic analysis of personal and place names from the earliest documents, and must be left to philologists, although it is obvious that the amount of material at present available is not sufficient for any revealing analysis. The archaeologist, however, has his part to play, for we have not so far investigated on any effective scale the material remains of the settled communities during the third millennium. The excavation of the Ninevite V levels on one or more of the well-sited and obviously important mounds in the region between Nineveh and Sinjar would yield the evidence for a full definition of this culture, and might produce some written records.

Excavation alone can provide further evidence on the problems of the second millennium. Even in the two centuries covered by the Cappadocian and Mari archives we have very little idea of the physical setting of life in Assyria, and we lack even such basic historical data as the limits of the territory of Aššur before the time of Šamši-Addu. What happened to the outlying cities during the domination of Mitanni is completely unknown, nor can we trace on the map the revival of Assyrian independence under Aššur-uballit and his successors. For the early part of the period these and cognate questions might be answered by the archives and the archaeological record of one of the cities in the plains south or north of Jebel Sinjar; the former are more promising, since they lie in an area more sensitive to political change, and the sparsity of later occupation has left their early levels more readily accessible. Ekallātum, Išme-Dagan's capital, would seem an obvious target if it can be firmly identified, but experience elsewhere suggests that the early levels might prove both expensive to uncover and disappointing in their yield, for it was a Late Assyrian site of some importance and the great mud-brick platforms of Late Assyrian buildings effectively obliterate earlier occupation. The same consideration applies to most of the significant sites of Middle Assyrian date, when the geographical limits of sedentary life seem to have coincided with those of subsequent periods.

None the less this problem must at some time be faced, since only the excavation of a stratified site can fill one of the most important lacunae in our essential information about the archaeology of the area, the sequence of pottery types in use throughout the Assyrian period, without which no accurate dating of the sites is possible. Even the Late Assyrian material is surprisingly little known, because excavation has been concentrated on palaces and public buildings in which no occupation debris was permitted to accumulate, and the renewal of the structure was a radical operation which left little trace of earlier remains. On such a site stratification in the usual sense does not exist, and it is characteristic that of the many hundreds of pottery types classified at Nimrud, only a very few can be dated before the last quarter of the seventh century when the buildings were destroyed. For this purpose the great city is useless. We need a town of medium size without the prestige of royal occupation to inflate the dimensions of its buildings and impose a preternatural cleanliness on their inhabitants; it is a pity that the possibilities of Tell Billa could not be further explored.

The excavation of smaller sites might also clarify our understanding of the Late Assyrian empire. One has only to compare the history of this period with that of the Roman Empire to realize how exclusively the former is based on documentary evidence. Owing to their unique character and power of survival the texts will always play a paramount part, but in this field the royal archives of Nineveh and Kalḫu would in many respects be easier to interpret if they were supplemented by the records and correspondence of a provincial governor. Many features of the system raise questions that can be answered only by archaeological evidence. The character, date, and distribution of Assyrian military posts and road stations, corresponding with, and in a sense the forerunners of, Roman *castella* and *mansiones*, would throw a flood of light on the organization to which the establishment registers from Kalḫu relate, and might also fill in the details of Assyrian history in the same way as the investigation of the Roman post at Ain Sinu has elucidated the course of events on the Severan frontier in Mesopotamia. In post-Assyrian archaeology we have everything to learn and there is little point in defining individual problems. Nimrud and Ain Sinu have contributed something to the identification of a pottery sequence, but their evidence covers in all a century and a half in a period of more than a thousand years, and they are both small sites from which we cannot expect a full picture. Clearly Hatra will make the most important addition now in prospect to our knowledge of the Parthian period, and our Iraqi colleagues are to be congratulated on their courage in undertaking, and the skill and assiduity with which they have pursued, such a formidable task.

Many decades of work lie before us. If these preliminary studies suggest a useful definition of some of the problems, or a fruitful line of approach, they will have served their purpose.

APPENDIX A

HELLENISTIC POTTERY

BLACK- AND RED-VARNISHED WARES[1]

THE Hellenistic levels at Nimrud contained virtually none of the pottery characteristic of that period at the Greek cities of the Eastern Mediterranean and at sites like Samaria and Dura. At Nimrud only a few fragments of the usual black- or red-varnished wares were found and there was no so-called 'Hellenistic Pergamene'. The absence of the latter ware is not surprising since it does not appear in Western Asia until the second half of the second century, and the Nimrud village probably came to an end sometime in the last quarter of the same century. The very few examples at Nimrud of the earlier red-varnished ware typical of sites like Tarsus and Antioch are all of a single type, bowls with an angular profile and with isolated palmette stamps in the base (type 9, Level 2, see also pl. XIV, 3). Only one true red-varnished sherd came from Level 3; it had a rather metallic black varnish on the interior with a matt red varnish outside. Six black-varnished sherds were found, two with a poor matt varnish, now cracked and peeling (types 48, 66). At Tarsus the varnish is said to degenerate to a 'thin, matt, cracked, and peeling coat which, by the top of the top level of the Middle Hellenistic Unit (early second century), is more like a paint in texture than a glaze';[2] this description fits the Nimrud sherds precisely. One unusual black-varnished sherd is a small fragment of a bowl with what appears to be both moulded and impressed decoration, although the fragment is too small to judge with certainty (Level 4). The other three fragments all have a very fine, lustrous, slightly metallic coating and, like the red-varnished examples, are ring-based bowls with rouletting and isolated palmette stamps (pl. XIV, 1, 2).[3] One other black-painted or 'varnished' fragment, a two-handled jar illustrated on pl. XV, should be mentioned. It was probably imported as both the shape and decoration are unusual, although the flaky matt paint is more like that of the locally, made painted bowls than the other imported pieces. A cruder version of the impressed concentric circle and dot decoration on this jar was found in Level 1 and at Nineveh.[4]

The rarity of true black varnish in Mesopotamia makes it quite certain that such pottery was never manufactured there, as it was in the regions of Tarsus and Antioch. At Dura too the black-varnished pottery constituted a relatively small proportion of the varnished wares, and it seems probable that the Greek predilection for black pottery never caught on in Mesopotamia, where an earlier tradition of red wares may have influenced later tastes. On some of the locally manufactured red-painted ware (see below) one occasionally finds bands of black paint that are obviously the result of firing. One such piece is illustrated on pl. XIV, 10. A number of locally made bowls are fired a rich brown inside and are black on the rim and exterior. It is impossible to say whether or not these colour variations are intentional, but their relatively small proportion suggests an accident of firing.

---

[1] 'Varnish' is not an accurate description, but is used here as the best available term to describe the often shiny appearance of the wash that was applied and to distinguish it both from the true glazes which were used at this period and the carelessly applied matt red wash of the locally manufactured pottery. The latter is referred to here as 'paint', again to dis-tinguish it from over-all washes that were occasionally employed.

[2] *Tarsus*, i. 153.

[3] A more detailed description of the Nimrud pottery can be found in *Iraq*, xx (1958), 124–53.

[4] See also p. 125.

RED-PAINTED WARE

By far the most distinctive type of pottery from the Hellenistic village at Nimrud is a red-painted ware that is known also from Nineveh, Tell Halaf, Sultantepe, Tell Billa, Balawat, Abu Sheetha, and a number of small sites in the Nimrud area.[1] The clay is buff with coarse to fine grit temper; the surface is usually wet-smoothed, though sometimes a wash or light slip is applied. The most characteristic feature is the careless application of red paint generally around the rim and occasionally almost covering the entire bowl. The paint colour varies with the firing and thickness from orange through red to dark brown and even purple. Sometimes the bowl is dipped into the paint, first on one side, then on the other, producing a scallop effect (see type 4). The paint is often allowed to trickle down the sides of the bowl or jar producing a very uneven line. When thickly applied, it has a tendency to flake off.

To a great extent the shapes appear to imitate those of the Attic-inspired varnished pottery common in Hellenistic levels at sites such as Tarsus and Antioch. It would seem, in fact, that the Nimrud painted bowls are the Mesopotamian version of the varnished wares that were so popular throughout the Hellenistic world. It is significant that the usual unpainted bowls with in-turned rim of this period at Nimrud (for example, type 30) are flat-based, whereas the painted examples are all ring-based like the black- and red-varnished examples further west. At Nimrud the paint is always matt; there is no attempt to simulate the glossy surface of the better varnished wares as there was at Alishar Hüyük, where the matt-painted surfaces of some of the moulded bowls were actually polished.[2] The most popular shape at Nimrud as well as at the sites with varnished ware is the bowl with an in-turned rim (types 14–16). Second in popularity at Nimrud are the bowls with an angular profile (types 8–11). This type again has western connexions. Most of the examples from Nimrud are mere fragments, but the only two large sherds of local ware with this profile have a very stylized palmette stamp in the base (types 8, 11). That this is in origin a palmette and not, as appears at first sight, a *caduceus* stamp is shown by the fragment illustrated on pl. xiv, 3, possibly imported, on which the palmette design is unmistakable. In this connexion it is interesting to note that this type at Antioch and Tarsus has stamped palmettes and rouletting on the floor, often like that on the imported black-varnished sherds at Nimrud (pl. xiv, 1, 2). The one fairly complete fragment of an imported red-varnished bowl which is, as mentioned above, of the same type, shows a trace of a similar palmette stamp on the broken edge of the base, in contrast to the very conventionalized stamps on the locally made bowls.

Almost equally common at Nimrud are the painted 'fish plates' (types 2–4). A type that is popular at Tarsus, in fact second only to the bowls with in-turned rims, is the bowl with a 'thickened interior rim'; it ranks fourth at Nimrud where it is apparently confined to Level 3 (type 5). Bowls in the traditional Mesopotamian shapes also are painted, but are found in far smaller quantity than the Greek-inspired types. An example is the carinated bowl type 36; bowls of this general shape are very common in Assyria throughout the first millennium.

A very distinctive type of painted bowl, found also at Sultantepe,[3] Nineveh, Abu Sheetha, and Balawat, is type 25, an open bowl decorated with vertical grooving. It seems probable that these bowls are local imitations of 'Hellenistic Pergamene';[4] they occur very late in the Hellenistic sequence (all from Level 1 with a possible stray in Level 3), which places the appearance of the type after the introduction of 'Hellenistic Pergamene' further west. The shapes as well as the decoration resemble those of the western ware. The vertical grooves were cut after the pot had been partially dried.

A unique fragment is type 18, a portion of a baby's feeding bottle. The decoration is impressed and

[1] R. C. Thompson, 'The Excavations on the Temple of Nabu at Nineveh', *Archaeologia*, lxxix. 138; R. W. Hamilton in 'Excavations on the Temple of Ishtar at Nineveh', *AAA*, xix. 82 and pl. lii; von Oppenheim, *Tell Halaf*, trans. G. Wheeler, pp. 313–15; S. Lloyd, 'Sultantepe', *AS*, ii. 13–14; iv. 101–4.

[2] *OIP*, 30, *Alishar*, iii, note by Waagé, p. 80.

[3] *AS*, iv. 101, fig. 1: 52, 53, 56.

[4] Cf. *Tarsus*, i. 293–5.

incised, and suggests an eastern imitation of the *ovolo* or bud pattern so common on moulded 'Megarian' bowls.[1] The identification of this type as a feeding bottle is confirmed by some from the Agora that show teeth marks on the 'nipple' and by the representation of a small child crawling, on another example in the Fitzwilliam Museum.[2] The top of the Nimrud bottle is covered with red-brown paint. Type 17 is the only other example from Nimrud with a combination of painted and incised decoration. At Nineveh a number of red-painted bowls with elaborate moulded or impressed ornament were found.[3]

Unfortunately we have at Nimrud no date for either the beginning or the end of the red-painted ware. It is found in all Hellenistic levels, and the fact that it occurs in greater quantity in 4–2 merely reflects the greater amount of pottery in those levels.

UNPAINTED PLAIN WARES

By far the most common fabric is a rather coarse plain buff or reddish-buff ware. The surface is generally wet-smoothed; occasionally a light slip is applied. Most of the storage jars, numerically the most common type of vessel, and the unpainted bowls and bottles are of this ware, as are, in fact, the locally manufactured painted bowls. The storage jars, as would be expected, are much coarser than the small bowls, some of which are made of a fine grit-tempered clay, rather sandy in texture. The most popular bowl type is small, flat-based, with an in-turned rim (type 30). Ring-based, unpainted bowls also occur frequently, those with carinated shoulders (types 36, 37) being the most common. Small jars, beakers, single- and two-handled bottles, and pitchers also are found. Storage jars generally have a folded rim, often with an indentation on the side (types 74, 75). An unusual vessel is the 'sprinkler' from Level 2 (type 88).

A few bowls are made of a well-levigated clay that has been fired hard, producing pottery rather like the very finest hard thin Achaemenian and Parthian wares known from the south. The clay is generally grey-buff, occasionally reddish. One yellow body sherd from Level 4 is almost identical with the southern pottery of this date. Type 46 is the finest of these bowls; the only nearly complete example is from a grave. Type 45 is of a comparable ware, although not so well finished and slightly coarser. Again the only nearly complete example is from a grave. Both these bowls have light pink bands around the shoulder or rim, although so light as to suggest a stain rather than paint. These seem intentional and not accidental, however, as such pink bands are found on a number of sherds of this type from Levels 3 and 4. The Assyrian prototype of this bowl is always made of the finest 'palace ware'.[4] In Levels 4 to 6, a few beaker rims and dimpled body sherds of a dark greenish-buff pottery resembling rather heavy Assyrian 'palace ware' were found. No complete examples of such beakers were found in the Hellenistic village, but type 138 came from a late Achaemenian or early Hellenistic context.

Another ware found in the trenches in and below Level 4 (one example from Level 2 is probably a stray) is made of a distinctive, rather coarse grit-tempered reddish clay with a very light, almost white slip.

STAMPED AND INCISED WARES

Another distinctive feature of the Hellenistic pottery at Nimrud is the use of impressed stamp decoration. Such ornament is found, though rarely, in the Assyrian period at Nimrud.[5] In the south

---

[1] Cf. *Tarsus*, i, fig. 129; *Antioch*, iv, fig. 9.

[2] *CVA*, Cambridge, Fitzwilliam Museum, ii, pl. 26, 4 and p. 47.

[3] *AAA*, xix, pl. lii: 16–18, 20, 21. These have obvious prototypes in the moulded bowls from sites further west. Unfortunately the lack of description makes it impossible to say whether the Nineveh bowls were imported or locally made, although the description of the

'red wash' and its application (p. 82) suggests the latter.

[4] See Rawson, 'Palace Wares from Nimrud', *Iraq*, xvi (1954), 168 ff.; also *Iraq*, xxi (1959), 135–6.

[5] The Assyrian stamps were generally rosettes, but on one elaborately ornamented jar from Ezida were found stamped pomegranate buds and blossoms, castellations, and tiny rosettes.

its use is characteristic of the Achaemenian period, and at Nimrud the Achaemenian types of stamp are found throughout the Hellenistic levels. In the south the stamps are often shallowly impressed on a knob pushed out by the pressure of the fingers inside the bowl. The Nimrud stamps are never 'pushed out' to the extreme found in the south, although finger indentations are noticeable. Such indentations are less marked in Level 2 than in the earlier levels. A fondness for stamped ornament is noted also at Tell Halaf, where 'triangles, circles, spirals, angles, and especially conventional palm leaves' are mentioned.[1]

Several types of stamps are illustrated on pls. xiv, xv. Impressed triangles, crescents, and circles are used in conjunction with the various stamps, particularly on the large jars. The use of palmette stamps on varnished and painted bowls has been discussed above in the section on red-painted pottery.

A rare type at Nimrud is the small bottle from Level 1 (pl. xiv, 13), decorated with an incised dot and line pattern and incised concentric circles. A possible prototype for this decoration is the imported painted two-handled jug illustrated on pl. xv, a, a unique piece at Nimrud. The concentric circle pattern is common in late Roman and Parthian contexts[2] and appears at Nimrud for the first time at the end of the Hellenistic occupation. Bottles of this shape are known from Nineveh, as is this type of decoration, sometimes painted.[3] A few sherds with incised zigzags and incised comb decoration, common in Parthian and later contexts, were found in Level 1. A grey-ware sherd with similar zigzags (pl. xiv, 16) is considerably earlier. A large ring-based glazed bowl, from Level 2, has a rosette stamped in the base (pl. xiv, 12), and a glazed bottle with an unusual stamped decoration (type 92) was found in Level 1.

Type 40, an open bowl decorated with incised ornament, found at Abu Sheetha, is of particular interest as the only specimen with a Greek potter's mark (XP). An identical bowl from Nineveh also bore traces of such a mark.[4] The Greek language is known to have been used at Nineveh, which was obviously an important centre in the Hellenistic period, and it is reasonable to suppose that these bowls were of local manufacture.

GLAZED POTTERY

Although the glazed pottery from Nimrud superficially resembles that from sites in Southern Mesopotamia and from Dura, the actual shapes are slightly different. The glazed bottles at Dura and Seleucia, for example, show a tendency to widen at the base in contrast to the more globular Northern Mesopotamian types. It must be remembered, of course, that most of the pottery published from Dura and Seleucia, the two sites that afford the largest body of comparative material, is considerably later than the Nimrud Hellenistic occupation. There is, in fact, very little well-stratified material of comparable date, but what there is seems to confirm the impression that in the glazed as well as the painted and unpainted pottery, the Northern Mesopotamian potters, although influenced by other areas, followed a course of their own.

The actual glazes used appear to have been much the same over a wide area, north and south. The usual glaze at Nimrud was originally a deep blue-green which in weathering produces a surface varying from blue-green to light blue and even a rather silvery blue that is at times almost white. No true dark green glazes have been found. A yellow glaze is sometimes used (type 95). The clay is often yellow in colour and of a very soft granular texture.

The glazed bottle with impressed decoration (type 92) is the only one of its kind from Nimrud, as is the ribbed bowl (type 44). The usual bowl type is 43, and several bottles resembling types 95 and 96 have been found, often in graves. The glazed pottery constitutes a very small proportion of the

---

[1] See von Oppenheim, *Tell Halaf*, p. 314.

[2] At Ain Sinu such decoration was dated A.D. 235, see p. 148; cf. *Tarsus*, i. 168.

[3] See *Iraq*, xx (1958), 129, n. 4.

[4] *AAA*, xix, pl. lii: 16; pl. lxiii: 7, with the potter's mark H, appears also to be the same type.

Hellenistic pottery, glazed bottles and bowls occurring with about equal frequency; glazed pilgrim flasks are rarer still. These types occur, for the most part, from Level 4 onwards and are most common in Levels 1 and 2. A few glazed twisted handles also came from Level 1. The only glazed vessel from Level 6 is a jar with small loop handles. The relatively small quantity of pottery from Levels 5 and 6, however, makes it dangerous to draw any conclusions about the chronological distribution of glazed pottery at Nimrud; we can say only that bowl and bottle types usually considered typical of the Hellenistic and Parthian periods are well established by the third quarter of the second century B.C.

Type 135, a common Assyrian and Neo-Babylonian polychrome glazed jar, is included in the catalogue because it was found in a Hellenistic inhumation grave.[1] It was not uncommon to place 'antiques' in Hellenistic graves; at Nimrud one such grave contained a large number of cylinder seals, one dating from the Akkadian period.

COARSE COOKING-WARE

Sherds of coarse, gritty, dark brown clay occur frequently in Levels 1 and 2 and are found also in Levels 3–5. Many of them are fire-blackened. No complete vessels were found in the Hellenistic levels, but an undoubtedly Hellenistic two-handled round-bottomed cauldron of this ware with a rim similar to type 79 was found in upper fill in an Assyrian building. Type 73 is the most common cooking-ware type in the upper levels. Type 79 is made of the same ware. All those examples that were sufficiently preserved to show the method of manufacture were hand-made. In Levels 3 and 4 a tan version of this coarse pottery occurred; the clay was grey with large white grits and the tan surface had been produced in the firing.

GREY WARE

At Sultantepe bowls of grey clay with light grits occurred with the red-painted ware. At Nimrud only four grey sherds were found in the Hellenistic levels: a flat plate with a rim like type 51 from Level 1, a heavy thick-walled bowl and the rim of a carinated bowl from Level 4, and the unusual sherd decorated with grooves and zigzag incision (pl. XIV, 16), probably Level 6 or earlier.

UNGUENTARIA

Only one complete example of this characteristic Hellenistic type (103) has been found at Nimrud. Such bottles are apparently not so common in Northern Mesopotamia as, for example, at sites like Tarsus, but a number are known from Tell Billa.[2] One example from the latter site is covered with dark red paint.

LAMPS

By far the most common type of lamp is the so-called pipe lamp which is well known in the Assyrian period. The Hellenistic examples are almost indistinguishable from the earlier ones, although the rim is usually folded slightly less than on the Assyrian versions.[3] One pipe lamp from Level 6 had a small handle on the shoulder, a type also known from Nineveh and Seleucia.

An unusual variety of lamp is type 101. The elaborate palmette handle is not known from Hellenistic levels at Tarsus or Antioch, but a somewhat similar type was found at Samaria.[4] Type 101 is from Balawat; one very like it was found at Nimrud by Layard.[5] Several lamps of this type are known from Nineveh, covered with red paint as is the one from Balawat.[6] A cruder example of the same general type was found in Level 4 of the Nimrud village (pl. XIV, 22).

[1] See *Iraq*, xx (1958), 130–1.
[2] The Billa examples are unpublished, in the Iraq Museum; see also *AS*, iv, nos. 49, 50; *Tarsus*, i, pl. 135.
[3] Type 141 is identical with the Assyrian type; it is probably late Achaemenian. See also *Archaeologia*, lxxix, pl. lv; and N. C. Debevoise, *Parthian Pottery from Seleucia*, pp. 403–6.
[4] *Samaria*, pp. 319–20 and fig. 191: 11a.
[5] *Monuments of Nineveh*, pl. 95a: 16.
[6] *Archaeologia*, lxxix, pl. lv: 209–10.

Type 102 is the only example of its kind from Nimrud. Lamps with a single side lug are found at Tarsus in the Middle Hellenistic Unit and in the lowest level of the Hellenistic–Roman Unit. None, however, is like the Nimrud example, the closest Tarsus type being no. 39, which has a smaller lug. It is dated about the end of the second century and is the only example of this particular variation of the lug-handled lamps from Tarsus. This group of lamps seems to be Eastern Mediterranean in origin and has no Corinthian counterpart.[1] The usual types of Hellenistic lamps are not represented at Nimrud with the exception of one piece, a fragment of a rosette-decorated base found in unstratified fill in the Nabu Temple (pl. XIV, 21).

KEY TO CATALOGUE OF HELLENISTIC POTTERY

FURTHER details, including find-spots, excavation catalogue numbers, and fuller descriptions of wares and types, will be found in the catalogue published in *Iraq*, xx (1958), 137–53. The omission of references to Levels in the following catalogue indicates that the piece was found in disturbed or unstratified context; exact find-spots for all the pottery can be found in the *Iraq* article.

Diagonal hatching indicates red paint.

ABBREVIATIONS

B   diameter of base
D   diameter of rim
H   height
Sultantepe   see *AS*, iv, 101 and fig. 1.
For other abbreviated references, see p. 167.

DATES OF LEVELS

6   ends about 225 B.C.
5   begins about 215 B.C.
4   begins about 175 B.C.
3   after 150 B.C., a late phase of 4, not always present
2   begins about 145 B.C.
1   after 140 B.C.

PLATE XIV. *Examples of Hellenistic stamped, painted, and glazed sherds, Nimrud*

1. Imported varnished sherd. Fragment of a ring-based bowl with rouletting and isolated palmette stamps in the base. Well-levigated grey-buff clay, deep rich brown varnish with a metallic lustre. Level 4. See discussion p. 122.

2. Imported varnished sherd. Fragment of a ring-based bowl with rouletting and isolated palmette stamps in the base. Well-levigated pink clay, rich purple varnish with a metallic lustre. *c.* Level 3–4. See p. 122. Cf. *Antioch*, iv, fig. 4: 16, 17; *Tarsus*, no. 66.

3. Varnished sherd. Fragment of a bowl with a well-finished ring base, carination on outside just above base. Dark buff clay, fine grit temper. Varnish of relatively poor quality; fired a deep orange-brown inside and orange outside. Isolated large palmette stamps in the base. Probably an imported piece. Level 4. See p. 122.

[1] See *Antioch*, iii, figs. 74, 75; *Samaria*, fig. 192. An imported lamp found at Petra provides the closest parallel with the Nimrud lamp, although this too has a much smaller side lug. P. J. Parr, 'Petra I', *ILN*, 10 November, 1962, p. 747, fig. 8.

4. Fragment of a painted bowl with swag incision. See type 17.

5. Rim sherd of a painted bowl, type 10. Gritty buff clay, orange-red paint covering the inside of the bowl and carelessly applied outside.

6–8. Fragments of grooved bowls similar to type 25. Gritty reddish clay; all completely covered with flaky orange-red paint. All are from Abu Sheetha. See p. 123.

9. Long strap handle, painted. Gritty reddish-buff clay, buff slip, decorated with a ladder pattern in red-brown paint. Level 2.

10. Rim sherd of a red-painted bowl with in-turned rim. Reddish-buff clay, fine grit temper, buff wash, orange-red paint blackened in a band at the rim inside and with patches of black on the darker red paint outside. Level 4. See p. 122.

11. Fragment of glazed bowl, type 44, Level 2.

12. Glazed ring base decorated with impressed rosette. B. 9 cm. Gritty buff clay, blue-green glaze weathered pale green and silvery white. Low flat ring base, groove inside. Level 2.

13. Fragment of a small two-handled flask. Extant H. 8 cm. Gritty reddish clay, buff slip. The bottle was moulded in two halves, the decoration impressed, and the two halves joined. Level 1. See p. 125.

14. Sherd of a globular (?) jar with incised and impressed decoration. Gritty buff clay, wet-smoothed. Circle pattern formed by impressing two crescents. Level 4. This is the only example of its kind from Nimrud, but several bowls from Abu Sheetha were decorated in this fashion.

15. Jar sherd with incised zigzags. Gritty buff clay. A late type; with the exception of type 16, all examples come from Level 1.

16. Jar sherd decorated with grooves and incised zigzags. Gritty grey clay. Level 6 or earlier. See p. 125.

17, 18. Rim sherds, type 45, Level 2.

19. Rim of stamp-impressed bowl, type 42. D. 28 cm. Gritty buff clay, light wash. Leaf stamp alternating with a 'pinched trefoil' pattern. Level 3. Very shallow finger-imprints inside. See p. 124.

20. Fragment of large stamp-impressed jar. Gritty reddish clay, buff slip. Level 3. Deep finger-imprints inside. See p. 124.

21. Base of small moulded Hellenistic lamp. Extant length, 6·4 cm. Soft gritty reddish clay. Rosette on base. The only example of its kind from Nimrud.

22. Two fragments of a moulded lamp with a palmette-decorated handle. Gritty buff clay. Traces of red paint on the top. Double-grooved ring base. Level 4. See discussion p. 126.
 Cf. *Samaria*, fig. 191: 11a.

23. Sherd with incised 'comb' decoration. Very gritty buff clay. A rare type, confined to Level 1, and found also at Ain Sinu in the third century A.D. See p. 150, and *Iraq*, xxi (1959), 226.

PLATE XV. *Examples of Hellenistic stamped and painted sherds, Nimrud*

(a) Top of two-handled jar. D. c. 9·5 cm. Fine buff clay, matt black paint or 'varnish' shading to brown where thin, flaked, and worn. Impressed decoration. Level 2, but possibly in disturbed soil. An imported piece; the only example of its kind from Nimrud. See pp. 122, 125.

(*b*) 1. Sherd of stamp-decorated bowl, type 42. Gritty buff clay, wet-smoothed. Finger-impressions behind tear-shaped stamps. Balawat. See pp. 124–5.

2. Jar sherd, stamp-decorated. Greenish-buff clay. Very small deep finger-marks behind the tear-shaped stamps and simple finger-prints behind the smaller stamp. *c.* Level 4 or 5. See pp. 124–5.

3. Fragment of stamp-decorated jar. Greenish-buff clay. Deep finger-impressions behind stamps. Below Level 6. See pp. 124–5. (Nos. 2 and 3 are illustrated upside down.)

4. Fragment of very heavy strap-handled jar with stamped decoration. Coarse dark buff clay, buff wash. Deep finger-impressions behind the tear-shaped stamps, shallower ones behind the other stamps. *c.* Level 4 or 5, and Balawat.

CATALOGUE OF HELLENISTIC POTTERY

FIGURE 15. *Hellenistic painted and other small bowls, Nimrud.* Scale 1 : 4

1. Miniature saucer, painted. D. 10 cm. Buff clay, fine grit temper. Surface almost covered with red-brown paint by dipping sides of bowl into paint. Level 3.

2. Fish plate, painted. D. 14·3 cm. Buff clay. Almost entirely covered with red paint shading to black on the rim.
    Cf. *Sultantepe*, no. 54.

3. Fish plate, painted. D. 19·8 cm. Gritty buff clay; carelessly applied pink paint, shading to mauve. Level 4.
    Cf. *Tarsus*, 23; *Olynthus*, pls. 190–1. Examples from Olynthus date as early as the fourth century, and at Tarsus this type is found in the late fourth and in the third century.

4. Fish plate, painted. D. 19·4 cm. Gritty buff clay; sides of bowl dipped into brown paint. Levels 3–5. Similar rims, unpainted, have been found at Nimrud as late as Level 2, but there is only one painted example from this level.
    Cf. *Antioch*, iv, 10k; *Samaria*, fig. 174: 35–36.

5. Plate with thickened interior rim, painted. D. 22 cm. Gritty reddish-buff clay, red paint. A common painted type confined to Level 3.
    Cf. *Sultantepe*, fig. 1: 27; *Samaria*, fig. 174: 29; *Antioch*, iv. 17; *Tarsus*, i. 27–38. At Tarsus this is the second most popular type.

6. Shallow bowl, painted. D. 24·8 cm. Gritty pink clay; buff wash. Edge of bowl dipped into red-brown paint; redipped carelessly, producing a darker brown to black colour where the two coats overlap.

7. Deep bowl, painted. D. 14·5 cm. Reddish-buff clay, grit temper. Paint varies from dull brick-red to dark purplish-brown depending on the thickness. A common type at Nimrud, although apparently not found at sites like Antioch and Tarsus. A number of examples were found in Levels 1, 2, and 4.

8. Bowl with angular profile, painted. D. 13·2 cm. Gritty reddish clay; red paint. Stylized palmette stamp in base of bowl. Level 4.
    Cf. no. 11 and pl. XIV, 3.

9. Bowl with angular profile, painted or 'varnished'. D. 15 cm. Gritty pink clay; red 'varnish' with darker band at rim and below external rib. Level 2.
    The colour of the paint or 'varnish' on this fragment is very similar to that of the majority of the Nimrud Hellenistic painted wares, but the quality of the finish is very different, having a rather shiny appearance in contrast to the normal matt surface of the other painted bowls. It seems

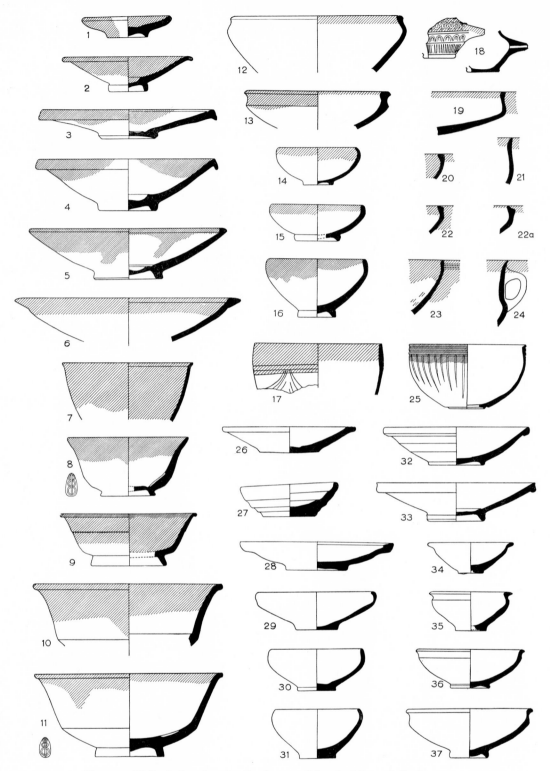

FIG. 15. Hellenistic painted and other small bowls, Nimrud. Scale 1:4

probable that this particular bowl was imported from some city further west where this type of red-varnished ware was the common pottery of the period. This suggestion would seem to be confirmed by the fact that at the broken edge of the base there is a small fragment of a palmette stamp of the type seen on pl. XIV, 1, 2, a variety never found on the locally manufactured bowls. Nos. 8 and 11, for example, are decorated with a very stylized version of the sort of palmette shown on pl. XIV, 3. All the bowls of this general type at Nimrud have some version of the palmette stamp in the base as do all the published bowls of this type at Tarsus (*Tarsus*, 41–49). The same association is observed at Antioch and other sites. (*Antioch*, iv, p. 12) 'Paint finger-prints' are found on the base of this bowl, a common feature at Tarsus not generally found at Nimrud.

10. Bowl with angular profile, painted. D. 21 cm. Coarse gritty buff clay; orange-red paint. Levels 1–5; Abu Sheetha; and 'Hellenistic house' (see pp. 140, 142).

11. Bowl with angular profile, painted. D. 21 cm. Gritty buff clay, red paint carelessly applied. Very stylized palmette stamp in base. Level 2.

12. Bowl with grooved bevelled rim, painted. D. 18·8 cm. Gritty reddish clay with a light wash or slip. Levels 3–4.

13. Carinated bowl, painted. D. 16 cm. Ware identical with no. 12. Levels 2–4.

    An identical painted sherd was found in unstratified fill, associated with a pilgrim's flask with a handle like one from Aššur (*Die Partherstadt*, pl. 47c), and a white-glazed bowl rim. Similar unpainted sherds came from Level 2. Carinated bowls are common at Nimrud in the Assyrian period and continue throughout the later occupations; see discussion of type 36.

    Cf. *Sultantepe*, 25, 33, 37.

14. Miniature bowl with in-turned rim, painted. D. 7·5 cm. Gritty buff clay, orange-red paint. Found in a Hellenistic grave.

15. Bowl with in-turned rim, painted. D. 9·9 cm. Gritty pinkish clay with buff wash; red paint.

16. Bowl with in-turned rim, painted. D. 10·6 cm. Gritty buff clay; red paint. Level 4.

    This is the most common of the painted bowl types at Nimrud, found in all levels in the Hellenistic trenches, but especially common in Levels 4–2. This is of little significance with regard to the distribution of the type, however, as there is far more pottery from these levels than from 5 and 6. This is also the most popular of the 'varnished' types from sites such as Antioch, Tarsus, and as far afield as Alishar (though attributed by Waagé to the Roman period at the latter site).

    Cf. *Tarsus*, pp. 156–7; *Antioch*, iv, p. 10; *OIP*, 30; at Samaria bowls of this shape are found in the Babylonian–Greek period (700–300 B.C.) covered with a red haematite wash and in later levels with black or red varnish.

17. Deep bowl, painted, incised decoration. D. 14 cm. Gritty buff clay, brown paint. Level 2.

18. Baby's feeding bottle, painted, B. 3·3 cm. Dark buff clay, fine grit temper; red-brown paint. Moulded in two halves. Incised and impressed decoration. c. Level 4–3. See pp. 123–4.

    Cf. *CVA*. Cambridge, Fitzwilliam Museum, ii, pl. 26, 4, and p. 47.

19. Bowl with angular shoulder, painted, fragment. Gritty reddish-buff clay, buff wash, brown paint. Levels 3, 4.

20. Bowl with thickened in-turned rim, painted, fragment. Gritty reddish-buff clay, buff wash; red paint with band of black along rim due to firing. c. Level 2.

21. Deep open bowl, painted, fragment. Light reddish clay, buff wash; paint fired dark brown inside and reddish-brown outside. Level 2.

22. Bowl with angular shoulder, painted, fragment. Gritty buff clay; red paint. Level 2.

22a. Bowl with angular shoulder, painted, fragment. Gritty buff clay; red paint. Level 4.

23. Open bowl, painted, incised grooves below rim; fragment. Buff clay, fine grit temper, buff slip; red paint. From Hellenistic pit, Balawat; Levels 1–3, Nimrud.

24. Deep bowl with handle, painted, fragment. Gritty reddish clay with distinctive light slip (see p. 124); red-brown paint. Grooved handle. Level 3.
    Cf. type 66.

25. Open bowl decorated with vertical incising, painted. D. 13 cm. Reddish clay, buff slip, red paint.
    A very distinctive Hellenistic type, found also at Sultantepe (p. 101 and fig. 1: 52, 53, 56), Nineveh (surface sherds), Balawat and Abu Sheetha. The vertical grooves are cut into the clay after partial drying. This type occurs only in Level 1 with the exception of one example, possibly a stray, in Level 3 (see p. 123). The shape is reminiscent of 'Hellenistic Pergamene' (cf. *Tarsus*, 293–5) as is the decoration. The Nimrud and Balawat bowls have either very low ring bases (as on no. 25) or rest on a simple ring formed by impressing a small disc at the base. The interior of most of these bowls is completely painted.

26. Plate with grooved lip. D. *c*. 15 cm. Coarse, gritty reddish clay; buff wash. Similar types, Levels 2–4.

27. Small open bowl. D. 11 cm. Gritty buff clay. Level 5.

28. Bowl with bevelled lip. D. 16·8 cm. Levels 3–6. A painted example with the inner edge of the rim more rounded and more deeply grooved was found at Balawat.

29. Bowl with in-turned rim. D. 12·6 cm. Slightly gritty reddish-buff clay, buff slip. Level 4.
    The rather pinched in-turned rim of this type is reminiscent of the late third- to early second-century bowls at Tarsus (cf. *Tarsus*, 72). The trend from the earlier bowls with only a slightly curved lip to the more pronounced curve is noted at about this date. (*Tarsus*, p. 157.) None of the Tarsus examples has the low flat base common to these small Mesopotamian bowls, but a development towards a very low foot is noticed. The bases of nos. 29–31 are string-cut and left unfinished.

30. Bowl with in-curved rim. D. 10·7 cm. By far the most common small bowl type in the Hellenistic levels at Nimrud. Found in great quantity in Levels 1 and 2, generally gritty buff clay, sometimes slightly reddish, often with a light slip wiped inside to give a 'reserve slip' effect. A few examples were found in Level 3, and the type is known from Balawat.

31. Bowl with in-curved rim. D. 9·8 cm. Gritty buff clay. Level 2.

32. Shallow plate with folded rim. D. 15·8. Dark buff or reddish-buff clay. Levels 1, 2.

33. Plate with enlarged folded rim. D. 17·1 cm. Dark buff clay. Levels 1, 2.

34. Miniature bowl with everted lip. D. 9·2 cm. Soft flaky badly fired reddish-brown clay. Level 1.

35. Small carinated bowl. D. 9·2 cm. Fine reddish or buff clay. Levels 3/4, 6.

36. Carinated bowl. D. 12 cm. Fine reddish-buff or coarse buff clay. Levels 2, 4.
    Carinated ring-based bowls of this general type are very common in the Hellenistic levels and are obviously related to similar types, generally of much better levigated clay, that are popular in the Assyrian period. In general the Assyrian bowls are more sharply carinated, but a great range of shapes is found in the Assyrian levels, and it is almost impossible to distinguish on the basis of shape alone between Assyrian and Hellenistic bowls of this kind.
    For Assyrian types, see *Iraq*, xxi (1959), pl. xxxv and types 32, 33.

37. Carinated bowl. D. 14 cm. Reddish-buff clay. Levels 3–5. See discussion of no. 36.

FIGURE 16. *Hellenistic bowls and plates, Nimrud.* Scale 1 : 4, except 42, 1 : 8

38. Plate. D. 26 cm. Gritty buff clay. Levels 2, 4.

39. Plate. D. 16·5 cm. Very gritty pink clay. Probably an early Hellenistic type, although no stratified examples have been found.

40. Open ring-based bowl, incised decoration. D. 19 cm. Buff ware. Abu Sheetha.

A Hellenistic type not found at Nimrud, but known from Nineveh (*AAA*, xix, pl. lii: 16). It is interesting that the Abu Sheetha bowl bore on its base the potter's mark XP, and the example from Nineveh is said to have the 'tip of an impressed Roman letter'. The only other Greek potter's mark illustrated from Nineveh (ibid., pl. lxiii: 7) appears to have come from the same type of bowl.

41. Open bowl with incised crescents. D. 16·8 cm. Hard thin ware, fine grit-tempered reddish clay, cream slip. Unstratified.

The use of incised crescents is common on Hellenistic pottery, and the shape of this bowl is almost identical with one type of painted grooved bowl from Balawat (pl. xiv, 7). Such decoration is not confined to the Hellenistic period, however; incised crescents are found in both Assyrian and Achaemenian levels. The ware is reminiscent of fine yellow Achaemenian ware from the south; it is in fact harder and finer than most of the pottery from the Nimrud Hellenistic village. Only a few of the finer buff-ware types are of similar quality. Type 41 is probably Hellenistic in date; it is late Achaemenian at the earliest. See discussion of type 109.

42. Bowl decorated with impressed stamps. D. 30 cm. Gritty buff clay.

An almost identical bowl was found at Balawat (see pl. xv, *b*, 1) and in Level 3 a bowl of the same shape was decorated with the leaf stamp alternating with a pinched trefoil imprint (pl. xiv, 19). The same pattern occurs on another jar from Balawat (pl. xv, *b*, 4) that is exactly paralleled at Nimrud. Other occurrences of impressed wares are: Level 2, a horseshoe-shaped stamp alternating with a radiate circle stamp similar to pl. xiv, 20, from the same level. The radiate circle stamp also occurs in Level 3, and in Level 4 was used with simple wedges on a large storage jar that had impressed notches on the rim, as had type 110. In Level 5 was a large storage jar (type 75) decorated with a circular stamp with radiating lines and two small concentric circles in the centre. In unstratified fill was found a sherd decorated with a circular stamp like the latter, but with radiating teeth rather than simple strokes. This was undoubtedly Hellenistic as it was associated with a red-painted beaker and the light slip on reddish ware which is found in the lower levels of the Hellenistic trenches.

43. Glazed bowl. D. 18·9 cm. Blue-green glaze. Inside the bowl and in the base are remains of the three clay supports which were used to separate a stack of bowls in the kiln.

Glazed bowls of this type were common in Levels 1 and 2, but rare earlier. There was one fragment in Level 3 of a large example and a single glazed ring base from Level 4. See also pl. xiv, 12. In the Hellenistic pit at Balawat a minature glazed bowl of this type was found: H. 3·1 cm., gritty yellow paste, glaze weathered green, two grooves inside the base.

44. Glazed bowl with raised ribs. D. 22 cm. Blue glaze weathered to yellow-green. Level 2.

This is a unique piece at Nimrud, and the type is not among those published from either Dura or Seleucia. See also pl. xiv, 11.

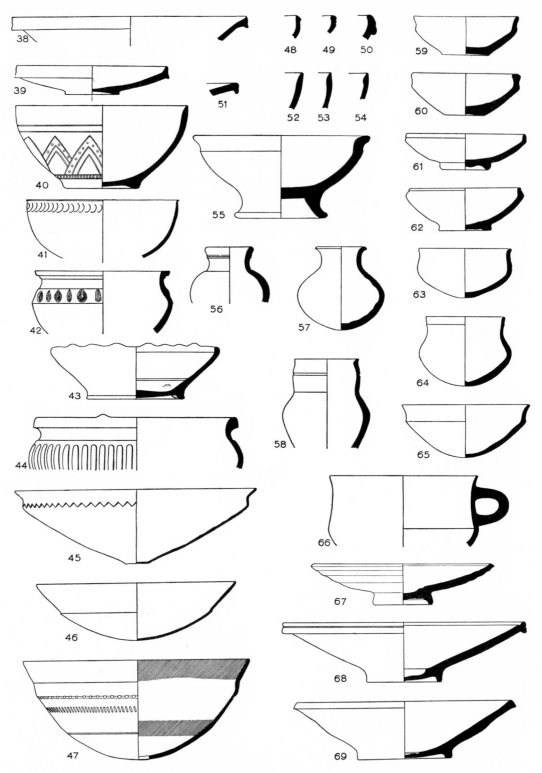

FIG. 16. Hellenistic bowls and plates, Nimrud. Scale 1:4, except no. 42, 1:8

45. Bowl with notched decoration on shoulder. D. 27·2 cm. Fine buff ware. Pink band around shoulder. Found in a Hellenistic inhumation grave with the polychrome glazed jar (type 135) and a bronze ladle.

    Sherds of similar bowls of identical ware were found in Level 1 only. See pl. xiv, 17, 18.

46. Shallow bowl. D. 22·9 cm. Very fine buff clay, fine grit temper, light greenish-buff wash, slight trace of pink bands (paint?) inside rim. Exterior of bowl shaved down when partially dry. Grave dug from Level 3.

    Identical rim sherds with the same pink 'paint' have been found in Level 3/4. Assyrian 'palace ware' provides a prototype for type 46, see *Iraq*, xxi (1959), type 28.

47. Deep decorated bowl. D. 24·9 cm. Fine gritty buff clay, purplish-brown paint at rim, band of very thin orange-red paint below, impressed decoration on shoulder. Level 2.

    Cf. Alishar (*OIP*, 29), fig. 59: 2, a similar rim, fine grey-buff clay with a thick purplish-brown wash, dated 'second half of the first millennium'.

48. Rim sherd of a black-varnished bowl. Fine gritty clay, very flaky matt varnish. *c*. Level 2.

    This piece must have been imported from some western site; the shape, however, is not one of those published from Tarsus or Antioch.

49. Rim sherd of a small bowl. Buff clay, pinkish slip. Level 2.

50. Rim sherd of deep bowl with folded rim. Gritty buff clay. Level 3, and Abu Sheetha.

    A similar heavier rim was found just below Level 2, light slip on coarse reddish clay (see p. 124), and a simple folded rim of this sort without the indentation came from Level 4. This type is indistinguishable from its Assyrian prototype.

51. Rim sherd of glazed plate. Dark blue or blue-green glaze weathered to yellow-green and very pale blue. Sandy yellow clay. This example is from Balawat.

    A common glazed type found in all levels except 6. The one Level 5 example had a brown, and the one from Level 4 a yellowish, glaze. Type 51 occurred unglazed in Levels 1–2.

52. Rim sherd, open bowl. Gritty buff clay. Level 1, and Abu Sheetha.

53. Rim sherd, open bowl. Gritty buff clay. Level 1, and Abu Sheetha.

    An example of type 25 with a rim like 53 was found in Level 1.

54. Rim sherd, open bowl. Gritty buff clay. Level 1, and Abu Sheetha.

55. Open bowl with high ring base. D. 20 cm. Coarse reddish clay, greenish-white slip (see p. 124).

56. Globular jar. D. 5·0 cm. Salmon clay, light buff slip. Level 2.

57. Globular jar. D. 5·7 cm. Gritty reddish-buff clay; buff wash. Level 3.

58. Ovate jar with cylindrical neck. D. 7 cm. Gritty buff clay.

    A number of unstratified examples were found, with one each from Levels 3 and 4. In Level 2 a jar of this shape was found with actual perforations at the line of the groove.

59. Small bowl with angular shoulder. D. 11 cm. Gritty reddish clay, light cream slip.

60. Small bowl with angular shoulder. D. 11·6 cm. Coarse reddish clay with light slip. Levels 3–4. There is an Assyrian prototype.

61. Shallow bowl with grooved in-turned rim. D. 13·2 cm. Greenish buff clay, fine grit temper, wet-smoothed, base pared down. 'Hellenistic house', see pp. 140, 142.

62. Carinated bowl with groove below rim. D. 13 cm. Gritty reddish clay, buff slip.

63. Bowl with flared rim. D. 10·1 cm. Pinkish clay, fine grit temper, pale wash. Level 3.

64. Bag-shaped bowl. D. 8·6 cm. Dark buff clay. Levels 2–5.

65. Open bowl. D. 14·2 cm. Coarse reddish clay with white slip (see p. 124).

66. Deep bowl with handle. D. 16·2 cm. Gritty buff clay. *c.* Level 3.
    Cf. type 24. There is a black-varnished example from Level 4 with a smaller handle and a much shorter neck. The 'varnish' is a flaky, matt black on the exterior and is fired chocolate-brown to black on the interior.

67. Plate. D. 20 cm. Gritty reddish clay, buff slip. A painted rim of similar shape came from Level 4.

68. Fish plate. D. 26·5 cm. Gritty buff clay. Level 2.
    A bowl of similar shape glazed (blue-green) came from Level 3.
    Cf. *Antioch*, iv. 17 n.; *Tarsus*, 23.

69. Plate. D. 23·6 cm. Gritty buff clay. Levels 1, 2.
    A similar rim of fine gritty pinkish clay with traces of red paint was found in Level 2.

FIGURE 17. *Hellenistic jars and jugs, Nimrud.* Scale 1 : 4, except 78, 82, 85, 86, 1 : 8

70. Beaker. H. 6·7 cm. Gritty buff clay. Level 4. This type of beaker or *istikan* developed from a very common Assyrian type. A rounded *istikan* base, also similar to an Assyrian type, also came from Level 4.
    Cf. *Iraq*, xxi (1959), pl. xxxvi.

71. Beaker. H. 10·3 cm. Gritty reddish-buff clay. Level 2.

72. Beaker. H. 10·3 cm. Gritty reddish clay. Level 2.

73. Rim sherd of two-handled cauldron. Very coarse brown clay. Level 1.
    Sherds of this extremely coarse clay are common in Levels 1 and 2 and are also found in 3–4. Many of them are fire-blackened. In the earlier levels in particular, sherds of this ware with plain flared rims similar to type 79 occurred.

74. Sherd of large jar. Coarse gritty buff clay. Abu Sheetha, and Levels 1–3.
    Types 73 and 74 are very common jar types; see also fig. 19.

75. Sherd of heavy storage jar. Coarse dark buff clay. A very common type in Levels 1–2 and also found in 3–5.
    Occasionally made of better quality gritty reddish-buff clay with a buff wash. There is one example in Level 5 with a strap handle, decorated with radiate circle stamps on the shoulder. Also from Level 5 was a similar strap-handled jar made of gritty 'cooking-ware'.

76. Sherd of large jar. Gritty buff clay. Abu Sheetha and Level 1.

77. Sherd of globular jar. Pinkish gritty clay, buff wash. Level 2.

78. Pot stand. H. 12·9 cm. Dark buff gritty clay. Level 2.

79. Flat-based jar. H. 16 cm. Coarse brown cooking-ware, hand-made.
    In Level 3 a large cooking-pot with a rim similar to this one and vertical loop handles from the rim to the shoulder was found (D. 25 cm.).

80. One-handled bottle, painted. H. 16 cm. Orange-brown clay, brown paint. Level 5.
    In Level 4 another type of painted bottle with a thin strap handle was found, very fine sandy buff clay, brown paint. The shoulder was more sharply defined than on the examples illustrated

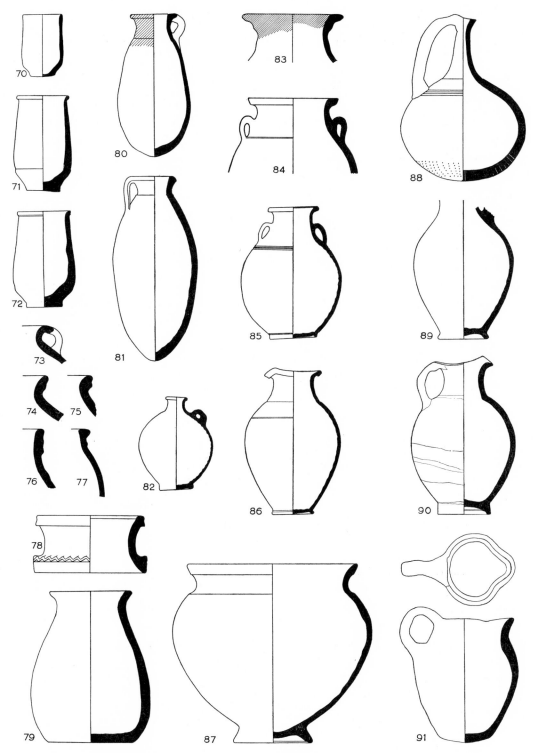

FIG. 17. Hellenistic jars and jugs, Nimrud. Scale 1:4, except nos. 78, 82, 85, 86, 1:8

here, and the top of the cylindrical neck flared out and then in slightly, forming a 'cup' at the rim. Painted plain flared rims of small bottles or jars were also found. For other painted examples see type 81.

81. Elongated bottle with handle. H. 20 cm. Gritty buff clay. Level 2.
    Painted examples of this type, slightly larger and with shorter necks, fine gritty buff clay, were found in Levels 4, 6.

82. Jug with handle on shoulder. H. 19 cm. Gritty buff clay. Level 2.

83. Rim of large painted jar. D. 11·3 cm. Gritty buff clay, buff wash, brown paint. Level 4.

84. Rim of two-handled jar. D. 10 cm. Gritty buff clay. Level 2.

85. Two-handled jar. H. 27 cm. Gritty reddish-buff clay, buff wash. Level 2.

86. Jug with pouring lip. H. 30 cm. Gritty buff clay. Levels 2, 3.

87. Deep tureen. H. 19 cm. Gritty buff clay. Level 2.

88. Sprinkler with handle. H. 18 cm. Gritty reddish-buff clay. Level 2.

89. Fragment of jug with single handle. Extant H. 14·8 cm. Fine gritty reddish clay, pale buff wash. Level 2.

90. Pitcher. H. 16·5 cm. Gritty pinkish clay, buff wash.

91. Pitcher. H. 13 cm. Coarse drab clay, hand-made. Surface; and 'Hellenistic house' (see pp. 140, 142).

FIGURE 18. *Hellenistic flasks, bottles, and lamps, Nimrud.* Scale 1 : 4, except 99, 106, 1 : 8

92. Glazed bottle. H. 22·2 cm. Blue-green glaze. Impressed decoration on one side of the bottle. Level 1.
    Cf. Nineveh, *AAA*, xix, pl. lii: 13.

93. Glazed bottle. H. 12·5 cm. Surface weathered green.

94. Glazed bottle. H. 12 cm. Cream glaze, soft yellow paste.
    Unfortunately this unique bottle is not stratified and therefore cannot be assigned with certainty to either the Achaemenian or Hellenistic period. The shape of both the body and the handles is different from the usual Hellenistic glazed bottles, yet the rim reminds one of type 92 and some of the Parthian glazed bottle rims from Dura. (N. Toll, *The Green-Glazed Pottery*, fig. 23). Except for the rim and ring base this bottle is very like an unpublished Neo-Babylonian one from Nippur.

95. Small glazed bottle. H. 7·5 cm. Yellow glaze. From a grave, found with a coin of Alexander I Bala (150–146). There is very little published material with which to compare the Nimrud ring-based two-handled glazed bottles. The general type is known from Nippur (blue-green glaze). J. P. Peters, *Nippur*, ii, pl. vii: 1, 3–5. Nos. 1 and 4 were found in a grave which from the description could well be Hellenistic or Parthian rather than Babylonian as Peters suggests. At Seleucia none was found in the Hellenistic level (Level IV), but there was relatively little pottery of this date. The published two-handled bottles are from Levels I–II, A.D. 43–200. (N. C. Debevoise, *Parthian Pottery from Seleucia*, pp. 99, 101). Most of the Dura material is also later. (N. Toll, *The Green-Glazed Pottery*, fig. 23.) See also p. 125.

96. Glazed bottle. H. 16 cm. Yellowish body clay, blue-green glaze. From a Hellenistic grave. This type of very low ring base, semi-flat, is less common at Nimrud than the ring base of types 92, 93,

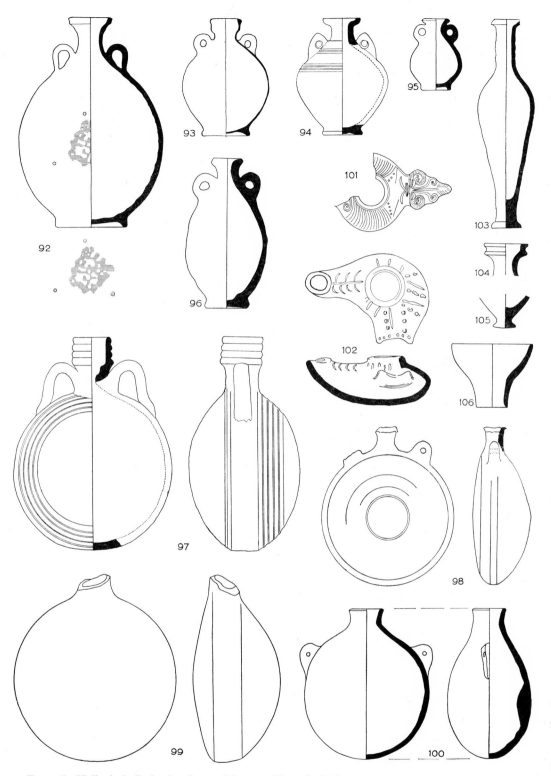

FIG. 18. Hellenistic flasks, bottles, and lamps, Nimrud. Scale 1:4, except nos. 99 and 106, 1:8

and 95; but it is the usual type in the south where ring bases on glazed two-handled bottles seem to be rare. (Cf. N. C. Debevoise, *Parthian Pottery from Seleucia*, pp. 99, 101; also Dura, N. Toll, *The Green-Glazed Pottery*, fig. 23; R. F. S. Starr, *Nuzi*, pl. 135: C, D, G.)

97. Pilgrim flask. H. 23 cm. Buff clay.

Though unstratified, this is obviously a Hellenistic type. There were no complete pilgrim flasks in the Hellenistic levels, but a number of fragments were found, sometimes blue-glazed, particularly in Levels 2–4. The most common type had a simple rolled rim (cf. *Dura*, fig. 25: 1, 2; *Seleucia*, no. 303). There were no examples of type 97 in the stratified levels.

98. Pilgrim flask. Extant H. 17 cm. Coarse orange clay, shiny grits. An unglazed example was found in Level 6. One from Level 4 had painted handles, dark brown gritty clay, dark purplish-brown paint.

99. Pannier water bottle. Extant H. 40 cm. Gritty buff clay. Level 2.

100. Pilgrim flask. H. 17·5 cm. Gritty buff clay. Large circular knob inside, about which that half of the flask was turned.

A fragment of a flask similar to this one with a handle identical to one from Aššur (*Die Partherstadt*, pl. 47c), grey gritty clay with a red slip, was also found.

Cf. also *Seleucia*, no. 306.

101. Lamp with palmette handle, painted. Extant length 13 cm. An unusual type from Balawat that is paralleled by a cruder specimen from Level 4 (see pl. XIV, 22). Gritty reddish clay, red paint.

The Balawat lamp is almost identical with one from Nimrud found by Layard (*Monuments of Nineveh*, pl. 95a: 16). The type is known also from Nineveh (R. Campbell Thompson, 'The Excavations on the Temple of Nabu at Nineveh', *Archaeologia*, lxxix, pl. lv: 209–10). See also *Samaria*, pp. 319–20, fig. 191: IIa.

102. Pipe lamp with projecting lug. H. 5·3 cm. Dark grey clay, burnished surface blackened. Decorated with incised lines and dots. See discussion p. 126.

103. Unguentarium. H. 22 cm. Heavy coarse buff clay. From a Hellenistic grave. Very characteristic of the Hellenistic period, although this is the only example from Nimrud. Cf. *Sultantepe*, nos. 49–50; *Tarsus*, pp. 171–2 and pl. 187.

The Tarsus type closest to the Nimrud example is no. 235, dated to the second quarter of the second century (pp. 31, 230). Cf. also *Samaria*, fig. 178: 1 from a 'vault cist'. In the Iraq Museum is a painted example from Tell Billa.

104. Rim sherd of flask. D. 4·8 cm. Gritty buff clay. *c.* Level 3.
Cf. *Dura*, fig. 25: 3; *Seleucia*, 305.

105. Base of small bottle or jar. B. 2·6 cm. Light buff clay, fine grit temper, light slip. Level 2.

106. Funnel. H. 13·6 cm. Coarse reddish clay, white slip (see p. 124).

FIGURE 19. *Hellenistic storage jars, Nimrud*. Scale 1 : 8, except 117, 1 : 4; 110, 114, 1 : 10; 109, 119, 1 : 20

Note: Nos. 107, 109, 111–13, 115, 116, 120 are from an outlying Hellenistic house (see *Iraq*, xix, pls. ii, vi: 1, and p. 10; also note on pl. xxvii, *Iraq*, xx (1958), 150). In spite of the occurrence of one painted sherd, of a type present in Level 5 and subsequently common (type 10), and generic resemblances in the jar rims, there is a marked difference between the pottery from this house and that found

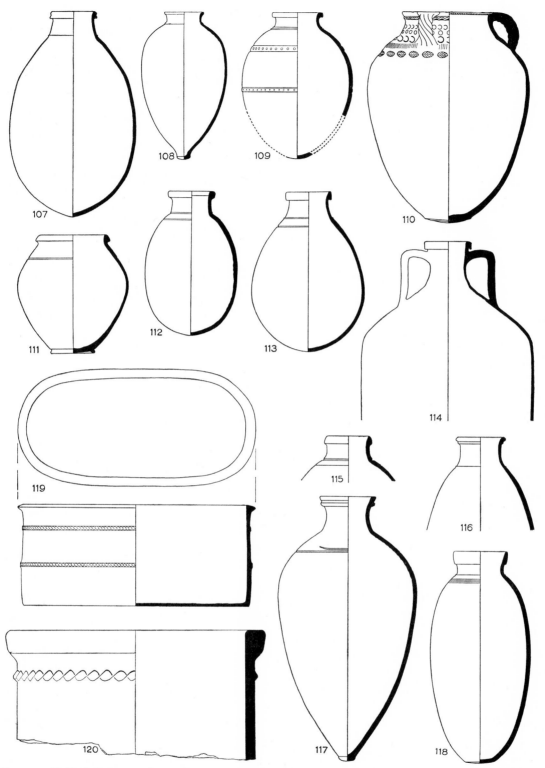

FIG. 19. Hellenistic storage jars, Nimrud. Scale 1:8, except no. 117, 1:4; nos. 110, 114, 1:10; 109 and 119, 1:20

in the Hellenistic village. It must be emphasized, however, that the amount of material from Levels 5 and 6 is insufficient to provide a true basis for comparison, and it is possible that the house dates from this time. It may be earlier, but cannot be later. A further group of pottery (137–44) from a post-Assyrian level beneath the house floor cannot be dated with certainty, but may be tentatively ascribed to the Achaemenian period.

107. Large storage jar. H. 44·1 cm. Gritty buff clay. 'Hellenistic house' (see note above). This type of folded indented rim is very typical of the Hellenistic period.

108. Storage jar. H. 32 cm. Gritty buff clay. Levels 1, 2 and 'Hellenistic house' (see note above).

109. Large storage jar. H. 77·5 cm. Gritty brick-red clay, grey-buff wash or slip. Occasional vertical incisions on the two ribs at the base of the neck; two bands on the body of the pot decorated with impressed circles. This jar is illustrated in the photograph of the 'Hellenistic house' floor, *Iraq*, xix, pl. vi: 1.

An identical storage jar was found in fill in the Nabu Temple, associated with sherds of the distinctive light slip on coarse reddish ware (p. 124). Type 41 was found at about the same level.

110. Large storage jar, decorated with stamped impressions. H. 56·5 cm. Three twisted handles. Gritty buff clay. Levels 1, 2.

111. Jar. H. 25·4 cm. Coarse brown clay with lighter wash. 'Hellenistic house' (see note above).

112. Globular storage jar. H. 31 cm. Dark buff clay with light wash. 'Hellenistic house' (see note above).

113. Globular jar. H. 34·5 cm. Dark buff clay, light wash. 'Hellenistic house' (see note above). The very slight depression inside the rim (see also 115) is characteristic of jars in this period.

114. Cylindrical-bodied jar with two handles. Extant H. 47·5 cm. Gritty reddish clay, buff slip. Level 6.

115. Jar rim. D. 9·2 cm. Gritty brick-red clay, buff slip. 'Hellenistic house' (see note above). The indentation on the inside of the rim is very characteristic of the pottery from this level.

116. Fragment of storage jar. D. 11 cm. Gritty reddish clay with buff wash or slip. 'Hellenistic house' (see note above) and Level 6.

117. Jar. H. 28 cm. Buff clay. Level 4.

118. Elongated storage jar. H. 45 cm. Gritty buff clay. Level 4.

119. Coffin. H. 54 cm. Gritty buff clay. See *Iraq*, xx (1958), pl. xxx, d; also *Iraq*, xix, pl. vi, 2.

120. 'Tub' fragment. D. 56·4 cm. Gritty dark buff clay. 'Hellenistic house' (see note above).

FIGURE 20. *Miscellaneous bowls and jars, Nimrud*. Scale 1 : 4, except 121, 136, 137, 142 143, 1 : 8

Nos. 121–129 are all from the 'Hellenistic house' referred to in the note on the previous plate. Also in this group were bowl type 50, bottle type 81, and a stone tripod bowl. Nos. 137–144 are from the second level referred to. Found with the latter group was a long tear-shaped bottle decorated with bands of red paint. Extant H. 18 cm. Greenish-buff clay.

121. Pot stand. H. 13 cm. Gritty buff clay, buff slip. 'Hellenistic house.' See *Iraq*, xix, pl. vi, 1.

122. Bottle rim. D. 3·4 cm. Salmon-coloured clay, buff slip. 'Hellenistic house.'

123. Cylindrical bottle. D. 2·7 cm. Salmon-coloured clay, buff slip. 'Hellenistic house.'

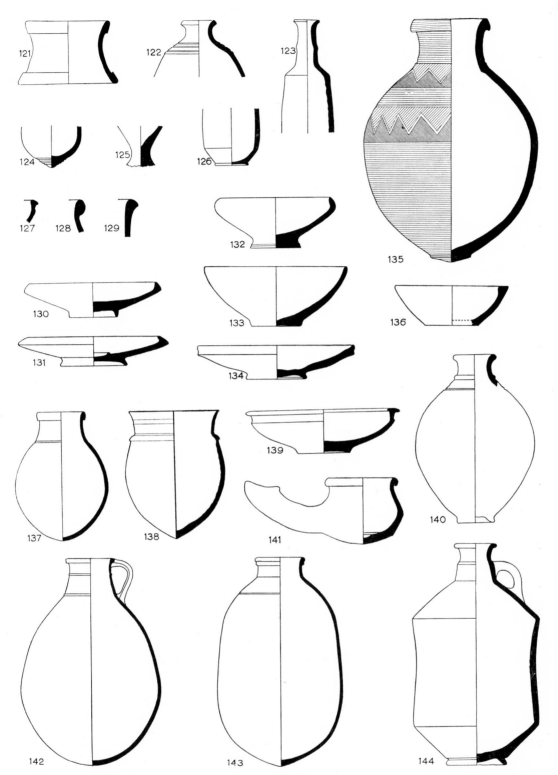

FIG. 20. Miscellaneous bowls and jars, Nimrud. Scale 1:4, except nos. 121, 136, 137, 142, 143, 1:8

124. Bottle base. Extant H. 4·6 cm. Salmon-coloured clay, buff slip. 'Hellenistic house.'

125. Fragment of pedestal base. Extant H. 4·7 cm. Buff clay. 'Hellenistic house.'

126. Fragment of base of small jar. B. 3·9 cm. Salmon-coloured clay, buff slip. 'Hellenistic house.'

127. Rim fragment of bowl with carinated shoulder. Extant H. 2·7 cm. Salmon-coloured clay. 'Hellenistic house.'

128. Jar rim. Extant H. 3·4 cm. Brick-red gritty clay, buff slip. 'Hellenistic house.'

129. Jar rim. Extant H. 3·9 cm. Buff clay. 'Hellenistic house.'

130. Shallow bowl with angular shoulder. D. 16 cm. Gritty buff clay. Possibly Hellenistic; late Achaemenian at the earliest (cf. no. 131).

131. Shallow bowl with angular shoulder. D. 14·4 cm. Gritty buff clay. Surface, associated with painted bowls. Probably Hellenistic.

132. Deep bowl. D. 12 cm. Gritty buff clay. Probably Achaemenian. See *Iraq*, xx (1958), 119.

133. Hemispherical bowl. D. 15·9 cm. Greenish-buff clay. Probably Achaemenian, see ref., type 132, and cf. a 7th–6th-century bowl from Susa, R. Ghirshman, *Village Perse-Achéménide, Mémoires de la Mission archéologique en Iran*, xxxvi, pl. xxv: 1.

134. Plate. D. 16·9 cm. Gritty pinkish clay, light wash. Probably Achaemenian. See ref., type 132. This plate, however, is not unlike several from the Hellenistic levels.

135. Polychrome glazed jar. H. 26 cm. Blue glaze; upper section of zigzag band, yellow glaze; lower, orange; zigzags separated by a narrow white glazed band; band of blue glaze between the two sets of zigzags outlined in white glaze. From a Hellenistic inhumation grave. This jar must be of considerably earlier date than the grave; see discussion, type 45, and *Iraq*, xx (1958), 123, 130 f.

136. Large flat-based bowl. D. 25·6 cm. Dark buff clay, light slip. Levels 3, 4, and probably earlier.

137. Globular jar. H. 27·6 cm. Buff clay with greenish-buff slip. Probably Achaemenian.

138. Beaker. H. 13·8 cm. Buff clay, larger and heavier than Assyrian 'palace ware' beakers, but obviously derived from the type. See *Iraq*, xxi (1959), pl. xxxvii. Probably Achaemenian.

139. Bowl with carinated shoulder. D. 16·9 cm. Greenish-buff clay. Level 6; and probably Achaemenian.

140. Globular ring-based bottle. H. 18 cm. Light buff clay. Probably Achaemenian.

141. Pipe lamp. D. 6·6 cm.
    Pipe lamps are common in the Assyrian period at Nimrud, and equally common in the Hellenistic levels, although usually with less marked rims. A pipe lamp from Level 5 had a handle (cf. *Seleucia*, 403) and a large one from Level 4 was about twice the size of the illustrated example.

142. Storage jar. H. 44·2 cm. Greenish-buff clay. Probably Achaemenian.

143. Storage jar. H. 44·2 cm. Buff clay. Probably Achaemenian. A considerable number of jars of this type were also found in levels 2–3.

144. Jug with single handle. H. 23·8 cm. Greenish-buff clay, wash. Probably Achaemenian.
    A jug very like this, but rounded where this example is sharply carinated, is said to have come from a Parthian grave at Aššur (*Die Partherstadt*, pl. 4: d, 15755a). The actual find-spot is unfortunately not given (*Die Gräber und Grüfte*, p. 192).

APPENDIX B

PARTHIAN AND ROMAN POTTERY FROM AIN SINU—ZAGURAE

THE pottery from Ain Sinu can be dated to the first third of the third century A.D. Most of that reproduced here comes from rooms excavated near the north gate of the *castellum* where thick deposits of sherds on the floor marked the destruction of that building, probably by Ardashir I in A.D. 237. Sherds from the barracks, which appear to have been dismantled before the fall of the *castellum*, may perhaps be dated a few years earlier, but in general it is safe to say that the pottery we have recovered spans a very short period of time up to A.D. 237.

It is for the most part Parthian in character, and is virtually identical with that found by the Iraq Antiquities Department in their excavations at Hatra.[1] We have already observed that Hatra was in alliance with Rome during the last few years of the occupation of Ain Sinu, but there is no reason to suppose that the use of local pottery in the Roman frontier posts was greatly affected by political considerations. It is more probable that we have here and at Hatra a typical sample of North Mesopotamian pottery of the latest Parthian period, which was sufficient in both quality and quantity to make the import of western products unnecessary.

LAMPS (Fig. 21, 1–4)

The lamps show more western influence than any other group of objects from Ain Sinu, but even these are very provincial products and are, with one or two exceptions, without parallel elsewhere. In general they have heart-shaped nozzles, lug handles, and large filling holes, and are ornamented with rather dull geometric patterns. The upper and lower portions were moulded separately, and the decoration was both impressed and moulded. In some cases the top of the lamp and filling hole are level (type 1), and in others the rudimentary discus is depressed (type 4).

As far as we know, with the exception of a single example from Nineveh,[2] no other lamps identical with those from Ain Sinu have been found at other eastern sites from which third-century material has been excavated. Lamps with handles and heart-shaped nozzles normally have small filling holes in contrast to the large ones at Ain Sinu. This type occurs at Dura and even as far east as Nineveh, where such lamps were probably imported from Syria or Cilicia.[3] There is at Dura a third-century type with large filling hole and heart-shaped nozzle, but this is invariably handleless. The simple geometric motifs employed to decorate these and similar plain-nozzled lamps of the same date are, however, very like those found on the Ain Sinu examples.[4] Handles are entirely lacking on Roman lamps from Antioch in the second and third centuries. The closest parallel to the Ain Sinu type is a single lamp from Dura with lug handle, large filling hole, and what appears to be an elaborate heart-shaped nozzle. This specimen has been classified with a type dated to the fourth and fifth centuries, but it seems possible that this particular lamp is to be dated earlier than the others in the group, perhaps in

---

[1] We wish to thank the Directorate-General of Antiquities, Baghdad, for their kind permission to examine the unpublished pottery and small finds from Hatra that are in store in the Iraq Museum.

[2] *AAA*, xix, pl. lxv: 17.

[3] *Dura, Lamps*, no. 401; *Archaeologia*, lxxix, pl. lv:

216 (vi, 6), 217.

[4] *Dura, Lamps*, no. 303. The moulded ornament on a fragment of a light buff lamp found in the *castellum* at Ain Sinu is very like *Dura* 287, but with a laurel wreath rather than a rosette pattern on the rudimentary discus.

the third century, closer to the date of the Ain Sinu lamps it so closely resembles. The latter may, in fact, prove to represent yet an earlier stage in the development of this so-called 'provincial' type at Dura and Antioch, the evolution of which has puzzled the excavators at both sites.[1] The heart-shaped nozzle is a very distinctive feature of third-century lamps, although its origins go back to the Augustan period.[2]

A number of lamp fragments other than those illustrated were found at Ain Sinu. Several of these had incised palm fronds below the nozzle, and three sherds from flat grooved lamp bases showed remains of elaborate moulded potters' or workshop marks. Unfortunately these were too fragmentary to enable us to reconstruct the monogram or design. Some handles were moulded with the lamp, and some appear to have been added later when the two halves were joined.

One surprising fact is that no examples of the so-called Mesopotamian or Parthian type of lamp, so common at sites like Dura, Nineveh, and Seleucia were found at Ain Sinu.[3] These lamps have a long history in Mesopotamia and are ultimately derived from the Assyrian and Babylonian 'pipe lamp' (see p. 126), not as some authors have supposed from moulded Hellenistic lamps, although the latter did, of course, influence some of the Parthian forms.

A fragment of a clay lantern was found at Ain Sinu. Only a portion of the body was preserved, but this is identical with the body of a lantern from Dura.[4]

GLAZED POTTERY (Fig. 21, 5–29)

Glazed pottery is extremely common at Ain Sinu, the glaze for the most part being brilliant blue-green or turquoise. The colour in fact varies from bright blue to near-green, but no specimens of the true green colours known from Seleucia and Dura were found. Unfortunately we have not as yet been able to have the Ain Sinu glazes analysed, so we cannot say how far these colour variations are the result of different chemical composition, intentional or otherwise, or of firing conditions. One would expect, however, to find an alkaline glaze coloured by cupric oxide, and if this were the case, variations in the amount of iron and copper present would account for the range of colours found.[5] The paste itself varies from a rather hard, fine, grit-tempered buff clay to a much softer yellow body. The surface of the glaze is generally crazed. A few white-glazed sherds were found (e.g. type 22).

By far the most frequent glazed vessels were plates and shallow bowls, types already well known from sites such as Dura.[6] What is surprising at Ain Sinu is the almost total absence of the one-, two-, and three-handled vases and jugs that are so characteristic of Parthian glazed pottery at Seleucia and Dura. Only four fragments of glazed jars or bottles were recovered at Ain Sinu (types 25–27); these were all flat-based. The only glazed vessel at all comparable with the well-known Parthian types was one that must have been similar to the unglazed type 49. Only four small fragments of this jar (type 28) were found, the body sherds being decorated with diamond stamps and a vertical band of impressed ornament in the same fashion as type 49. One sherd was found from a glazed bowl, the interior of which had been decorated with impressed triangles and an incised wavy line (type 29); this and type 28

---

[1] *Dura, Lamps*, no. 408 and p. 84. The tendril decoration on the Dura lamp does, of course, suggest a somewhat later date than the Ain Sinu lamps, but the general similarity of the two types is so close as to suggest some relationship between them. Waagé, *Antioch*, i. 65 f., writes, 'The presence of the handle, quite lacking in the Roman lamps of the second and third centuries at Antioch, is the surest proof that the type did not evolve there.'

[2] *Antioch*, i. 63. For a general discussion of heart-shaped lamps, see A. B. Walters, *British Museum Catalogue of Lamps*, pp. 167–81.

[3] *Dura, Lamps*, nos. 348–400 and p. 83; *Archaeologia*, lxxix, pl. lv; N. C. Debevoise, *Parthian Pottery from Seleucia on the Tigris*, pp. 119–29.

[4] *Dura, Lamps*, no. 421.

[5] For an extremely useful discussion of the Dura green glazes, see *Dura*, pp. 1–5 and 81–95 ('Technological Notes on the Pottery' by F. R. Matson).

[6] *Dura*, type XI–F, fig. 28, cf. Ain Sinu 8, 14–17; type XI–H, fig. 29, cf. Ain Sinu 5, 6, 10–13.

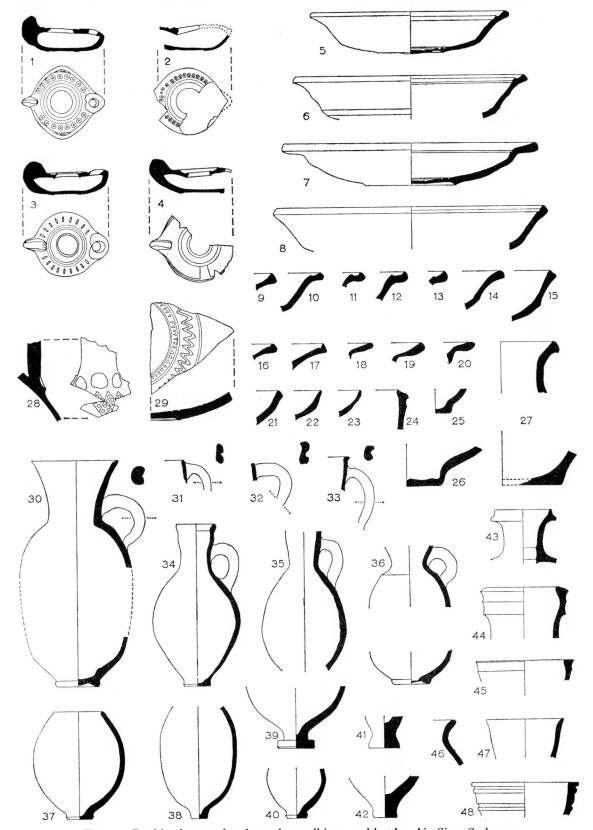

FIG. 21. Parthian lamps, glazed vessels, small jugs, and bottles, Ain Sinu. Scale 1:4

represent the only decorated glazed ware from Ain Sinu. One fragment of a glazed plain double handle was also found.[1] No glazed pilgrim flasks were recovered, nor were there any of third-century date from either Seleucia or Dura.

In view of the comparative rarity of the finer decorated and glazed wares among the published pottery of this date from Aššur and Nineveh, it seems that their absence from Ain Sinu reflects not merely the poverty of a small site, but a real difference between the pottery of Northern Mesopotamia on the one hand, and of the Euphrates and Southern Mesopotamia on the other. Certainly the much greater use of glazed wares in the south and the Euphrates valley, in contrast with the highly ornate but unglazed northern pottery, is a marked feature of the Early Islamic period.

STAMPED AND INCISED WARE (Fig. 22; Pl. XVI, 4, 5)

The most distinctive pottery from Ain Sinu is a group of two-handled jars decorated with impressed diamonds (types 49–55). Such pottery is common at Hatra, and was found at Nuzi.[2] A single sherd was found on the surface of Tell Ibra (Vicat), but so far none has been published from any other site in the Eastern Roman Empire. In general the jar shapes recall those of the Parthian green-glazed types, and it is quite obvious that at Hatra and Ain Sinu these are the local substitute for the more ornate green-glazed wares, the absence of which at Ain Sinu has already been remarked.

There is a considerable variation in both ware and stamp. The most common stamp impression is divided into four compartments by transverse ridges with a small circular knob in each compartment; there appear to be two sizes, the side of one measuring 10 mm., and the other, 8 mm. The larger size is often smoothed over so that the knobs appear very flat and the ridges fade out in the middle of the impression. These stamps are applied to the pot either in groups forming a series of pendant diamonds (types 49, 50) or in solid diagonal rows (type 54). The former groups often alternate with vertical rows of crescents as on type 49, or a quadruple row of small impressions forming a vertical band (28 is of this type). A less common form has nine knobs without separating ridges (type 55). Again there are two sizes, one measuring 11–12 mm. on a side, and the larger, 15–16 mm. These jars were made of clay which varied from an extremely well-levigated pale cream or green, with a smoothed surface, sometimes with a slip, to a very gritty greenish paste. Several examples of a coarser reddish clay were also found. The interiors of some of the jars were sealed with thin coats of bitumen.

The necks of these stamped two-handled jars were usually covered with shallow ribbing, and further incised or stamped decoration on the neck was common, the diamond pattern being confined, however, to the body of the jar. The decorated handle of type 54 and the appliqué pellets on types 54 and 53 are a further parallel with the green-glazed vases of Dura.[3] It has been suggested that the appliqué pellet ornament is derived from metal prototypes, but so far no comparable metal vessels have been found. Types 51–53 have been restored from fragments, and there is no extant evidence for handles. They are so like the stamp-decorated types, however, that we have restored handles and included them in the general group of diamond-stamped vessels; there seems very little doubt that this is where they belong. It is possible that type 59 should be included in the same category.

Type 55 (pl. XVI, 4) is a unique specimen and is, to the best of our knowledge, without parallel elsewhere.[4] The shoulder is decorated with a horizontal band of incised zigzags, below which is a rather irregular band of incised ornament consisting of semicircles of zigzags in which are either diamond stamps or swags of radiating lines.

Less common than the diamond stamp was one composed of four or five concentric circles, isolated

[1] Cf. *Dura*, fig. 20, D, E.
[2] R. F. S. Starr, *Nuzi*, pl. 135: F.
[3] Cf. *Dura*, fig. 10.

[4] One sherd from what may have been a similar type of jar was found at the north gate of the barracks, and a single sherd from Hatra may also be of this type.

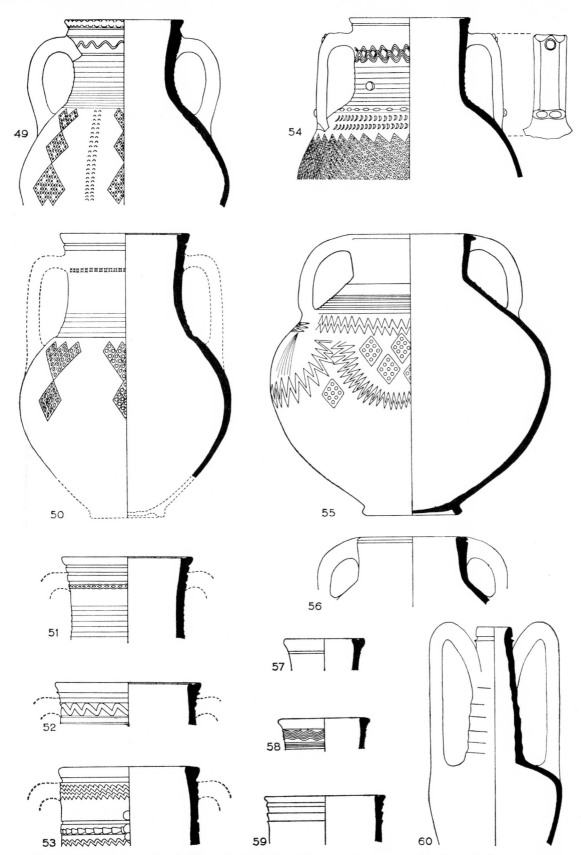

FIG. 22. Parthian two-handled jars with incised and impressed ornament, Ain Sinu. Scale 1:4, except no. 60, 1:8

examples of which decorated type 55. All the other examples of this type of stamp impression from Ain Sinu, however, occurred on sherds more or less completely covered with the stamped pattern, the impressions sometimes overlapping one another; no complete vessels ornamented in this fashion were found. Similar stamped ware was picked up at Tell Ibra (Vicat) and is known at Tarsus, although at the latter site a single impression appears between large leaf stamps, more in the manner of the ornament on 55.[1] A very early Parthian example of incised concentric circle ornament is known from Nimrud (see p. 125 and pl. XIV, 13).

Incised wavy lines and zigzags are common at Ain Sinu. They range from very wide sweeping bands to the fine wavy comb incision on type 58. One example is decorated with irregular wavy comb incision of a type usually dated much later; this particular jar was in fact found at a high level just inside the wall of the *castellum* and was thought at first to be Islamic. A sherd with identical decoration and of the same ware was found in wall plaster in the barracks, however, and is thus certainly to be dated to the early third century at the latest.[2]

COOKING WARE (Fig. 23, 75–85; Pl. XVI, 1, 2)

The cooking-vessels at Ain Sinu are made of one of the most distinctive wares found on the site. It is an extremely thin, hard, very gritty, ribbed, red ware, obviously designed to withstand heat. The paste is usually brick-red in colour, some examples being very dark red. A purplish-brown slip is often, though not always, applied to the exterior of the vessel. There were three major types, and these were found in great numbers, although generally badly smashed because of the thin, brittle nature of the ware. These were a two-handled cauldron (type 81), a single-handled jug (type 85), and a shallow two-handled dish resembling a casserole, though apparently lidless (type 77). The rim of one cooking-ware jar was found (type 76) and a fragment of what may have been a deep bowl or perhaps another type of jug or jar similar to type 85 (type 75). The Hatrene cooking-ware is identical with this, and sherds of the same type have been picked up at Tell Hayal (Alaina) and Tell Ibra (Vicat). The Dura cooking-ware also is said to be identical with that from Ain Sinu.[3]

Kitchen vessels such as the ribbed two-handled cauldron have a wide distribution both in time and space, but the third-century Parthian variety in Mesopotamia is easily recognized by its very thin walls and fine ribbing. The closest published parallel is from Petra, a first century A.D. Nabataean cauldron. The ribbing, however, appears to be much more clumsily executed than on the Ain Sinu examples.[4] Kitchen ware of third-century date from Tarsus is much heavier and coarser, although some of the types superficially resemble those from Ain Sinu.[5]

PAINTED DECORATION (Fig. 24, 97–102; Pl. XVI, 3)

A number of single-handled water jars decorated with wide bands of red-brown paint, one wide wavy band encircling the body of the jar, were found (type 97). A larger type without handles, but with the same type of painted ornament, also occurred (type 98). Types 99–102 are rim sherds from painted jars of these types. All of these jars are made of coarse grit-tempered buff to reddish-buff clay. Traces of brown or reddish-brown paint were found on a number of other jar rims, e.g. types 61, 64.

A curious black 'paint' is occasionally found, in particular on the interior of open bowls (e.g. types 68, 70). It is possible that this is some sort of bitumen coating, but it appears much harder and more

---

[1] *Tarsus*, i, pl. 164, B. The usual Ain Sinu ornament is applied more in the manner of pl. 168, C.

[2] See *Iraq*, xxi (1959), pl. lv, 9. A very early Parthian example of incised and wavy comb ornament was found at Nimrud, see p. 125 and pl. xiv, 23.

[3] We are indebted to Mr. F. R. Matson for this information.

[4] P. Parr, 'Excavations at Petra II', *ILN*, 17 November 1962, p. 790 and fig. 3.

[5] *Tarsus*, i, fig. 162: 797; figs. 204–6. Cf. also the 'Roman Pergamene' cauldron, fig. 160: 758.

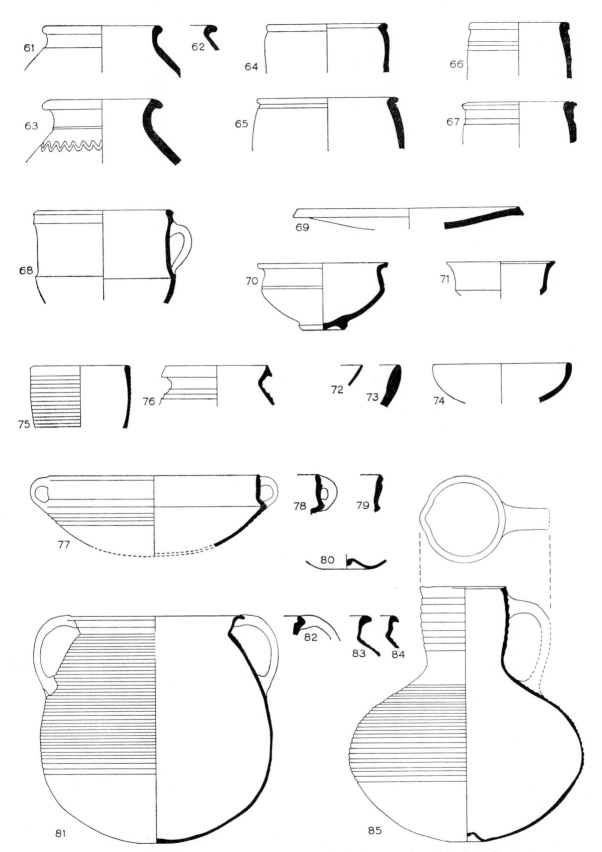

FIG. 23. Parthian bowls, cooking-ware vessels, and miscellaneous jars, Ain Sinu. Scale 1:4

shiny than the usual bitumen sealing found inside some of the large jars. One sherd in particular from the north gate of the *castellum* is covered on the interior with a thick lustrous black coating that resembles black glaze; a red wash was smeared over the exterior of the vessel. The unusual rim sherd type 89 is coated on the top and interior with a similar, though duller, thick black 'paint'. One bowl (type 74) was covered with an unusual dark red slip, but no other examples were found.

UNDECORATED WARE

Into this category fall a large number of small jugs and bottles, a few bowls, and a miscellaneous assortment of jars, most of which unfortunately are represented only by rim sherds.

The absence of small glazed jars, jugs, and bottles of the types so common at other Parthian sites has already been noted. At Hatra and Ain Sinu these are apparently replaced by plain single-handled jugs (types 30–36) that are in general more slender in shape than their glazed counterparts. Only type 36 seems to approach the pear-shaped glazed types. At Hatra some of the small jars were decorated with the same impressed diamonds as the larger two-handled jars at Ain Sinu (types 49, 50), but none of the Ain Sinu examples found thus far was so ornamented. In general the small jugs and bottles were made of well-levigated buff or greenish-buff clay, sometimes with a light wash or slip.

Surprisingly few unglazed bowls were found (types 69–74). These were made of a variety of wares (described in the catalogue, p. 157). Two examples of the single-handled cup (type 68) occurred.

A wide range of jar rims was discovered (types 45, 48, 57–59, 61–67, 90–96). Like the bowls, these were made of a number of different wares. The finest quality was of well-levigated buff or greenish-buff clay, often with a light wash, but coarse grit-tempered brick-coloured clay was also common. Fine grit-tempered buff and reddish clays were employed as well. Short-necked jars with everted rims (types 61–63) were common, as were types 64–67. Types 92, 93, and the painted types 97–102 illustrate the most common type of large jar rims. Only two examples of type 103, a large two-handled water jar, were found. The high-necked amphora (type 60) is a unique find; it was made of bright orange coarse grit-tempered clay, the corrugated neck resembling water-pipe.[1]

The barrel-shaped water bottle (type 86) is also represented by a single specimen. We know of no parallel for it in Parthian pottery where its function is performed by the pilgrim flask. It is obviously designed to be carried slung about the body and looks like a piece of military equipment, perhaps of Roman origin, although we have not been able to find a published example from a Roman site.[2]

KEY TO CATALOGUE OF PARTHIAN AND ROMAN POTTERY, AIN SINU

THE only designation of find-place made in this catalogue is either AS I, the barracks, or AS II, the *castellum*. Precise find-spots and a photograph of the more complete specimens can be found in the more detailed catalogue published in *Iraq*, xxi (1959), 228–37 and pl. lv. The abbreviations and conventions are the same as those used in Appendix A.

FIGURE 21. *Parthian lamps, glazed vessels, small jugs, and bottles*. Scale 1:4

1. Lamp. H. 2·1 cm., width 7 cm. Low ring base, rounded shoulder. Large filling hole surrounded

---

[1] See *Iraq*, xxi (1959), pl. lv, 4. A very similar type was found in the Athenian *agora*, where it is dated to the mid-third century. H. S. Robinson, *The Athenian Agora*, v, pl. 15, k 113.

[2] In the Iraq Museum is a slightly larger two-handled bottle from Level 1 at Seleucia which closely resembles the Ain Sinu specimen (20 × 15 cm., IM 33863). It is certain, however, that the Ain Sinu example had only one handle.

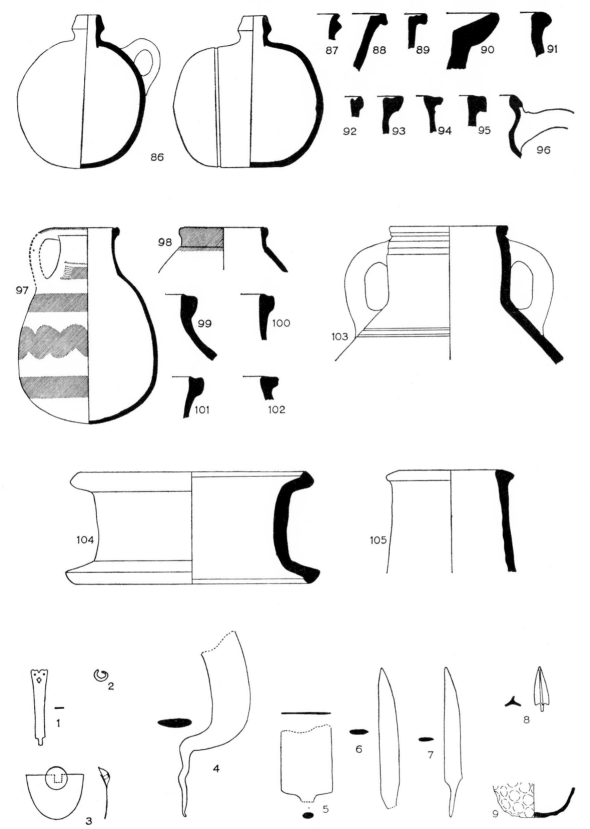

FIG. 24. Parthian painted and miscellaneous jars; metal objects; Ain Sinu. Scale 1:4, except 97 and 98, 1:8

by two ribs; top decorated with band of impressed circles. Handle pinched in at sides; nozzle surrounded by heart-shaped rib. Reddish clay, badly fired, very soft. AS II. (*Iraq*, xxi (1959), pl. lv, 14.)

2. Lamp, incomplete. H. 2·3 cm., width 6·7 cm. Slightly indented flat base. Sloping sides and shoulder, flat top. Large filling hole surrounded by wide ridge, groove, and smaller ridge. Top decorated with band of impressed circles stopping at handle, where there are traces of impressed ovals parallel to long axis of lamp. Handle and nozzle missing. Incised palm frond on lower part of lamp below nozzle. Buff clay. AS II. Three fragmentary examples; one with extant heart-shaped nozzle.

3. Lamp H. 2·3 cm., width 6·3 cm. Indented flat base with four concentric grooves, one in the centre and three at the edge, forming a low double ring. Sloping sides, rounded shoulder. Top decorated with radiating grooves; two ridges at edge of depressed surround of large filling hole, rib at edge of hole. Shallow striations on front of handle, heart-shaped nozzle, the base of which has two grooves at either side. Buff clay. AS II.

4. Lamp, incomplete. H. 2·5 cm., width 7·2 cm. Slightly indented base with groove at edge, slanting sides, carinated shoulder, flat top with rib at edge of depressed surround of large filling hole, ridge at edge of hole. Top of lamp undecorated except for a plain ansate plaque in relief at the side. Undecorated handle, nozzle missing. AS II; two examples.

5. Glazed bowl. H. 4·2 cm. Dark buff paste, greenish-blue glaze inside and out, weathered yellow over most of surface. AS II. (*Iraq*, xxi (1959), pl. lv, 5.)

6. Glazed bowl, incomplete. D. 24 cm. Fine buff paste, blue-green glaze. AS I, II; a common type.

7. Glazed plate. H. 4·1 cm. D. 26 cm. On one example, which lay as it had fallen, face downwards in the soil, the interior glaze was a deep brilliant turquoise, obviously a close approximation to the original colour. On the exposed outer surface the glaze had weathered to the usual blue-green where it was preserved, and yellow where it had worn thin. Buff paste. AS II. A common type. (*Iraq*, xxi (1959), pl. lv, 11.)

8. Glazed bowl, incomplete. D. 28 cm. Buff paste, blue glaze weathered silvery blue to almost white. AS II; a common type.

9. Rim sherd of glazed bowl. D. *c.* 30 cm. Light buff paste, blue-green glaze on yellow surface. AS I.

10. Rim sherd of glazed bowl. D. *c.* 28 cm. Buff paste, blue glaze weathered silvery blue. AS II; common type.

11. Rim sherd of glazed bowl. D. 28–30 cm. Buff paste, light blue-green glaze. The rib on the interior near the rim is decorated with radial incisions 3–5 cm. apart. AS I.

12. Rim sherd of glazed bowl. D. 22–24 cm. Buff paste, blue-green glaze weathered silvery green. AS II.

13. Rim sherd of glazed bowl. D. 27 cm. Buff paste, blue-green glaze. AS II.

14. Rim sherd of glazed bowl. Reddish-buff paste, blue glaze weathered yellow. Upper edge of rim decorated with radial grooves at 7–10 mm. intervals. AS II.

15. Rim sherd of glazed bowl. Dark buff paste, turquoise glaze. A number of examples of this type were found in AS II.

16. Rim sherd of glazed bowl. D. 28–30 cm. Buff paste, yellow surface, light blue-green glaze. AS I.

17. Rim sherd of glazed bowl. D. *c.* 28 cm. Buff paste, pale blue glaze. AS I.

18. Rim sherd of glazed bowl or plate. D. over 24 cm. Buff paste, blue-green glaze weathered yellow. AS II.

19. Rim sherd of glazed bowl or plate. D. *c.* 28 cm. Buff paste, blue-green glaze. AS I.

20. Rim sherd of glazed bowl. D. 22–30 cm. Blue-green glaze. AS II.

21. Rim sherd of glazed bowl. D. *c.* 30 cm. Buff paste, green glaze. AS II.

22. Rim sherd of glazed bowl. D. *c.* 11 cm. Fine gritty dark buff paste, white glaze. AS II.

23. Rim sherd of glazed bowl. D. *c.* 10 cm. Buff paste, blue-green glaze. AS II.

24. Rim sherd of glazed jar (?). D. 11 cm. Blue-green glaze. AS I.

25. Base of glazed jar. B. 3·2 cm. Fine grit-tempered buff paste, blue-green glaze. AS II.
    Cf. *Dura*, figs. 23–24.

26. Base of glazed jar. B. 7 cm. Dark buff paste, green glaze inside and out. AS II.

27. Rim and base of glazed jar. D. 12 cm. Dark green glaze on exterior (but not base) and inside neck of jar. AS II.

28. Fragment of handle and shoulder of glazed stamp-decorated jar. Extant H. 7·9 cm. Yellow paste, blue-green glaze. Three thumb impressions at base of handle, diamond stamp below. AS II.
    Several other fragments, probably from the same jar, were decorated with incised crescents and diamond stamps in the same manner as type 49.

29. Fragment of glazed decorated bowl. Extant D. 8·2 cm. Dark buff paste, green glazed interior, dark buff exterior with only faint traces of glaze. Incised and impressed decoration. AS II.

30. Single-handled jug, incomplete. Estimated H. 22·1 cm. D. 8·5 cm. Well-levigated buff clay. AS II.

31. Rim sherd of single-handled jug. D. 3·5 cm. Greenish-buff clay. AS II.

32. Fragment of neck and handle of single-handled jug or bottle. Greenish-buff clay. AS II.

33. Rim sherd of single-handled jug or bottle. D. 4–5 cm. Well-levigated buff clay, light wash or slip. AS II.

34. Single-handled jug, incomplete. H. 16 cm. Well-levigated buff clay, lighter wash. AS II. (*Iraq*, xxi (1959), pl. lv, 7.)

35. Fragment of single-handled jug. Extant H. 13·5 cm. Greenish clay, dark buff slip. Flat strap handle with slight groove. AS II.

36. Single-handled jug, incomplete. Greenish-buff clay, buff wash or slip. Handle grooved in middle. AS II.
    Cf. *Dura*, fig. 24.

37. Bottle. H. 10·2 cm. Well-levigated dark buff clay, greenish-buff wash. Rim rounded off as though bottle were unfinished. AS II.

38. Body of bottle, incomplete. Extant H. 10·9 cm. Brick-red, fine grit-tempered clay, buff slip. AS II.
    A bottle of similar shape, but made of well-levigated reddish clay with a buff slip, with ribbing all the way up the sides, was also found (AS II).

39. Bottle base. Extant H. 6 cm. Gritty dark buff to reddish clay, warm buff slip. AS I, II.

40. Bottle or jar base. Extant H. 4·8 cm. Dark buff clay. AS II.

41. Jar base. Extant H. 3·1 cm. Dark buff clay. AS II.

42. Jar or bottle base. Extant H. 4 cm. Dark buff clay. AS II.

43. Rim sherd of large bottle or pilgrim flask. D. 5·5 cm. Fine grit-tempered pinkish-buff clay, buff slip. AS I.

44. Rim sherd from large bottle or jar. D. 9 cm. Fine grit-tempered reddish clay, buff slip. AS II.

45. Rim sherd, large jar (?). D. 10 cm. Fine grit-tempered pink to buff clay, light wash. AS II.

46. Rim sherd, small bottle. Fine grit-tempered greenish clay. AS I.

47. Rim sherd of jug or bottle. D. 8 cm. Fine grit-tempered buff clay, buff slip. AS I.
    Cf. type 30.

48. Rim sherd, jar. D. 11 cm. Light buff clay, wash. AS I.
    An identical sherd was found at Tell Hayal (Alaina).

FIGURE 22. *Parthian two-handled jars with incised and impressed ornament, Ain Sinu.* Scale 1:4, except no. 60, 1:8

49. Two-handled stamp-decorated jar, incomplete. D. 11·6 cm. Fine grit-tempered dark buff clay. Edge of rim chipped, apparently intentionally. Deeply incised wavy line on neck; body decorated with vertical rows of diamond stamps and crescent impressions. AS II (*Iraq*, xxi (1959), pl. lv, 6).

50. Two-handled stamp-decorated jar, incomplete. D. 12·9 cm., reconstructed H. 27·3 cm. Well-levigated greenish clay with pink core, pale greenish-buff wash. Decorated rib on neck, diamond stamp impressions on body. AS II.

51. Fragment of two-handled jar. D. 13 cm. Pale greenish clay. Cable ornament below rim. AS II.

52. Rim sherd of two-handled jar. D. 14·5 cm. Well-levigated buff clay, light slip. Incised zigzag around neck. AS I.

53. Fragment of two-handled jar. D. 14 cm. Pale greenish clay and slip. Double band of deeply incised zigzags just below rim, band of impressed ornament and another row of zigzags below. Appliqué pellets. AS II.

54. Two-handled decorated jar, incomplete. D. 12 cm. Fine grit-tempered greenish-buff clay. Two overlapping bands of incised wavy decoration below rim. Incised 'chain' and two bands of impressed crescents on upper shoulder. Occasional appliqué knobs on neck. Upper portion of body completely covered with diagonal rows of diamond stamp impressions. Flat strap handles ornamented at the top with two applied discs over an oval lump of clay, with a depression at either side; similar oval appliqué at base of handle. AS II. (See pl. xvi, 5; a similar jar from Hatra.)

55. Stamped and incised two-handled jar. H. 26·8 cm. Fine grit-tempered salmon-coloured clay, traces of black paint or bitumen on rim and interior. Shoulder decorated with horizontal band of incised zigzags, below which is a rather irregular band of incised ornament consisting of semi-circles of zigzags, open upwards, in which are either diamond stamps or swags of radiating lines. The latter also occur between some of the semicircles of zigzags. Miscellaneous decoration of impressed concentric circles and diamond stamps also occurs. A unique specimen from AS II (pl. xvi, 4).

56. Rim sherd of two-handled jar. D. 11 cm. Fine grit-tempered dark buff clay, light wash. AS II.
    Possibly the same general type as 55.

57. Rim sherd of jar (handles?). D. 8 cm. Gritty brick-coloured clay, buff wash. AS I.

58. Rim sherd of jar (handles?). D. 9 cm. Well-levigated buff clay, light wash. Incised wavy lines on neck. AS II.

59. Rim sherd of jar, probably two-handled. D. 12 cm. Well-levigated reddish clay, light wash. AS II. Probably a variant of types 49–50.

60. Large high-necked amphora, incomplete. Extant H. 42 cm. D. 7 cm. Corrugated neck resembling water-pipe. Coarse grit-tempered bright orange clay, inside blackened. AS II (*Iraq*, xxi (1959), pl. lv, 4).
    The only example of this type of water-jar found at Ain Sinu. (See p. 152, n. 1.)

FIGURE 23. *Parthian bowls, cooking-ware vessels, and miscellaneous jars, Ain Sinu.* Scale 1:4

61. Rim sherd, jar. D. 12 cm. Fine grit-tempered greenish-buff clay, traces of brown paint or slip inside and out. AS I, II.

62. Rim sherd, jar. D. *c.* 11 cm. Flaky coarse-tempered brick-coloured clay. AS II.

63. Rim sherd, jar. D. 12·2 cm. Fine grit-tempered buff clay with reddish exterior, red slip (?), surface badly salted. Incised wavy line ornament on shoulder. AS II.

64. Rim sherd, jar. D. 12 cm. Fine grit-tempered buff clay, light wash, traces of reddish-brown paint on rim. AS I, II.
    A number of sherds of this type were found.

65. Rim sherd, jar. D. 14 cm. Fine grit-tempered brick-coloured clay. AS II.

66. Rim sherd, jar. D. 10 cm. Fine grit-tempered dark buff clay, light wash. AS I.

67. Rim sherd, jar. D. 11·5 cm. Fine grit-tempered buff clay with reddish exterior, buff wash. AS II.

68. Strap-handled cup, incomplete. Extant H. 9·5 cm. D. 14 cm. Gritty light brick-coloured clay, light slip, interior covered with black paint (?) (cf. 55, 70). AS II.

69. Flat plate, fragment. D. 23 cm. Gritty brick-coloured clay, buff wash on inner surface. AS I, II.
    This resembles an earlier type more commonly found glazed.

70. Small bowl, incomplete. H. 6·4 cm. Fine grit-tempered brick-coloured clay, red-brown slip on interior covered with black paint or bitumen (?), light slip on exterior. AS II. (See pp. 150, 152 and *Iraq*, xxi (1959), pl. lv, 13.)

71. Small bowl, fragment. D. 11 cm. Gritty dark buff clay. AS I.

72. Rim sherd, bowl. Very fine greenish-buff clay, smooth grey-green surface. AS I.
    The only sherd of this type from Ain Sinu.

73. Rim sherd, coarse bowl. D. greater than 32 cm. Straw- and grit-tempered coarse buff clay, surface eroded. AS I.

74. Small bowl, fragment. D. 14 cm. Fine grit-tempered buff clay, traces of dark red slip or paint on interior and exterior, surface badly salted. AS II.
    The only example of this deep red slip or paint from Ain Sinu.

75. Deep bowl (?); or rim of large jug similar to type 85 (?). D. 10 cm. Thin gritty ribbed red ware. AS II.

76. Rim sherd, jar. D. 11 cm. Thin gritty ribbed red ware, dark core, light brown wash on exterior. AS II.

77. Shallow two-handled cooking vessel. H. 7·8 cm. D. 20·6 cm. Hard gritty red cooking-ware, darker exterior, fire-blackened. AS II.

  A very common and distinctive type. Types 78–79 illustrate variations of type 77. (See *Iraq*, xxi (1959), pl. lv, 17, 18.)

78. Rim sherd of cooking-ware vessel, variant of type 77. Exterior covered with purplish-brown slip. AS II.

79. Rim sherd of cooking-ware vessel, variant of type 77. D. 24 cm. Brown surface. AS I.

80. Cooking-ware base, probably type 85. Brown surface. AS I.

81. Two-handled cooking-ware cauldron. H. 22 cm. D. 17·6 cm. Purplish-brown slip on exterior. AS I, II (pl. xvi, 2).

  A very common type, variations of which are shown in types 83, 84, and 82 (?).

82. Rim sherd of two-handled cooking-ware cauldron (?). Exterior covered with purplish-brown slip. AS II.

83. Rim sherd of cooking-ware cauldron, variant of type 81. D. 18 cm. Dark brown surface. AS I.

84. Rim sherd of cooking-ware cauldron, variant of type 81. D. 18 cm. AS II.

85. Single-handled cooking-ware jug, incomplete. H. 24·4 cm. D. 8·4 cm. Gritty hard brick-red ware, dark surface; rim, neck, and shoulder covered with dark brown slip. AS II (pl. xvi, 1).

FIGURE 24. *Parthian painted and miscellaneous jars; metal objects; Ain Sinu. Scale 1:4, except 97, 98, 1:8*

86. Water bottle. D. 2·7 cm., D. of bottle 11·5 cm. Grit-tempered greenish-buff clay. Neck made separately and inserted into barrel. AS II.

  The only barrel-shaped water bottle found at Ain Sinu. See also p. 152, n. 2.

87. Rim sherd, large jar (?). D. *c.* 22 cm. Coarse light brick-coloured clay, badly eroded surface. AS II.

  Similar rims occur on green-glazed jars at Dura, but the Ain Sinu example belongs to a type of vessel with a much wider neck.

88. Rim sherd, deep bowl (?) D. *c.* 28 cm. Grit-tempered dark brick-coloured clay, dark core. AS II.

89. Rim sherd, deep bowl (?). D. 22–24 cm. Gritty dark buff clay, traces of black paint in grooves on rim. AS II.

  Several painted examples were found.

90. Rim sherd, large bowl or wide-mouthed jar. D. at least 32 cm. Straw-tempered slightly gritty pinkish-buff clay, buff wash. AS II.

91. Rim sherd, large bowl (?). D. *c.* 42 cm. Fine grit-tempered reddish-buff clay, buff wash. AS I.

92. Rim sherd, jar. D. 12 cm. Grit-tempered buff clay, light slip. AS II.

  Cf. painted jar types 97–101.

93. Rim sherd, jar. D. *c.* 13 cm. Very coarse grit-tempered brick-coloured clay. AS I, II.

94. Rim sherd, jar. D. 14–16 cm. Gritty dark buff clay, buff wash. AS I.

95. Rim sherd, jar. D. over 30 cm. Straw- and grit-tempered dark pinkish-buff clay, buff surface. AS II.

96. Rim sherd, one- or two-handled jar. Gritty buff clay. AS I.

97. Single-handled painted jar, incomplete. H. 38·4 cm. D. 13·5 cm. Grit-tempered dark buff clay, decorated with bands of reddish-brown paint. AS II (pl. XVI, 3).

98. Large painted storage jar, incomplete. D. 17 cm. Gritty dark buff clay, light wash, decorated with wavy and plain bands of orange paint in the same fashion as type 97. AS II.

99. Rim sherd, painted storage jar. D. 16 cm. Gritty brick-red clay, traces of red paint on exterior and top of rim. AS II.
    Possibly a variant of type 98.

100. Rim sherd, painted jar. Gritty reddish clay, trace of red paint in groove on top of rim. AS I.
    Variant of type 97 or 98.

101. Rim sherd, painted jar. D. c. 16 cm. Gritty buff clay, traces of red paint on top of rim. AS I, II.

102. Rim sherd, painted jar. D. 12–14 cm. Fine grit-tempered reddish-buff clay, buff wash on exterior, traces of dark red paint on top and exterior of rim. AS I.

103. Two-handled water-jar. Extant H. 13·5 cm. D. 12 cm. Gritty dark buff clay, buff slip. Round handles. AS II.

104. Pot-stand. H. 10·7 cm. Coarse grit-tempered reddish-buff clay. AS II. (See *Iraq*, xxi (1959), pl. lv, 5, 10.)

105. Neck of large jar, incomplete (handles?). D. 13 cm. Coarse grit-tempered brick-coloured clay, buff wash. AS II.

METAL AND GLASS OBJECTS

1. Strip of bronze with holes pierced for decoration, and perhaps also for riveting, at one end, and a projecting tongue bent over to form a loop at the other. Width at pierced end 17 mm., tapering to 9·5 mm. at shoulder above loop; average thickness 1·4 mm. Use unknown, perhaps a pendant. AS II.

2. Bronze ear-ring, crescent-shaped with in-turned points. D. 13 mm., maximum thickness 3 mm. Two specimens. AS II.

3. Semi-elliptical bronze plate, with domed head of bronze stud for attachment. Plate 43 mm. long, 57 mm. wide. Perhaps epaulette or decoration for armour. AS II.

4. Iron sickle-blade, broken. Surviving length 120 mm., rectangular section. AS II. (*Iraq*, xxi (1959), pl. lv, 19.)

5. Iron spear-blade, broken. Surviving length of blade 65 mm., flat section 2·2 mm. thick. Tang of oval section, 11 by 6 mm., broken close to blade. AS II.

6. Iron knife-blade, straight-backed, slightly convex cutting edge. Length of blade 120 mm., maximum width 21 mm. tapering to a point. Tang broken. AS II.

7. Iron knife-blade, straight-backed, slightly convex cutting edge. Length of blade 118 mm., maximum width 18 mm. tapering to a point. Tang of square section maximum 6 by 6 mm., tapering to a point. AS II.

8. Iron arrowhead, three-bladed, slightly barbed. Length of head 36 mm., barbs offset 5·5 mm. from tang of round section AS II, two examples.
    Identical arrowheads have been found at Hatra.

9. Base of glass bowl, fragment, surviving H. 30 mm., decorated externally with circular depressions 11 mm. in diameter covering the whole of the visible surface. Thickness 4 mm. AS II.

    A fragment of a glass cup decorated with vertical grooves in the style of Hellenistic small bowls (see pl. XIV, 6) was also found (AS II).

    A number of square glass bottles were found at Hatra, but none was discovered at Ain Sinu.

LIST OF ABBREVIATIONS

AAA	*Annals of Archaeology and Anthropology* (University of Liverpool).
AASOR	*The Annual of the American Schools of Oriental Research* (New Haven).
AfO	*Archiv für Orientforschung* (Berlin).
AGH	*Admiralty Intelligence Division, Geographical Handbook, Iraq and the Persian Gulf* (London, H.M.S.O., 1944).
ANET	Pritchard, J. B., ed. *Ancient Near Eastern Texts Relating to the Old Testament* (Princeton University Press, 2nd ed., 1955).
AOS	*American Oriental Series* (New Haven).
ARMT	*Archives royales de Mari*, texts in transliteration and translation (Paris, 1950–).
AS	*Anatolian Studies* (London, British Institute of Archaeology at Ankara).
BASOR	*Bulletin of the American Schools of Oriental Research* (New Haven).
Belleten	*Türk Tarih Kurumu, Belleten* (Ankara).
BMC, Arabia	Hill, G. F. *Catalogue of Greek Coins in the British Museum, Arabia* (London, 1922).
BSOAS	*Bulletin of the School of Oriental and African Studies* (London).
CAH	*Cambridge Ancient History.*
CIG	*Corpus Inscriptionum Graecarum.*
CIL	*Corpus Inscriptionum Latinarum.*
CVA	*Corpus Vasorum Antiquorum.*
Dessau	Dessau, H. *Inscriptiones Latinae Selectae* (Berlin, 1954–5).
Dura, Coins	Bellinger, A. R. *The Excavations at Dura-Europos, Final Report*, vi. *The Coins* (New Haven, Yale University Press, 1949).
Econ. Geog.	*Economic Geography* (Worcester, Mass.).
Geog. Jl.	*Geographical Journal* (London, Royal Geographical Society).
Hoffmann, *Auszüge*	Hoffmann, G. 'Auszüge aus syrischen Akten persischer Märtyrer', *Abhandlungen für die Kunde des Morgenlandes*, vii (1880).
HSS	*Harvard Semitic Series* (Cambridge, Mass.).
HUCA	*Hebrew Union College Annual* (Cincinnati).
ILN	*Illustrated London News* (London).
JADD	Johns, C. H. W. *Assyrian Deeds and Documents* (Cambridge, 1901–23).
JAOS	*Journal of the American Oriental Society* (New Haven).
JCS	*Journal of Cuneiform Studies* (American Schools of Oriental Research, New Haven).
JESHO	*Journal of the Economic and Social History of the Orient.*
JNES	*Journal of Near Eastern Studies* (Department of Oriental Languages and Literature, University of Chicago).
LAR	Luckenbill, D. D. *Ancient Records, Assyria* (Chicago, 1926).
LSS	*Leipziger Semitistische Studien.*
MJ	*University of Pennsylvania Museum Journal* (Philadelphia).
OIP	*Oriental Institute Publications* (University of Chicago Press).

PBA	*Proceedings of the British Academy* (London, Oxford University Press for the British Academy).
RA	*Revue d'Assyriologie* (Paris).
RCAE	Waterman, L. *Royal Correspondence of the Assyrian Empire* (Ann Arbor, University of Michigan Press, 1930–6).
SAOC	*Studies in Ancient Oriental Civilization* (Chicago).
Tribus nomades	*Les Tribus nomades et semi-nomades des États du Levant.* (Haut-Commissariat de la République française, Beyrouth, 1930).
WVDOG	*Wissenschaftliche Veröffentlichungen der Deutschen Orient-Gesellschaft* (Leipzig).
ZA	*Zeitschrift für Assyriologie* (Berlin).

SELECTED BIBLIOGRAPHY

A. CHAPTERS I–III

ADAMS, ROBERT M. 'Early Civilizations, Subsistence, and Environment', in *City Invincible* (University of Chicago Press, 1958).

—— 'Salt and silt in ancient Mesopotamian agriculture', with T. Jacobsen, *Science*, 128 (Washington, 1958).

—— 'Agriculture and Urban Life in Early South-western Iran', *Science*, 136 (1962).

Admiralty Intelligence Division, Geographical Handbook, *Iraq and the Persian Gulf*, (London, H.M.S.O., 1944).

ANDRAE, W. *Das wiedererstandene Assur* (Leipzig, 1938).

Archives royales de Mari (texts in transliteration and translation), i–ix, xv (Paris, 1950–60), under the direction of A. Parrot and G. Dossin.

BACHE, C. 'University of Pennsylvania Museum—Baghdad School Expedition at Billah', *BASOR*, 40 (1930), with E. A. Speiser.

—— 'The first Assyrian Level at Tell Billa', *MJ*, xxiv (1935).

BALKAN, K. 'Observations on the Chronological Problems of the Kārum Kaniš', *Türk Tarih Kurumu Yayınlarından*, vii/28 (Ankara, 1955).

BELL, GERTRUDE. *Amurath to Amurath* (London, 1924).

BRAIDWOOD, ROBERT J., and HOWE, BRUCE. 'Prehistoric Investigations in Iraqi Kurdistan', *SAOC*, 31 (University of Chicago Press, 1960).

BUDGE, E. A. WALLIS. *By Nile and Tigris* (London, 1920).

DAVIES, D. H. 'Observations on Land Use in Iraq', *Econ. Geog.* 33 (1957).

DRIVER, G. R. *Aramaic Documents of the Fifth Century B.C.* (Oxford, 1957).

DUSSAUD, R. *Les Arabes en Syrie avant l'Islam* (Paris, 1907).

The Economic Development of Iraq, International Bank for Reconstruction and Development (Baltimore, 1952).

FIELD, HENRY. *An Anthropological Reconnaissance in the Near East* (Cambridge, Mass., Peabody Museum, 1950).

—— *The Anthropology of Iraq*, pt. 1, 1 (Peabody Museum, 1940); pt. 2, 1 Peabody Museum, 1951).

FORRER, E. *Die Provinzeinteilung des assyrischen Reiches* (Leipzig 1921).

GADD, C. J. 'Tablets from Chagar Bazar and Tall Brak', *Iraq*, vii (London, 1940).

GELB, I. J. 'Two Assyrian King Lists', *JNES*, xiii (1954).

—— 'The Early History of the West Semitic Peoples', *JCS*, xv (1961).

GOETZE, A. 'An Old Babylonian Itinerary', *JCS*, vii (1953).

—— 'The Laws of Ešnunna', *AASOR*, xxxi (1956).

—— *Kleinasien* (1957).

GRANT, C. P. *The Syrian Desert* (London, 1937).

HALLO, W. H. 'Zariqum', *JNES*, xv (1956).
—— 'The Road to Emar', *JCS*, xvii (1964).

HITTI, P. K. *History of the Arabs* (London, 1953).

JACOBSEN, T., and LLOYD, S. 'Sennacherib's Aqueduct at Jerwan', *OIP*, 24 (1935).
—— and ADAMS, R. M. 'Salt and silt in ancient Mesopotamian agriculture', *Science*, 128 (1958).

JOHNS, C. H. W. *An Assyrian Doomsday Book* (1901).
—— *Assyrian Deeds and Documents* (Cambridge, 1901–23).

KRAELING, C. H., and ADAMS, R. M., edd. *City Invincible* (University of Chicago Press, 1960).

KUPPER, J.-R. *Les Nomades en Mésopotamie au temps des rois de Mari* (Paris, 1957).
—— 'Le rôle des nomades dans l'histoire de la Mésopotamie ancienne', *JESHO*, ii (1959).
—— 'Northern Mesopotamia and Syria', *CAH*, II. i (1963).

LAESSØE, J. 'Akkadian Annakum: "Tin" or "Lead"?', *Acta Orientalia*, xxiv (Budapest, 1959).
—— 'The Shemshara Tablets', *Arkaeologisk-kunsthistoriske Meddelelser Dan. Vid. Selsk.* 4, no. 3 (Copenhagen, 1959).

LANDSBERGER, B. 'Assyrische Königsliste und "Dunkles Zeitalter",' *JCS*, viii (1954).

LAYARD, A. H. *Nineveh and its Remains* (London, 1849).
—— *Nineveh and Babylon* (London, 1853).

LEEMANS, W. F. 'Foreign trade in the Old Babylonian Period', *Studia et Documenta ad Iura Orientis Antiqui pertinentia*, 6 (Leiden, 1960).

LEES, G. M., and FALCON, N. L. 'The Geographical History of the Mesopotamian Plains', *Geog. Jl.*, 118 (1952).

LE STRANGE, G. *Lands of the Eastern Caliphate* (Cambridge, 1905).

LLOYD, SETON. 'Sennacherib's Aqueduct at Jerwan', *OIP*, 24 (1935), with Jacobsen, T.

LUCKENBILL, D. D. *Ancient Records, Assyria* (Chicago, 1926).

LUKE, H. C. *Mosul and its Minorities* (London, 1925).

MALLOWAN, M. E. L. 'Excavations at Brak and Chagar Bazar', *Iraq*, ix (1947).
—— Excavations at Nimrud, preliminary reports, annually in *Iraq*, xii–xvi, xviii–xxi (1950–9).

MUSIL, A. *The Middle Euphrates* (New York, 1927).
—— *Northern Nejd* (New York, 1928).

OATES, D. Excavations at Nimrud, preliminary reports, annually in *Iraq*, xviii–xxi, xxiii–xxv (1956–9, 1961–3).

OPPENHEIM, A. L. 'The Seafaring Merchants of Ur', *JAOS*, 74 (1954).

PARKER, B. Administrative and economic tablets from Nimrud, *Iraq*, xvi (1954), xix (1957), xxiii (1961).
—— 'Economic Tablets from the Temple of Mamu at Balawat', *Iraq*, xxv (1963).

POEBEL, A. 'The Assyrian King List from Khorsabad', *JNES*, i (1942), ii (1943).

PRITCHARD, J. B., ed. *Ancient Near Eastern Texts Relating to the Old Testament* (Princeton University Press, 1955).

ROWTON, M. B., in 'Chronology: Egypt, Western Asia, and the Aegean Lands', *CAH*, i, vi (1962).

SAFAR, FUAD. 'Sennacherib's Project for supplying Erbil with water', *Sumer*, iii (1947).

SAGGS, H. W. F. 'The Nimrud Letters, 1952', i–vi, *Iraq*, xvii, xviii, xx, xxi, xxv (1955–63).

SMITH, SIDNEY. Chs. i–v in 'The Assyrian Empire', *CAH*, iii (1925).
—— *The Early History of Assyria* (London, 1928).
—— *Alalakh and Chronology* (London, 1940).

SPEISER, E. A., and BACHE, C. 'University of Pennsylvania Museum—Baghdad School Expedition at Billah', *BASOR*, 40 (1930).

Les Tribus nomades et semi-nomades des États du Levant (Haut-Commissariat de la République française, Beyrouth, 1930).

WATERMAN, L. *Royal Correspondence of the Assyrian Empire* (Ann Arbor, University of Michigan Press, 1930–6).

WISEMAN, D. 'The Nimrud Tablets, 1950', *Iraq*, xiii (1951), with J. V. Kinnier Wilson.
—— 'A New Stela of Aššur-naṣir-pal II', *Iraq*, xiv (1952).

B. CHAPTERS IV–V

AMMIANUS MARCELLINUS. Loeb Classical Library, ed. and trans. J. C. Rolfe (London, 1950, 1952).

ANDRAE, W. *Das wiedererstandene Assur* (Leipzig, 1938).
—— and LENZEN, H. 'Die Partherstadt Assur', *WVDOG*, lvii (1933).

ARRIAN. *Parthica*, ed. A. G. Roos (1928).

ASSEMANUS. *Bibliotheca Orientalis*, i (1719).

BAR HEBRAEUS. *Chronicon Ecclesiasticum*, ed. Abbeloos and Lamy, iii (1877).

BAUR, P. V. C., ROSTOVTZEFF, M. I., and others. *Excavations at Dura-Europos, Preliminary Reports* (New Haven, Yale University Press, 1929–39).

BELLINGER, A. R. *The Excavations at Dura-Europos, Final Report*, vi. 'The Coins' (New Haven, Yale University Press, 1949).

BERCHEM, D. VAN. 'Recherches sur la chronologie de Syrie et de Mésopotamie', *Syria*, xxxi (1954).

BURY, J. B. *History of the Later Roman Empire* (London, 1923).

BUTLER, H. C. *Early Churches of Syria* (1929).

CASKEL, W. 'The Beduinization of Arabia', *American Anthropological Memoirs*, 76 (New York, 1954).

CASTELIN, K. O. 'The Coinage of Rhesaena in Mesopotamia', *Numismatic Notes and Monographs*, 108 (New York, 1946).

CHAPOT, V. *La Frontière de l'Euphrate* (Paris, 1907).

CHRISTENSEN, A. *L'Iran sous les Sassanides* (Copenhagen, 1944).

CROWFOOT, J. W. *Early Churches in Palestine* (Schweich Lectures, British Academy, London, 1941).

DEBEVOISE, N. C. *A Political History of Parthia* (University of Chicago Press, 1938).

DEVRÉESSE, R. *Le Patriarchat d'Antioche* (1945).

DUSSAUD, R. *Topographie historique de la Syrie antique et médiévale* (Paris, 1927).

GABRIEL, A. *Voyages archéologiques dans la Turquie orientale* (1940).

HILL, G. F. *Catalogue of Greek Coins in the British Museum, Arabia* (London, 1922).

HITTI, P. K. *History of the Arabs* (London, 1953).

HOFFMANN, G. 'Auszüge aus syrischen Akten persischer Märtyrer', *Abhandlungen für die Kunde des Morgenlandes*, vii (1880).

JOHN OF EPHESUS. *Ecclesiastical History*, trans. R. Payne Smith (Oxford, 1860).

JONES, A. H. M. *The Later Roman Empire* (Oxford, 1964).

LABOURT, J. *Le Christianisme dans l'empire perse* (Paris, 1904).

LAMMENS, H. *L'Arabie occidentale avant l'Hégire* (1928).

LASSUS, J. *Sanctuaires chrétiens de Syrie* (Paris, 1947).

LEPPER, F. A. *Trajan's Parthian War* (London, 1948).

LE STRANGE, G. *Lands of the Eastern Caliphate* (Cambridge, 1905).

LEVI DELLA VIDA, G. 'Pre-Islamic Arabia', in *The Arab Heritage* (1944).

MAGIE, D. *Roman Rule in Asia Minor* (Princeton University Press, 1950).

McEWAN, CALVIN W., and others. 'Soundings at Tell Fakhariyah', *OIP*, 79 (University of Chicago Press, 1958).

NAU, F. *Les Arabes chrétiens de Mésopotamie et de Syrie du VIIe au VIIIe siècle* (1933).
—— (ed. and trans.) 'History of Mar Ahudemmeh', in *Patrologia Orientalis*, iii.

NÖLDEKE, T. *Geschichte der Perser und Araber zur Zeit der Sasaniden aus der arabischen Chronik des Tabari* (1879).

POIDEBARD, A. *La Trace de Rome dans le désert de Syrie* (Paris, 1934).

PROCOPIUS. *Wars*, i. Loeb Classical Library, ed. and trans. H. B. Dewing (London).

Ravennatis Anonymi Cosmographia, ed. M. Pinder and G. Parthey (Aalen, 1860).

REITLINGER, G. 'Medieval Antiquities West of Mosul', *Iraq*, v (1938).

ROSTOVTZEFF, M. I. *Excavations at Dura-Europos, Preliminary Reports* (1929–39), with Baur and others. (New Haven, Yale University Press.)
—— *Social and Economic History of the Hellenistic World* (Oxford, 1941).
—— *The Excavations at Dura-Europos, Final Reports* (1943–   ), with Bellinger, A. R.; Brown, F. E.; and Welles, C. B., edd.

SEGAL, J. B. 'Mesopotamian Communities from Julian to the Rise of Islam', *PBA*, xli (London, 1955).

SPANNER, H., and GUYER, S. *Rusafa* (1926).

TCHALENKO, G. *Villages antiques de la Syrie du Nord* (Paris, 1953).

URE, P. N. *Justinian and his Age* (Harmondsworth, 1951).

Weltkarte des Castorius, ed. K. Miller (1888).

C. APPENDIXES A and B

Alishar, ii. OSTEN, H. H. VON DER. 'The Alishar Hüyük, Seasons of 1930–32', pt. ii, *OIP*, 29 (Chicago, 1937).

Alishar, iii. Ibid., pt. iii, *OIP*, 30 (Chicago, 1937).

ANDRAE, W., and LENZEN, H. 'Die Partherstadt Assur', *WVDOG*, lvii (1933).

Antioch, i. ELDERKIN, G. W., ed. *Antioch-on-the-Orontes*, i, 'The Excavations of 1932' (Princeton University Press, 1934).

Antioch, iii. STILLWELL, R., ed. *Antioch-on-the-Orontes*, iii, 'The Excavations of 1937–1939' (Princeton University Press, 1941).

Antioch, iv. WAAGÉ, F. O., ed. *Antioch-on-the-Orontes*, iv, Pt. 1. 'Ceramics and Islamic Coins' (Princeton University Press, 1948).

Dura. TOLL, N. *The Excavations at Dura-Europos, Final Report*, iv, pt. i/1. 'The Green Glazed Pottery' (New Haven, Yale University Press, 1943).

Dura, Coins. BELLINGER, A. R. *The Excavations at Dura-Europos, Final Report*, vi. 'The Coins' (New Haven, Yale University Press, 1949).

Dura, Lamps. BAUR, P. V. C. *The Excavations at Dura-Europos, Final Report*, iv, pt. iii. 'The Lamps' (New Haven, Yale University Press, 1947).

HAMILTON, R. W. 'Excavations on the Temple of Ishtar at Nineveh', *AAA*, xix (1932).

LLOYD, SETON. 'Sultantepe', *AS*, ii–iv (1952–4).

OPPENHEIM, Baron M. VON. *Tell Halaf*, trans. G. Wheeler (London, 1933).

Samaria. REISNER, G. A., FISHER, C. S., and LYON, D. G. *Harvard Excavations at Samaria* (Harvard University Press, 1924).

Seleucia. DEBEVOISE, N. C. *Parthian Pottery from Seleucia on the Tigris* (Ann Arbor, University of Michigan Press, 1934).

STARR, R. F. S. *Nuzi* (Cambridge, Mass., Harvard University Press, 1939).

Sultantepe. LLOYD, S. *AS*, iv (1954), p. 101 and fig. 1.

Tarsus, i. GOLDMAN, H. ed. *Excavations at Gözlü Kule, Tarsus*, i. 'The Hellenistic and Roman Periods' (Princeton University Press, 1950).

THOMPSON, R. C. 'The Excavations on the Temple of Nabu at Nineveh', *Archaeologia*, lxxix (London, 1929).

INDEX

THE Index should be used in conjunction with the Table of Contents. In the transliteration of ancient and modern names I have endeavoured to follow common usage in existing books and maps and to render them intelligible to an English reader even when this involves inconsistency. I am indebted to Mr. Jonathan Hodgkin for his help in compiling the index.

PLATE I

a. The plain west of Aššur. A line of greener vegetation marks the trough of the ancient road from Aššur to Hatra

b. The approach to the foothills: Dohuk valley, *c.* 60 km. north of Mosul

PLATE II

a. The western exit of the Negūb tunnel, which supplied water from the Greater Zab to the Kalḫu canal

b. The Kalḫu canal beside the Greater Zab just below the tunnel

PLATE III

a. The Negūb tunnel from the west

b. Sluice openings in the east shaft of the Negūb tunnel

PLATE IV

a. Jebel al-Qosh from the south, showing Bandwai village and the head of the canal leading to Wadi al-Milh

b. The canal south of Bandwai. The figure is standing in its bed

PLATE V

a. The entrance to Karsi gorge on the north side of Jebel Sinjar

b. Karsi valley within Jebel Sinjar. Traces of a road terrace appear on the extreme right

PLATE VI

a. The modern village of Majnuniye from the top of Tell Hayal; Jebel Sinjar in the background

b. The *wadi* of Tell Afar from the slope of the ancient tell; on the right, ruined towers of the medieval citadel

PLATE VII

a. Beled Sinjar from the west

b. The Roman extension of Beled Sinjar, looking west across the watercourse

PLATE VIII

a. Beled Sinjar: bastion no. 21, just east of the watercourse

b. Beled Sinjar: the Roman south gate

PLATE IX

a. Beled Sinjar: the south-west wall from bastion no. 7. The scale in the foreground marks the jamb of a postern gate

b. Beled Sinjar: bastions nos. 6 and 7 from the south

PLATE X

a. Beled Sinjar: the entrance to bastion no. 5 from within. The small door is of recent date

b. Beled Sinjar: the west wall of bastion no. 5 from within. The arch on the left is a recent addition

PLATE XI

a. Beled Sinjar: bastion no. 6 from the south

b. Beled Sinjar: masonry of the scarp on the north side of bastion no. 7

PLATE XII

b. Beled Sinjar: exterior of a window-slit, bastion no. 6

a. Beled Sinjar: the north gate. Half of a medieval bitumen pavement has been
removed to show the Roman paving beneath

PLATE XIII

a. Qasr Serīj: the west façade and the apse from the south-west

b. Qasr Serīj from the south-east

c. The west end of the north aisle

d. The semi-dome of the apse

PLATE XIV

Examples of Hellenistic stamped, painted, and glazed sherds, Nimrud

PLATE XV

Examples of Hellenistic stamped and painted sherds, Nimrud

PLATE XVI

Parthian pottery from Ain Sinu and Hatra

Photographs by A. Robertson-Pearce. Courtesy Iraq Museum